S0-AXP-617

21149

Skillstreaming
the Elementary School Child

A Guide for Teaching Prosocial Skills

THIRD EDITION

Ellen McGinnis

Education Resource Center
University of Delaware
Newark, DE 19716-2940

RESEARCH PRESS
PUBLISHERS

2612 North Mattis Avenue ■ Champaign, Illinois 61822 ■ [800] 519-2707 ■ www.researchpress.com

P G
14 4599
2012

RESEARCH PRESS
PUBLISHERS

Copyright © 2012 by Ellen McGinnis

5   4   3   14   15

All rights reserved. Printed in the United States of America.

Skillstreaming is the registered trademark of Research Press.

In this volume, Tables 1 and 2, skill outlines and homework reports in Part 2, and the program forms in Appendixes A and B may be reproduced with proper credit to the source for noncommercial use by the original purchaser only, not to extend to reproduction by other parties. Excerpts may be printed in connection with published reviews in periodicals without express permission. No other part of this book may be reproduced by any means without the written permission of the publisher.

Copies of this book may be ordered from Research Press at the address given on the title page.

Composition by Jeff Helgesen
Cover design by Linda Brown, Positive I.D. Graphic Design
Printed by McNaughton & Gunn, Inc.

ISBN: 978-0-87822-655-9
Library of Congress Control Number 2011932202

To Alex Smith, always a source of encouragement

Contents

PART 2
Skill Outlines and Homework Reports

Homework Reports follow each skill.

Appendixes

Figures and Tables

Preface

Skillstreaming is now over 30 years old. Starting with its introduction in 1973 as one of the very first social skills training approaches, it has been widely used in the United States and beyond and is now in place in hundreds of schools, agencies, and institutions serving children and youth. This third edition of *Skillstreaming the Elementary School Child* integrates what has been learned from research investigations over the past 10 years with training recommendations provided by many of the hundreds of teachers, administrators, youth care workers, and other practitioners who have used Skillstreaming.

The origins and development of the Skillstreaming approach afford an interesting context with which to understand the 21st-century incarnation of the program described in this book. The prevailing therapeutic approaches of the 1950s and 1960s (psychodynamic, nondirective, and behavior modification) held that an individual possessed effective, satisfying, or healthy behaviors but that these behaviors were simply unexpressed. In contrast, Skillstreaming represents a psychoeducational approach, viewing the individual in educational terms, as a person in need of help in the form of skills training. Instead of providing therapy, the task of the skills trainer or teacher is the active and deliberate teaching of desirable behaviors to replace those less productive in nature.

Skillstreaming differs from the approaches of behavior theorists such as Albert Bandura (1973), who described the processes of modeling, behavioral rehearsal, and reinforcement implicit in the Skillstreaming approach but who emphasized operant procedures such as prompting and shaping of behaviors. Although a strictly behavioral approach increases the frequency of a behavior, that behavior must already be within a person's repertoire. If the person does not have a grasp of the needed skill, operant procedures are insufficient to add that skill to the person's behavioral options.

The deinstitutionalization movement of the 1960s, which resulted in the discharge of approximately four million persons from mental health and other institutions into local communities, set the stage for acceptance of an alternative way of providing treatment. The realization was that the more traditional therapeutic interventions, which focused on looking inward to correct one's nonproductive actions (i.e., insight-oriented approaches), were ineffective for many individuals from lower socioeconomic environments, who constituted the majority of individuals discharged from institutions. The lack of effective methods to reach this population led Dr. Arnold P. Goldstein to develop Structured Learning Therapy (Goldstein, 1973), the precursor to Skillstreaming. Structured learning methods approached aggression, withdrawal, and other nonproductive patterns in a new way—as learned behaviors that can be changed by teaching new, alternative skills.

In addition to the growing importance of such structured learning methods in applied clinical work and as a preventive focus in community mental health, parallel developments in education clearly encouraged skills training. Specifically, a number of other approaches grew from the personal development context of certain educational movements—for example, progressive education (Dewey, 1938) and character education (Chapman, 1977). The goal of these approaches was to support the teaching of concepts and behaviors relevant to values, morality, and emotional functioning—in particular, values clarification (Simon, Howe, & Kirschenbaum, 1972), moral education (Kohlberg, 1973), and affective education (Miller, 1976). These three approaches, as well as other personal growth programs, combined to provide a supportive climate and context for skills training. These programs share a concern for personal development, competence, and social effectiveness. Clearly, education had been broadened well beyond basic academic content to include areas traditionally the concern of mental health practitioners.

Since its initial development as an intervention prescriptively targeted to low-income adults deficient in social skills, Skillstreaming has increasingly been used with many other populations. In the 1980s and beyond, Dr. Goldstein's skills training program, now known as Skillstreaming, was adapted to meet the needs of adolescents (Goldstein, Gershaw, Klein, & Sprafkin, 1980; Goldstein & McGinnis, 1997), elementary children (McGinnis & Goldstein, 1984, 1997), and preschool and kindergarten children (McGinnis & Goldstein, 1990, 2003) who exhibited aggression and other problematic behaviors. In addition to its use with children and adolescents, the Skillstreaming approach has been employed successfully with elderly adults, child-abusing parents, industrial managers, police officers, and others. Over more than 30 years of program use, a considerable amount of evaluation research has been conducted and reported. The results of these studies support the efficacy of Skillstreaming and have suggested means for altering and improving its procedures and materials. An annotated bibliography detailing Skillstreaming research is available on the Skillstreaming website (www.skillstreaming.com).

Acknowledgments

During the more than 40 years of his professional life, Arnold P. Goldstein (1934–2002) was a professor at Syracuse University, director of the Center for Research on Aggression, and wrote or coauthored over 90 peer-reviewed articles and 50 books. In the final year of his life, Dr. Goldstein founded the International Center for Aggression Replacement Training (ICART), which leads research and provides information and training to professionals throughout the world. At this point, Dr. Goldstein's work, including Skillstreaming, is used throughout the United States and in at least 16 other countries. Many people, myself included, cannot thank him enough for his efforts to help youth and adults with aggression problems and other challenging behaviors change to improve their lives and the lives of those who interact with them.

Three other persons share major responsibility for bringing Skillstreaming into existence and nurturing its development over these many years. Robert P. Sprafkin and N. Jane Gershaw originally helped codevelop the program and were prime contributors to enhancing both its early application and its initial evaluation. Barry Glick fully shared the effort to expand its boundaries to include especially difficult-to-reach adolescents. These colleagues well deserve special thanks and appreciation.

Thanks also to Shawnda Gorish and Julianne Woodhouse from Des Moines Public Schools, who provided many of the real-life scenarios included in the suggested content for modeling displays, and to Knut Gunderson, Sandnes, Norway, for his thoughtful review and suggestions from his training experience.

Gail Salyards and Russ Pence from Research Press provided the encouragement and understanding needed to complete this revision. Special appreciation and thanks to Karen Steiner, my editor, for her careful and sensitive reviews, changes, and recommendations, and for understanding the need to represent Arnie's spirit in this work.

Introduction

Today's elementary students deal with the same behavioral concerns students experienced decades ago—noncompliance, peer confrontations, failure to participate in academic or social activities, and so forth. Although these concerns continue, classrooms include increasingly violent and aggressive students, as well as students who in their profound social isolation lack a sense of belonging. It is not uncommon to hear teachers comment that students come to school with more problems than ever before and further ask, "How can we even begin to address these concerns?" School administrators often lament the amount of time they spend on student discipline, wondering where they will find the time for proactive leadership. And, in tough economic times, when parents must come to the school for a midday conference due to their child's inappropriate behavior or stay home because their child has been suspended, they understandably worry they may lose their jobs. Community members are involved as well, most frequently when violent incidents occur, and it is now somewhat common to read news reports about school violence.

In addition, the current generation of elementary schools has a much higher expectation to enhance services to all students. Federal legislation requires increased accountability for schools to advance student achievement, to close achievement gaps between groups of students, and to set the stage for more students to become socially and academically successful in order to increase graduation rates. In an increasing number of schools across the country, teachers are held accountable for their students' individual test scores and student behavior through the teacher evaluation process.

Behavioral concerns in schools and other settings have a profound impact on the individual child who is struggling but also on the teacher, peers in the classroom, school leadership, parents, and the community. Such concerns are illustrated in the following real-life scenarios:

> In one elementary classroom, Ann's teacher often becomes irritated as Ann tries to get attention from others by laughing at classmates when they answer a question. She tries to join in the conversations and activities of other girls by making comments that are interpreted by her peers as rude. Ann spends recess time by herself, occasionally trying to join an ongoing activity by making an unrelated, silly remark. Ann's mother expresses her concern that Ann doesn't seem to have any friends.

> In a third-grade classroom, Enrique doesn't understand the school expectations. He struggles with following directions and fails to share materials to complete group projects. It seems he is always where he isn't supposed to be, wandering about the classroom. He doesn't return to his seat when asked to do so by his teacher. Classmates are beginning to tease him, and Enrique often pushes and pokes other students in response. He has also been in physical fights in the school hallway and playground. The teacher feels helpless because it seems no matter what

Enrique is asked to do, a classroom disruption will be forthcoming. Enrique's parents are concerned because they know the importance of his success in school.

In still another elementary classroom, Mario is very quiet in class, his academic work is average, and he does not listen to what the teacher asks him to do. His teacher has noticed that Mario is often alone in social situations and seems to withdraw if a peer challenges him. One day at recess, Mario takes a knife from his backpack and threatens a student who apparently has provoked him. Mario's teacher is alarmed at this action. Mario is suspended from school, and Mario's father must miss work to supervise him at home.

WHY TEACH SOCIAL SKILLS?

How can teachers deal with these typical types of student concerns? Can teaching social skills change such scenarios? Research has demonstrated benefit for students across age and skill levels. For example, instruction in social skills has been shown to positively impact elementary-age children (Denham, Hatfield, Smethurst, Tan, & Tribe, 2006; Maddern, Franey, McLaughlin, & Cox, 2004), elementary-age students (Gresham, Van, & Cook, 2006; Lane, Menzies, Barton-Arwood, Doukas, & Munton, 2005; Lo, Loe, & Cartledge, 2002), and adolescents (Cook, Gresham, Kern, Barreras, & Crews, 2008). Benefit has also occurred for students with disabilities (Maag, 2006), including learning disabilities (Kavale & Forness, 1996), and those with emotional and behavioral disorders (Cook et al., 2008; Gresham, Cook, Crews, & Kern, 2004). Additional evidence supports social skills instruction for individuals with lower incidence disabilities, such as traumatic brain injury (Dykeman, 2003), schizophrenia (Kurtz & Mueser, 2008), and Asperger's syndrome (Lopata, Thomeer, Bolker, & Nida, 2006; Tse, Strulovitch, Tagalakis, Meng, & Fombonne, 2007).

Social skills deficits have been the target of considerable research scrutiny, and it is well accepted today that a child's lack of social competence relates to later negative outcomes (Walker, Ramsey, & Gresham, 2004). For most students, because of the length of time they spend in the school setting, the majority of socialization occurs in school (Schoenfeld, Rutherford, Gable, & Rock, 2008). A positive relationship between social skills and school success has been repeatedly demonstrated (Cartledge & Lo, 2006), and students who are socially competent have a greater likelihood of graduating high school (Caprara, Barbaranelli, Pastorelli, Bandura, & Zimbardo, 2000). Planned and direct instruction in social skills is of benefit to students themselves because it empowers them to get their needs met in desirable ways, helps them learn important social behaviors to deal effectively with increased social demands, and positively impacts their learning (Cartledge & Lo, 2006; Cook et al., 2008; Docksai, 2010). For peers and teachers, social skills instruction results in a more positive school climate and more time for teachers to spend on academic instruction instead of discipline, leading to a more rewarding learning and teaching experience.

WHAT IS SKILLSTREAMING?

Skillstreaming is an evidence-based strategy designed to systematically teach social skills to address the needs of students who display aggression, immaturity, withdrawal, or other problem behaviors. For elementary-age students, this means skills to successfully navigate their school environments, follow teacher expectations, deal with peer and adult conflict, and deal with the many feelings typical of students in this age group. The Skillstreaming process focuses on four principles of learning. These learning procedures—modeling, role-playing, performance feedback, and generalization training—have been used to teach a variety of behaviors, from academic competencies to sports, daily living skills, and vocational skills. They are applied in Skillstreaming to teach students desirable social behaviors.

Before discussing what Skillstreaming is in more detail, it is important to point out what it is not: Skillstreaming is not an affective education strategy that focuses primarily on discussion of feelings and the individual's strengths as a way to foster positive self-concept. Although discussion is a part, Skillstreaming engages students in active learning through role-playing and practice. Skillstreaming will not address all children's needs in every situation at all times. Instead, it is a well-validated instructional procedure that should be included with other techniques, such as behavior intervention planning, conflict resolution, and cooperative learning. Nor is Skillstreaming a procedure for teaching compliance skills, the focus of some skills-training programs. Although it will teach students the skills needed to follow school rules better, the program is mainly intended to teach students the skills needed to solve problems that occur in their daily lives, to be assertive in handling situations that cause them stress or unhappiness, and to increase the chance that they will have satisfying relationships with others.

A Skill-Deficit Model

The Skillstreaming model makes the assumption that the learner is weak in or lacks a behavioral skill or skills within his or her skill repertoire. The goal, then, becomes teaching desirable skills. This assumption is made for several very important reasons. First, the belief that most students do not know how to act productively in given situations lessens the frustration experienced by many teachers when a child seems continually to react in the same inappropriate way despite efforts to address the behavior. This assumption allows teachers to focus on proactive instruction instead of reacting to the child's misbehavior as if it were done purposefully to create problems. In addition, the assumption of skill deficit sets the stage for instruction in social skills that the student may actually use and that the teacher can therefore prompt. The assumption furthermore suggests to the student that the teacher and others will be patient and encouraging during the learning of these sometimes very difficult skills.

In Skillstreaming workshops for trainers, the skill-deficit model is readily illustrated by asking participants to think of a time they agreed to do something asked by a friend, relative, or acquaintance but which they really did not want to do. Most participants quickly identify situations in which, as adults, they have felt pressured into doing something they didn't want to do, whether it was allowing a neighbor to borrow the lawn mower or taking on extra job responsibilities. In a practice environment, group members are asked to respond to such requests by Saying No (Skill 55). The majority of participants experience difficulty with this skill, even in the practice setting! Yet many times the expectation is that students, even at the elementary level, will be able to resist peer pressure by quickly and emphatically expressing their feelings appropriately.

Researchers in the area of social skills training—for example Gresham, Sugai, and Horner (2001), Gresham (2002), and Gresham et al. (2006)—advocate that practitioners consider the difference between a skill deficit (can't) and a performance deficit (won't). These authors explain that a child with a skill deficit lacks the knowledge of how to perform a skill or how to select which skill is appropriate in a given situation. Other children, like the workshop participants just described, may know how to perform a skill but lack the fluency in skill use necessary to execute the skill in a competent manner. Others may experience competing problem behaviors, such as poor self-control, which inhibit their skill use. Still others may know how to carry out a skill but fail to do so because of lack of positive reinforcement (a performance deficit). Some children with increased social anxiety have a social information processing deficit (Crick & Dodge, 1994; Raine et al., 2006). In other words, they experience errors in how they think about and respond to social cues. In practice, acquisition (can't do), performance (won't do), fluency, and competing problem behaviors will be addressed within the context of a skill deficit, with particular emphasis placed on addressing the type of deficit throughout the Skillstreaming instructional process.

Planned, Systematic Instruction

Most educators recognize that the days of defining public education's goal only as teaching basic academic competencies are over. With increased emphasis on student achievement, instruction in social skills and social-emotional learning is gaining in acceptance (Docksai, 2010). Educators, counselors, and therapists have also increased their understanding that students or clients need to be taught desirable behaviors in the same planned and systematic way academic skills are taught (Maag, 2006). Incidental learning (discussing alternatives or telling students what to do) is insufficient for students to learn alternative behaviors, just as it is insufficient to tell students how to divide and expect that they will be able to complete division problems. Whatever the reason for a student's skill lack or weakness, schools must establish and implement procedures to teach these skills, just as they would in the case of academic deficits.

A Way to Improve School Climate

Creating a welcoming and positive school climate is recognized as a critical factor in increasing academic learning. Historically, educational interventions dealing with student behavior problems have concentrated on strategies to diminish or extinguish behaviors of concern (e.g., time-out, loss of privileges). Although reinforcement strategies are effective in increasing positive behaviors, it is necessary to wait until a behavior is displayed before it can be rewarded. Thus, many students with infrequent appropriate behaviors rarely receive positive reinforcement; in most cases, they receive an abundance of negative feedback. Although negative procedures may be useful as part of a comprehensive behavior intervention plan, overemphasis may further discourage children with behavior problems. For these students, positive feelings about school and learning itself are unlikely. Creating a better balance of positive to negative consequences is necessary to foster a positive school climate.

Teaching prosocial skills provides the elementary school child with opportunities to be successful in both hypothetical and real-life situations and lends a sense of balance to behavior management programs. Although inappropriate behaviors will continue to need intervention, through Skillstreaming, students have the opportunity to build alternative socially acceptable behaviors to increase their opportunities. Teachers and others will also find that prompting students to use a previously learned social skill when problematic situations arise in the classroom or in other school settings will often stop the student's inappropriate actions in midstream and channel his or her energies in a more prosocial direction. Like reminding a student to use a reading strategy to master unknown vocabulary, when given in a helpful and encouraging manner, such prompting fosters a positive classroom and school climate.

A Way to Enhance Self-Esteem

A description of an elementary-age child with difficult behaviors often includes the phrase "poor self-esteem." Counselors, teachers, and others often struggle to design interventions that improve the child's positive feelings about himself or herself. One way of addressing this issue is to teach the student to be more competent. The traditional focus on academic competence recognizes that such competence contributes to the child's positive feelings about self in relation to achievement. Likewise, increasing competence in a variety of socially related skills will improve an individual's self-concept.

Although behavior management programs are useful, necessary, and very often effective in reducing problem behaviors, emphasis on such programs alone may reinforce in students the idea that adults are the dispensers of all rewards and punishments. The child may learn to believe that whatever he or she might do or however he or she might act, the positive or negative results of these actions will be determined by someone else in power—a teacher, parent, or other adult. Such a belief, referred to as an *external locus of control,* can foster feelings of helplessness. When students learn, for example, to handle conflict in ways that yield approval from others, they also learn a sense of responsibility and control. They more easily make the connection between their actions (e.g., use of a skill) and positive consequences. When students learn that they have the skills and ability to effect change, their self-esteem is likely to improve.

Remediation and Prevention

The Skillstreaming approach provides remediation for students who are significantly deficient in prosocial skills whether or not they are receiving special education services. The student with a learning disability may need to learn the skill of Asking for Help (Skill 2), as well as organizational skills such as Following Instructions (Skill 5). The child with an identified attention deficit may have a particular need to learn the skills of Completing Assignments (Skill 6) and Ignoring Distractions (Skill 10). Children with more severe disabilities, such as autism or cognitive disabilities, can be taught a variety of social skills to enhance independence and to make their lives more satisfying. Those with emotional or behavioral disorders—whether characterized by withdrawal, aggression, or immaturity—continue to benefit from learning prosocial skills. Although aggression and violence are very visible and perhaps cause more stress to teachers, school administrators, parents, and others, teaching prosocial skills to the withdrawn child or the student who reacts immaturely or inadequately is also important.

Skillstreaming is also intended for the general education population—students whose behavior is not significantly problematic but who will increase their personal satisfaction and happiness by learning or improving upon prosocial skills. How many young people do we know who, when they reach adolescence, have significant problems dealing with stress or with interpersonal relationships when none were noticed in earlier grades? Many students may need help with skills to form satisfying interpersonal relationships, participate in problem solving, or deal productively with day-to-day stress. Undertaking instruction with students who do not yet experience significant problems offers the hope of preventing future difficulties.

A Strategy to Help Prevent Violence and Aggression

As discussed in more detail later in this introduction, a need exists to address the increase in school violence by teaching students prosocial ways of resolving conflict, proactive problem solving, and the social skills necessary to enhance self-esteem and engender a sense of belonging. Aggressive children, for example, learn quickly and at an early age that they can get what they want by hitting, pushing, biting, and so forth. Because aggression is a remarkably stable behavior and is unlikely to change without intervention, alternatives to aggression need to be taught early. Skillstreaming is one method of doing just that.

SKILLS FOR ELEMENTARY SCHOOL CHILDREN

Social skills, as defined by Gresham (1998a) are "socially acceptable learned behaviors enabling individuals to interact effectively with others and avoid or escape socially unacceptable behaviors exhibited by others" (p. 20). Caldarella and Merrell (1997) reviewed studies conducted using social skills rating scales or inventories and found five broad dimensions of social skills, including peer relation skills, self-management skills, academic skills, compliance skills, and assertion skills. Gresham et al. (2006) took a somewhat different perspective and identified two categories: *replacement behaviors,* which are the skills that serve the same function or purpose as the problem behavior, and *socially valid skills,* or those that include a set of competencies to enhance initiating and maintaining positive relationships, facilitate peer acceptance and friendships, contribute to satisfactory school adjustment, and allow students to cope with and adapt to the social demands of the given environment.

The 60 skills in this curriculum, shown in Table 1, involve those social behaviors believed to be related to peer acceptance (Dodge, 1983; Greenwood, Todd, Hops, & Walker, 1978); school success, including self-control and cooperation (Cartledge & Milburn, 1980; Lane, Givner, & Pierson, 2004; Lane, Wehby, & Cooley, 2006); and social success (Chen, 2006; Fox & Boulton, 2003; Spivack & Shure, 1974; Warden & MacKinnon, 2003), as well as those likely to enhance children's personal satisfaction (Goldstein & McGinnis, 1997). Additional prosocial skills have been selected to teach alternatives to the maladaptive behaviors often employed by unpopular or rejected children, such as poor cooperation (Coie & Kupersmidt, 1983; Meier, DiPerna & Oster, 2006), anxiety (Buhremester, 1982), disruptive behaviors (Dodge, Coie, & Bralke, 1982), poor interpersonal problem solving (Chen, 2006), and verbal and physical aggression (Dodge et al., 1982). In addition, social skills include those related to academic performance, such as the ability to work in groups and respond appropriately to adult correction and other feedback, and building and maintaining friendships (Gresham et al., 2001).

UNDERSTANDING VIOLENCE AND AGGRESSION

Although Skillstreaming is effective in changing the behavior of children and adolescents displaying a wide range of skill deficits, it is particularly effective in providing alternatives to aggression. Because aggression is such a problem among children and youth in schools and other settings, an overview of its causes and characteristics is important for teachers, support staff, administrators, and others involved in implementing Skillstreaming.

General factors associated with increased violence in schools and communities include frequent exposure to violence through the media, violent role models, health factors such as prenatal substance abuse, poverty, inadequate or abusive parenting, lack of social skills, discrimination, and lack of educational and job opportunities (National Association for the Education of Young Children, 1993). School demographics, such as the school level (elementary, middle, high school), neighborhood crime rate, and school location (city, urban fringe, rural), are additional factors impacting both crime and school disruptions (Nickerson & Martens, 2008).

Although a predisposition toward violent behavior may exist as a result of hereditary, hormonal, or biological factors (e.g., traumatic head injury), aggression is primarily a learned behavior. John Reid, clinical psychologist and director of the Oregon Social Learning Center in Eugene, has analyzed numerous studies suggesting that the two strongest predictors of violence and delinquency are ineffective, harsh, abusive, emotional discipline and lack of parental supervision (Bourland, 1995). Patterson, Reid, Jones, and Conger (1975) discuss these actions by describing a cycle of aggression that begins with coercive parenting. In this cycle, the parent reacts to the child in a hostile, threatening, or irritated manner. The parent is inconsistent in his or her discipline, at times providing very tight supervision and at other times providing almost no supervision at all. Discipline is characterized by yelling and corporal punishment. At times, the child will comply with the parent's coercion, providing a natural reward for the parent's disciplinary action. At other times, the child will act coercively in return—yelling, threatening, hitting, and so on.

As children so parented grow older, they deal with peer confrontations in a similar manner. If they want a toy, they take it. If they don't like something another child has said, they hit or kick. Other children (or these children's parents) react by not including aggressive children, thus limiting the positive models from whom aggressive children can learn alternative behaviors and leading to social isolation. As aggressive children reach school age, they fulfill their need to have friends by seeking out peers who react similarly.

Table 1: Skillstreaming Curriculum for Elementary Students

Group I: Classroom Survival Skills

1. Listening
2. Asking for Help
3. Saying Thank You
4. Bringing Materials to Class
5. Following Instructions
6. Completing Assignments
7. Contributing to Discussions
8. Offering Help to an Adult
9. Asking a Question
10. Ignoring Distractions
11. Making Corrections
12. Deciding on Something to Do
13. Setting a Goal

Group II: Friendship-Making Skills

14. Introducing Yourself
15. Beginning a Conversation
16. Ending a Conversation
17. Joining In
18. Playing a Game
19. Asking a Favor
20. Offering Help to a Classmate
21. Giving a Compliment
22. Accepting a Compliment
23. Suggesting an Activity
24. Sharing
25. Apologizing

Group III: Skills for Dealing with Feelings

26. Knowing Your Feelings
27. Expressing Your Feelings
28. Recognizing Another's Feelings
29. Showing Understanding of Another's Feelings
30. Expressing Concern for Another

31. Dealing with Your Anger
32. Dealing with Another's Anger
33. Expressing Affection
34. Dealing with Fear
35. Rewarding Yourself

Group IV: Skill Alternatives to Aggression

36. Using Self-Control
37. Asking Permission
38. Responding to Teasing
39. Avoiding Trouble
40. Staying Out of Fights
41. Problem Solving
42. Accepting Consequences
43. Dealing with an Accusation
44. Negotiating

Group V: Skills for Dealing with Stress

45. Dealing with Boredom
46. Deciding What Caused a Problem
47. Making a Complaint
48. Answering a Complaint
49. Dealing with Losing
50. Being a Good Sport
51. Dealing with Being Left Out
52. Dealing with Embarrassment
53. Reacting to Failure
54. Accepting No
55. Saying No
56. Relaxing
57. Dealing with Group Pressure
58. Dealing with Wanting Something That Isn't Yours
59. Making a Decision
60. Being Honest

From *Skillstreaming the Elementary School Child: Teaching Prosocial Skills* (3rd ed.), © 2012 by E. McGinnis, Champaign, IL: Research Press (www.researchpress.com, 800-519-2707).

Thus, the main characteristics of children who are the targets of coercive parenting are inadequate social skills and high levels of aggression both in and out of school.

A cycle similar to the one described by Patterson and colleagues (1975) in the home environment can often be seen in school. The child who refuses to follow directions in school may be yelled at by the teacher. The one who verbally threatens to hit a peer may be threatened with punishment. The teacher's aggression (e.g., yelling, punishing) may further intensify the student's anger and problem behavior (Gemelli, 1996). Adults displaying such actions provide a powerful negative model for dealing with conflict, inadvertently teaching undesirable behaviors.

Aggressive children have been found to generate fewer alternative solutions when presented with problem situations, and their repertoires of solutions include fewer nonaggressive options (Camodeca, Goossens, Schuengel, & Terwogt, 2003). Instead, aggressive children offer more action-oriented solutions, such as pushing and fighting (Asarnow & Callan, 1985). Further, aggressive children anticipate that more positive outcomes and fewer negative outcomes will occur after an act of aggression (Hubbard, Dodge, Cillessen, Coie, & Schwartz, 2001).

Dodge, Lockman, Harnish, Bates, and Pettit (1997) and Crick and Dodge (1996) distinguish between two types of aggression: reactive and proactive. *Reactive aggression* is a response to frustration and the result of a child's diminished capacity for self-control. Aggressive behavior thus serves as a defense against a peer who is perceived as harmful. As stated by Guerra, Boxer, and Kim (2005), "An aggressive child is more likely to attend to aggression-promoting cues (e.g., being bumped into by a peer) and less likely to properly address prosocial cues (e.g., the peer subsequently apologizing)" (p. 279). The child's perception of hostile intent in results in a retaliatory response often accompanied with anger and high levels of social anxiety. *Proactive aggression* is a less emotional and more object-directed and organized response, likely driven by the expectation of receiving a reward. Proactive aggression, used to coerce or influence another, has been associated with criminal behavior (Raine et al., 2006).

Crick and Dodge (1994) hypothesize that reactive aggression is the result of a child's social information processing deficit. In other words, there are errors in how a child thinks about and therefore responds to social cues. The child approaches social situations based on both biological capacity and "a database of memories of past experiences" (p. 76). The child's response is dependent upon how these cues or events are processed. In this model of social information processing, the child's ongoing social experiences will contribute to his or her social knowledge in both quantitative and qualitative ways. Therefore, it is important to build the child's social knowledge by teaching alternative prosocial options.

INCLUDED IN THIS BOOK

This book provides a clear guide to understanding and using the Skillstreaming program with elementary-age children. Part 1 includes chapters devoted to program content and implementation. Part 2 provides Skill Outlines and Homework Reports for each of the 60 skills in the curriculum.

Chapter 1, "Effective Skillstreaming Arrangements," describes the procedures necessary to plan and begin Skillstreaming at the elementary level. Discussion concerns the specific arrangements to maximize the effectiveness of Skillstreaming instruction and the settings in which it occurs. Specifically discussed are group leader selection and preparation; student selection and grouping; the role of support staff and parents in instruction; and specific instructional concerns such as skill selection, setting, materials, and instructional variations.

More than 30 years of research supports the individual components of modeling, role-play (behavioral rehearsal), feedback, and generalization training, as well as the positive results when the four components are implemented together. Chapter 2, "Skillstreaming Teaching Procedures," examines these four core teaching procedures of Skillstreaming, along with the nine-step sequence constituting the Skillstreaming teaching method.

Chapter 3, "Sample Skillstreaming Session," offers an edited transcript of an introductory Skillstreaming session with two leaders and a group of children in an elementary classroom. This transcript depicts the leaders introducing students to the group's purpose and procedures and follows the Skillstreaming teaching procedures discussed in chapter 2. The skill used for instruction is Responding to Teasing (Skill 38).

A challenge in intervention work is to match the intensity of the child's need to the type and amount of intervention. Chapter 4, "Refining Skill Use," describes factors that increase the effectiveness of Skillstreaming, as well as other skill-building strategies that may be incorporated for students with more intense behavioral concerns. Real-world use of this skill curriculum, especially in the face of difficult and challenging interpersonal circumstances, will require that students be skilled in employing skill sequences and combinations, also included in this chapter.

As evidence regarding Skillstreaming's effectiveness has accumulated, it has become clear that skill acquisition is a reliable finding. The main concern of any teaching effort is not how students perform in the teaching setting but how well they perform in their real lives. Chapter 5, "Teaching for Skill Generalization," examines approaches to enhance transfer and maintenance of skill learning.

Chapter 6, "Managing Behavior Problems," addresses issues in the group reflecting deficient motivation and heightened resistance and describes a framework of universal, targeted, and individual strategies for enhancing motivation and reducing resistance. Examination of individual strategies includes discussion of functional

behavioral assessment (FBA) and steps in creating a behavior intervention plan (BIP).

Establishing positive relationships between families and the school is necessary to improve student behavior, as well as academic skills. A positive working relationship with parents is important to Skillstreaming success. Therefore, this is the subject of chapter 7, "Building Positive Relationships with Parents."

Finally, chapter 8, "Skillstreaming in the School Context," reviews issues surrounding school violence and discusses Skillstreaming as a viable schoolwide intervention for reducing aggression and other behavior problems in schools. Specifically examined are such topics as integrating Skillstreaming in the curriculum and the role of Skillstreaming as it relates to inclusion, multitiered systems of support, positive behavior intervention and support (PBIS), and Response to Intervention (RTI).

Following these chapters, Part 2 presents Skillstreaming's 60 skills for the elementary-age child. Provided for each skill are a Skill Outline and two different Homework Reports. The Skill Outline includes the behavioral steps of the skill, notes for group leaders further explaining the steps, and suggested situations for modeling displays. Outlines and reports may be reproduced from this book or printed from the accompanying CD.

Three appendixes complete the book. Appendix A includes forms helpful in running the program in addition to the Skill Outlines and Homework Reports included in Part 2. These may be photocopied or printed from the CD at the back of this book. Recent research has pointed to the need to monitor the consistency and accuracy of program implementation. Appendix B therefore includes implementation checklists for leaders and those who supervise them, as well as for ensuring generalization integrity. Appendix C examines behavior management techniques based on behavior modification principles that are helpful in the Skillstreaming group and in general.

PART I

Skillstreaming Program Content and Implementation

CHAPTER 1

Effective Skillstreaming Arrangements

This chapter describes specific arrangements to organize and maximize the effectiveness of the Skillstreaming instructional environment. In particular, discussion concerns group leader selection and preparation; student selection, grouping, and preparation; the role of support staff and parents; specific instructional concerns such as skill selection and negotiation, setting, and materials; and instructional variations.

GROUP LEADER SELECTION AND PREPARATION

Since Skillstreaming began, hundreds of persons with a wide variety of backgrounds and positions have been effective group leaders. Teachers, counselors, and psychologists in the schools; youth care workers in treatment facilities and delinquency centers; and social workers in mental health and other community agencies are primary examples of such personnel.

In the school setting or in any instructional group focusing on skill building, several qualities of effective group leadership are apparent. Specifically, these include general teaching skills, knowledge and understanding of Skillstreaming procedures, skills in managing behavior problems, cultural understanding of group members, and motivation.

General Teaching Skills

In a Skillstreaming group, as in any learning environment, effective teaching skills are necessary.

First, the competent leader demonstrates good group-process skills. For example, rather than presenting a lecture, the leader listens to what the students are saying, gives feedback to let students know their viewpoints have been heard, and then adjusts instruction according to the needs of participants. Much of the Skillstreaming group can be directed by the students themselves (e.g., selection of topics, skill sequences, role-plays) with the group leader's acting as facilitator.

A second quality of effective group leadership, also a component of group processing, is the ability to manage any behavior problems that may arise throughout instruction. One child may persist in a lengthy discussion that bores the rest of the group, another student may have difficulty paying attention, and still another may refuse to participate at all. The skilled leader is able to respond to such events in a firm, helpful, and unobtrusive manner and to maintain the flow of instruction. Chapter 6 presents a number of techniques for preventing and reducing the frequency or intensity of problem behaviors. Effective leaders use these strategies while keeping in mind the goal of providing an encouraging environment for learning. The child's behavior, rather than the child himself or herself, is always the target.

The teaching agenda, as described in chapter 2, is delivered in a clear and organized fashion. Techniques that contribute to low aggression in the classroom are used in the group. Specifically, transitions from one activity to another are smooth, the lesson moves at an energetic pace, students are actively engaged, and the relevance of skills to students' real-life needs is emphasized.

Knowledge of Skillstreaming

In addition to general teaching skills, what specific knowledge is needed to make Skillstreaming instruction most effective? The following list describes the areas of preparation teachers or other leaders of Skillstreaming groups need, including skills and knowledge to implement procedures.

1. Knowledge of Skillstreaming background, goals, and procedures

2. Ability to orient participating children, support staff members, and parents to Skillstreaming

3. Ability to assess student needs and select skills relevant to children's real-life needs, emphasizing assertiveness and problem-solving skills

4. Ability to plan and present live modeling displays, including presentation of a coping model and verbal mediation techniques

5. Ability to initiate and sustain role-playing

6. Ability to present material in a sequential, clear, and detailed manner

7. Accuracy and sensitivity in providing encouragement and corrective feedback

8. Willingness to accept children's use of prosocial behaviors

9. Sensitivity to situations throughout the day in which skills could be used and prompting of appropriate skill use

Teachers and other group leaders may prepare for the Skillstreaming group in a variety of ways, depending on their own learning styles. Some may read and study this Skillstreaming program book, then be ready to begin. Others may read and study the Skillstreaming materials, then choose to attend a workshop or training session, finding that listening to others who have implemented the techniques successfully augments what they have read. Still others may rely on the demonstration of real-life groups in operation presented in *The Skillstreaming Video* (Goldstein & McGinnis, 1988).

Although there is no right or wrong way to prepare to teach a Skillstreaming group, many adult learners respond most effectively to what might be called an apprenticeship training sequence. Reading this book, viewing *The Skillstreaming Video,* and attending a workshop are first steps in this sequence. A good next step is the opportunity to participate first in a mock Skillstreaming group led by experienced trainers and made up of leaders-to-be pretending to be students. After one or more such role-play opportunities, the potential group leader can observe an experienced leader conduct an actual group, then co-lead a group with the experienced leader, and, finally, lead the group while being observed by the experienced leader. This incremental training sequence, each of its steps adjustable in duration, has proven to be most satisfactory in training Skillstreaming group leaders.

In a school setting, for example, school social workers, psychologists, or counselors often carry out Skillstreaming groups, pulling individual children from various classrooms, or a counselor may co-teach Skillstreaming with the general education teacher in the classroom. A group of classroom teachers might request staff development training, which would first include participation in a mock Skillstreaming group. During planning time, individual teachers could observe, then participate as co-leader in an ongoing skills group. Support staff could then assist teachers in beginning groups in their own regular or special classroom settings. Some support staff and teachers together have decided to continue this team arrangement, with the teacher running the group alone only when the other leader must be absent.

Managing the Group

A variety of activities included in Skillstreaming will keep the enthusiastic attention of most students within the recommended time frame

(25 to 40 minutes). If classroom rules have not been previously identified, they should be decided on prior to implementing Skillstreaming groups, discussed daily with the children to ensure understanding, and posted in the classroom. Rewarding such behaviors by praising children's efforts will help children feel positive about learning new prosocial behaviors.

Should behavioral concerns surface in the large group, a total-group management plan may be implemented. This type of plan might consist of a group checklist for desired behaviors, then providing a special activity for the entire group (e.g., extra recess) when goals are met. Such plans may motivate the group to work cooperatively and may also increase the children's individual motivation. Students who have disabilities relating specifically to behavior, as well as others who frequently exhibit behavior problems, may need an even more structured plan to reinforce desirable group behaviors.

Though a great many Skillstreaming groups have been productively led by one teacher alone, whenever possible, two staff members should work together. Skill-deficient children are often quite proficient in generating the behavior management problems that make successful training difficult. To arrange and conduct a role-play between two children while at the same time overseeing the attention of other, easily distractible group members is daunting for anyone. A much better arrangement involves two teachers (or one teacher and another adult, such as a paraprofessional, volunteer, or school support staff member). One stands at the front of the group and leads the role-play while the second sits in the group, preferably next to the child or children most likely to have attention problems or act disruptively.

Cultural Understanding

Skillstreaming group leaders need to demonstrate cultural proficiency. As defined by Robins, Lindsey, Lindsey, and Terrell (2006), "Cultural proficiency is a way of being that allows individuals and organizations to interact effectively with people who differ from them" (p. 2). Which specific behaviors ideally define a given Skillstreaming skill? Which skills are optimal for use in any given setting? Which teaching and learning processes will best be used to acquire a skill? The answers will vary from culture to culture. Whether culture is defined by geography, ethnicity, nationality, social class, gender, sexual orientation, age, or some combination thereof, for Skillstreaming to be meaningful it must be viewed and practiced within a multicultural context.

When teachers are members of or are only minimally familiar with different cultural groups, definitions and prescriptions may conflict. Learning goals may not be met. Teachers must be aware of cultural differences so they can determine which behaviors are in actuality social skills deficits and which behaviors are a part of the child's culture and should either be appreciated as they are displayed or be modified according to specific situations (Cartledge & Kourea, 2008; Cartledge & Lo, 2006; Cartledge & Milburn, 1996). For example, youngsters may engage in verbal bantering that appears to observers from a different cultural orientation to be aggressive, yet these behaviors may be common and acceptable in their culture. In such an instance, the behaviors themselves do not need to be changed; instead, instructional emphasis may need to be placed on when and where such verbal exchanges are appropriate within the school context. Typical examples of such differences include acceptability of assertiveness and nonverbal communication. For example, children from African American backgrounds tend to be more assertive, while individuals from Hispanic American, Native American, and Asian American backgrounds tend to be more passive, and Anglo students need more physical space between speakers than do other cultural groups (Elksnin & Elksnin, 2000). In contrasting Asian American culture with predominantly Western culture, Cartledge and Feng (1996) encourage teachers to "validate cultural background, making sure learners understand that certain situations will call for different responses, not that their ways of doing things are inferior" (p. 112). When we fail to address such cultural differences, students certainly will suffer. For instance, African American students are more frequently perceived by educators to have social difficulties (Harry & Klingner, 2006) and are more often identified for special education services than are students from other groups (Donovan & Cross, 2002).

Classrooms in this country are increasingly characterized by different languages, cultures, and learning styles. With the increase in diversity, Perea (2004) has aptly observed that "there is no longer a single American culture to assimilate into" (p. 36). To reach all students, group leaders will to the degree possible employ materials that are consistent with a diversity of backgrounds and learning styles (i.e., "appropriate") and that have been selected in active and continuing consultation with persons representing the cultural groups concerned (i.e., "appreciative"). In discussing social skills interventions and what educators can do to interact with a culturally diverse student population, Cartledge and Johnson (1997) state:

> Social skill interventions are not to be viewed as a means for controlling students for the comfort of teachers or for homogenizing students so they conform to some middle-class prototype designated by the majority group in this society. Inherent in the concept of culturally-relevant social skill instruction is a reciprocal process where the educator: (a) learns to respect the learner's cultural background, (b) encourages the learner to appreciate the richness of this culture, (c) when needed, helps the learner to acquire additional or alternative behaviors as demanded by the social situation, and (d) similarly employs and practices the taught behaviors. (p. 404)

Skillstreaming will be most effective when it is delivered in a manner appreciative of and responsive to such notions as skill strengths and differences versus skill deficits, differential teaching strategies and instructional methods, student channels of accessibility and communication styles, stereotyping of and by culturally different student populations, and culturally associated characteristics of the target students. Culturally proficient instructional strategies may include multiple response techniques, appropriate pacing, establishing a community of learners, use of models from the learner's cultural group, incorporating the learner's language into instructional scripts, and involving parents in support of the instruction (Cartledge & Kourea, 2008). Teacher knowledge, skill, and sensitivity are required.

Motivation

Effective group leaders believe in what they are teaching and demonstrate enthusiasm, thus conveying an excitement in learning. Believing in the efficacy of the intervention contributes to the fidelity of implementation (implementing the Skillstreaming teaching agenda as designed). Group leader motivation may be increased by a thorough understanding of the rationale for Skillstreaming presented in this book and by mastering the program procedures.

Generally, however, the decision to learn and teach this particular approach is typically motivated by the potential group leader's desire to enhance his or her own teaching or intervention skill to better serve children. Teachers and other professionals who work with children with behavioral problems typically do so to make a difference. Implementing Skillstreaming additionally will motivate both classroom teachers and administrators because reduced behavior problems will allow them more focus on teaching and learning. Teachers who implement Skillstreaming in their classrooms often hear positive comments from other school staff regarding their students' behavior. For example, one principal queried a special education teacher, "I rarely see any of your students in the office for discipline anymore. What is it you are doing in your classroom?" These types of rewards are immeasurable for both teachers and their students.

STUDENT SELECTION, GROUPING, AND PREPARATION

Student Selection

Skillstreaming is a method for teaching an extended curriculum of interpersonal, aggression management, and related skills to children who are weak or lacking in these competencies. The assessment task, therefore, is twofold: first, to identify those children who can benefit from direct instruction in skill building and, second, to determine the level of proficiency or deficiency in necessary skills. For a culturally diverse group, the assessment process will need to take into account "differences versus deficits" (Cartledge & Milburn, 1996).

The selection process for elementary school children may involve a number of assessment strategies, including sociometrics, role-play observations, behavior rating scales, naturalistic observations, and skill checklists. The two latter strategies are the most user friendly and are the ones that lead most directly from assessment to instruction. It is important to remember, however, that assessment results are most useful when more than one type of evaluation procedure is implemented (i.e., the assessment is multimodal) and when the child's strengths and deficits are assessed in a variety of situations and settings and by a variety of individuals—for example, peers, adults, parents (i.e., it is multisource). In most Skillstreaming programs, such assessment has typically involved each child's teacher and parent, as well as the child. It is common, however, for discrepancies between adult and child ratings to occur. Whether such a discrepancy reflects overconfidence, denial, blaming others, lack of ability to assess one's own skills, or some other process in the child's perception, it is important to get the perspective of each child on his or her own skill strengths and weaknesses. Teaching the skills the student believes necessary has proven to be a major motivational tactic.

Direct Observation

Direct, or naturalistic, observation involves observing what the child does at particular times or in particular situations. Such observations, easily implemented by a classroom teacher, might involve taking frequency counts (e.g., how often a child deals with being teased or reacts to frustration in a particular manner), recording duration (e.g., how long it takes for a student to decide on something to do or the length of a crying episode), or making anecdotal records (e.g., what specific behaviors are of concern and their antecedents and consequences). Direct observation is especially valuable if the person or persons who are planning to serve as group leaders (teachers, youth care workers, etc.) are the same persons who routinely see the child in interactions with others. In such circumstances, the behavioral observations can be frequent, take place in the child's natural environment, and reflect skill competence across diverse settings and situations.

Direct observation is one method that is also advocated in assessing the goal or purpose of the child's behavior, as in a functional behavioral assessment. Seeking to determine the student's motivation for engaging in a given maladaptive behavior will better help the adults who work with the child develop alternative, prosocial behavior plans, strategies, and skills to serve the same function for that child.

Skill Checklists

Skill checklists are designed to assess various individuals' perceptions of a student's skill proficiency. Checklists for teachers and other school staff, parents, and students are included in Appendix A. The Teacher/Staff Checklist is completed by a teacher or another person in the school environment who is familiar with the student's behaviors in a variety of situations. The rater is asked to gauge the frequency of a particular student's use of each of the 60 Skillstreaming skills. The checklist also provides an opportunity for the rater to identify situations in which skill use is particularly problematic, information that will be useful for later modeling scenarios. The numerical value assigned to each skill targets the most important skills for that child, leading to effective grouping of students and prioritizing of skills for instruction.

In situations in which whole-class instruction in Skillstreaming will be provided, the checklist may be used in two ways. First, a checklist may be completed for target students, those who demonstrated a high level of problem behavior. Second, checklists completed for all students can provide a picture of overall student behavior or the skills in which the majority of students in the classroom struggle. Both approaches provide additional guidance for skill instruction.

The Parent Checklist is completed by the student's parent in an attempt to assess the parent's perceptions of the child's skill levels in the home and neighborhood. As is the case for the Teacher/Staff Checklist, parents are asked to respond to descriptions of the 60 prosocial skills in terms of frequency of skill use. Even though information relative to the student's skill use outside of the school setting may be useful to the teacher in identifying specific skills, in planning modeling displays, and in encouraging role-play scenarios, some discretion in requesting a parent to complete this checklist is in order. As an alternative to requesting that a parent complete the entire checklist, specific questions on the checklist may be selected to assess the child's strengths and weaknesses in skill areas that are of concern in the school setting. Parents may also be asked to respond to portions of the checklist during an interview.

The Student Checklist is designed to assess students' perceptions of their own skill proficiency. Requesting students to complete this self-rating may enhance their awareness of the skills they need to learn. Their willingness to participate actively in the group will likely be increased if students see the relevance of the skills to their daily lives (e.g., as a way of having more satisfactory peer relationships). The checklist is written at a third-grade reading level and is suggested for independent administration at this level or higher. It may, however, be simplified and read individually or in small-group settings to younger students or to students less proficient in reading. Because of its length, the teacher may decide to give only a part of the checklist at one time. It may take two or more sessions spaced a day or so apart to complete the entire checklist.

Student Grouping

Once selected for participation, children are grouped according to two criteria. The first criterion is shared skill deficiency. It is useful to group students who share similar skill deficiencies or patterns of deficits. By doing so, instruction more intensely provides skill remediation in the areas of need for selected students. The Grouping Chart (Appendix A) is designed to summarize the scores on all 60 skills for entire classes, units, or other large sets of youngsters and can readily be used to identify shared skill deficiencies.

The second grouping criterion concerns the generalization-enhancing principle of *identical elements*. This principle is discussed at greater length in chapter 5, on generalization. The heart of this notion is that the greater the similarity between qualities of the teaching session and the real-world setting, the greater the likelihood that the student will use the skill outside the group. Cross-setting similarity is operationalized by constructing Skillstreaming groups from the same class, living unit, neighborhood, and the like. Classroom-based instruction is especially effective because of this important generalization principle, as well as because teachers are available to prompt skill use when situations in the classroom occur. When instruction is carried out in this manner, it functions as a universal intervention, reaching all students who may benefit. Some students may need more intense interventions (e.g., increased instructional time, additional interventions). In such cases, Skillstreaming in a whole-class model will be only a part of the behavior change plan.

Student Preparation

After student selection and grouping, the next task is preparing students for Skillstreaming group participation. Preparation is conducted first on an individual basis to provide information about the group routine and to motivate the student to participate by relating the process to his or her real-life needs. A similar introduction then occurs when the group first meets. This introduction to Skillstreaming covers the following topics.

Purposes

A description of the purposes of the group as related to the child's specific skill deficits comes first. For example, the teacher might say something like the following.

Individual student preparation

> Remember on Tuesday when you threw the rock at Sam when you were angry and then lost the privilege of being on the playground with your class? In this group, you'll learn skills to help you stay out of that kind of trouble so that you can have your recess with the others.

Group preparation

> Knowing how to deal with conflict with others requires us to learn some new skills. Remember how, as a class, we've talked about problems with name-calling and fighting? In this group you'll learn skills to handle problems with your friends and classmates in better ways so you won't get into trouble and will earn your privileges.

Statements such as these can serve both preparatory and motivational purposes.

Procedures

Next is a general description of the procedures involved in Skillstreaming. This might include something like the following.

Individual student and group preparation

> In order to handle difficult situations in ways that will keep you out of trouble but will still help you get what you need, we'll first show you a good example of the skill. Then you and the others in your group will take turns trying the skill in the group. We'll all talk about how well we did, and then you'll try out the skill on your own in a situation where you need to use it.

This brief description of modeling, role-play, feedback, and generalization procedures is illustrated more completely once students have actually participated in a Skillstreaming session.

Incentives

After the description of procedures comes an explanation of any incentive plans or systems in place in the class, school, agency, or institution. These include strategies such as token rewards, points, privilege/level systems, or other reinforcement plans. Although the relevance of skills to real life motivates most elementary-age children, in the initial stages of this type of group work it is often helpful to plan and implement a reinforcement system to help manage problem behaviors and encourage participation. Whether in the form of tokens, points, or verbal praise, frequent positive reinforcement is important in the initial stages of learning any new skill.

Rules/Expectations

Rules to guide student behavior have long been used in elementary classrooms. Chapter 6 presents a series of useful "rules for the use of rules" as they might be applied in the Skillstreaming group, among these that rules be few in number, negotiated with students, stated behaviorally, stated positively, posted in the classroom, and sent home to parents. All of these recommendations apply to the use of rules in the Skillstreaming group.

To develop rules for the group, the teacher might say something like the following:

> In this group, we want to encourage and help one another. There are some things we can all do that will be helpful. Let's come up with a number of helpful things we can do, and I'll list them on the board. Who can think of a helpful rule for the group?

Clearly defining rules in the early stages of group work may prevent many student behavior problems. In addition, providing positive reinforcement for obeying rules (e.g., "Thank you for waiting your turn to talk") will increase the likelihood that rules will be followed.

SUPPORT STAFF AND PROGRAM COORDINATOR ROLES

Support Staff

The effort to teach prosocial behavior should not go forward in isolation; teachers and their students are a part of a school, a center facility, or another institution. Discussion earlier in this chapter described ways to prepare staff members who will serve as Skillstreaming group leaders. What about the rest of the staff? They also have a meaningful role to play in this effort, even though they will not be serving as group leaders.

The goal of changing the behaviors of aggressive, withdrawn, or immature students often succeeds only at a certain time and in a certain place. That is, the program works but only at or shortly after the instruction and only in the same place. Thus, a program may make a child behave in more desirable ways during and immediately following the weeks of teaching in the classroom where it took place. But a few weeks later—or in the school hallway, outside on the playground, on a field trip, at home, or elsewhere outside the classroom—the child's behavior may be as problematic as ever.

This temporary success followed by a relapse to old, negative ways of behaving is a failure of generalization. Generalization failures are much more the rule than the exception with many children. During Skillstreaming instruction, students receive a great deal of support, encouragement, and reward for their efforts. However, between group sessions or after instruction ends, many students receive little support for skill use.

The common failure of generalization is not surprising. However, this outcome can be minimized. Newly learned and thus fragile skills need not fade away after Skillstreaming instruction has ended. Chapter 5 details ways to improve generalization outcomes. Briefly, however, if attempts to use skills in the real world are met with success (i.e., support, enthusiasm, encouragement, reward), children will be much more likely to continue using the skills. Teachers, school staff, community workers, parents, friends, counselors, peers, school administrators, and others who work directly with students are in an ideal position to promote continued skill use. All of these individuals can be powerful "transfer coaches," helping to make sure the Skillstreaming curriculum turns into long-term gain. Following are some specific ways these individuals can assist.

Learning the Program

All school or agency staff should become highly familiar with their institution's Skillstreaming program—its goals, methods, group leadership, and, especially, the skills themselves. Memos, faculty meetings, attendance at Skillstreaming workshops, hall corridor "Skill of the Week" posters, and other means should regularly be employed. In these ways, the transfer coach's prompting, encouraging, reassuring, and rewarding behaviors will more accurately target student skill needs.

Prompting

Under the pressure of real-life situations, both in and out of school, students may forget all or part of skills learned earlier. If their anxiety is not too great or their forgetting too complete, all they may need to perform the skill correctly is prompting. Prompting involves reminding students what to do (the skill), how to do it (the steps), when to do it (now or at another "good time"), where to do it (and where not to), and why the skill is useful (the positive outcomes expected). For example, the lunchroom supervisor may prompt a student to ignore distractions, in the school hallway the principal may suggest that a student avoid trouble or use self-control, and in the library the librarian may prompt a student to ask a question or offer help to a classmate. The school playground offers many opportunities for students to practice friendship-making skills and alternatives to aggression; playground supervisors need to take an active role in prompting skill use in such environments.

Encouraging

Offering encouragement to students assumes they know a skill but are reluctant to use it. Encouragement may be necessary, therefore, when the problem is lack of motivation rather than lack of knowledge or skill. Encouragement can often best be given by gently urging students to try using what they know, by showing enthusiasm for the skill being used, and by communicating optimism about the likely positive outcome of skill use.

Reassuring

For particularly anxious students, skill generalization attempts will be more likely to occur if the threat of failure is reduced. Reassurance is an effective threat-reduction technique. "You can do it" and "I'll be there to help if you need it" are examples of the kinds of reassuring statements the transfer coach can provide.

Rewarding

The most important contribution the transfer coach can make for skill generalization is to provide (or help someone else provide) rewards for correct skill use. Rewards may take the form of approval, praise, or compliments, or they may consist of special privileges, points, tokens, recognition, or other reinforcers built into a school's management system. For example, one school successfully enhanced skill generalization by having all staff in the school distribute "Gotcha Cards" whenever they observed a student using a prosocial skill. All such rewards will increase the likelihood of continued skill use in new settings and at later times.

The most powerful reward that can be offered, however, is the success of the skill itself.

For example, if a child practices Dealing with an Accusation (Skill 43), then a real-life interaction goes very well, that reward (the successful interaction) will help the skill transfer and endure more than any external reward can. The same conclusion, that success increases generalization, applies to all of the Skillstreaming skills.

It is important for all adults and peers to react with behaviors that signal awareness of effective skill use. If transfer and maintenance become schoolwide goals—supported by staff, administrators, students, and parents—and all make a concerted effort toward this end, fragile skills will become lasting skills, and Skillstreaming will have been successful.

Program Coordinator

Even if teachers, students, and support staff are prepared and motivated to begin a Skillstreaming program, the participation of one more professional helps ensure a successful outcome. Many effective programs involve the appointment of a program coordinator or master teacher. It is unfortunately common for Skillstreaming programs to begin with appropriate organization, good intentions, and adequate enthusiasm only to wind up being discarded a few months later because of a lack of oversight. The barrage of other responsibilities often placed on teachers and other front-line staff makes intervention programs more likely to fail in the absence of such guidance.

The program coordinator or master teacher should be well versed in both Skillstreaming and program management. His or her responsibilities may include providing staff development, observing sessions, monitoring schoolwide progress, setting up specific generalization-increasing efforts, motivating staff, facilitating the gathering and distribution of materials, and handling the many other details on which program success depends.

SPECIFIC INSTRUCTIONAL CONCERNS

Program planners and group leaders will need to consider the following factors, essentially the mechanics of the Skillstreaming group.

Skill Selection and Negotiation

Many children for whom Skillstreaming is appropriate attribute their negative and undesirable behavior to others. From this externalized perspective, rarely is anything their fault! Experience suggests that one of the most effective methods of student motivation is negotiating the skill curriculum, or selecting skills the students themselves say they need and want to learn. Students can identify which skills they feel they need by filling out all or part of the Student Checklist (Appendix A).

Teaching skills that provide students with positive alternatives for dealing with their immediate needs will increase their feelings of social competence and their desire to learn other skills. When students perceive a need to learn a new behavior, then have the opportunity to use that newly acquired behavior in situations that will benefit them, learning is likely to be far more effective and enduring. Teaching skills important to others (e.g., teachers and parents) is a program goal but is of secondary importance in determining the skill agenda.

Placement in the School Curriculum

In schools, Skillstreaming has found a place at various times—from homeroom at the beginning of the day to after-school detention at its end. Frequent placements include the resource room and in-school suspension. Sometimes Skillstreaming has been included in a school's regular curriculum—specifically, in subject areas that deal with personal or interpersonal development, such as social studies (e.g., family and community relationships), language arts (e.g., communication and problem-solving skills), and health (e.g., stress management, peer relationships). At the elementary level, social skills training and other relationship-based initiatives have more recently been recognized as deserving a place of their own. Including Skillstreaming as part of the regular curriculum increases the likelihood that students will use and retain the skills taught, thus enhancing the program's effectiveness as both intervention and prevention.

Instructional Setting

Whenever possible, the setting for Skillstreaming should be the classroom or other location where the students spend the majority of their time. Research provides two reasons in support of this recommendation. First, because the child's peers in this setting will also have received the instruction, they will be more likely to help the skill-deficient child perform the skill by providing encouragement and feedback as the child practices the newly learned behavior. Second, because generalization from the teaching setting to the application setting does not occur automatically, carrying out the instruction in the setting in which the child will most often need the prosocial skill (i.e., the natural environment) will help the learning to generalize. Alternative and typically less structured school areas—such as hallways, playgrounds, the school cafeteria, and the school bus—are good places to carry out instruction and practice sessions. When a given skill applies in an easily accessible school environment, modeling and role-playing should occur in that environment.

Occasionally, it may be necessary to provide skill instruction in another, more artificial environment, such as a counselor's office or a special education resource room. This can and should be done in cases in which the student needs additional guidance or practice to learn the skill, but such settings are not recommended either for ongoing instruction or as the only teaching environment.

A special group space should be provided in the classroom for the majority of group instruction. Ideally, chairs will be positioned in a semicircle in an area that allows all students to view group leaders' modeling displays and participants' role-plays. In some large-group settings, this may not be possible. In such cases, alternatives may include having students sit on the floor or at their desks, arranged in a semicircle.

Time Factors

Frequency and Length of Sessions

At the elementary level, Skillstreaming sessions are best held three to five times per week. They should be frequent enough for a series of skills to be taught and far enough apart for the students to have opportunities to complete assigned homework between sessions. Specific Skillstreaming procedures should be followed for at least three sessions per week; the other two sessions might consist of work on specific skill steps, such as relaxation training, asking on-topic questions, or using a game-type format to review a group of previously learned skills.

Throughout the school day in both structured and unstructured settings, teachers may prompt, encourage, reassure, and reward students' use of prosocial skills. When a situation suggesting instruction in Skillstreaming arises, teachers may choose to provide additional group or individual sessions. From this viewpoint, Skillstreaming is an ongoing effort, the initial instruction occurring at the time set for the group with additional learning and transfer-enhancing procedures taking place throughout the school day.

Sessions of approximately 25 to 40 minutes each are suggested, with the shorter time period for students in the lower elementary grades and increased time for older students, as their behavior, interest, and attention span permits. The upper time limit of the group is clear when several children become restless and inattentive. It is important to maintain the students' interest for subsequent Skillstreaming sessions, and sessions should therefore be planned in the future to end slightly before students become restless. As with any lesson, teachers will need to adjust the session's length to respond to a variety of factors, some of which include students' behavioral needs.

To facilitate the continued use of newly learned skills, an additional 5 to 10 minutes at the end of the school day can be allotted for students to chart the skills they have practiced throughout the day.

Program Duration

Skillstreaming programs have been as brief as two days, as long as three years, and just about all lengths in between. The two-day programs take place in in-school detention rooms, in which detained students are taught a single skill. Three-year and other lengthy programs are open Skillstreaming groups, adding new members one at a time as older members "graduate" or otherwise leave. A more typical program lasts the school year, although students may participate over consecutive school years.

Another way of defining duration of program, beyond days or months of meetings, concerns the number of skills taught. The goal of Skillstreaming is teaching prosocial skills so they are not only learned (acquired) but are also used (performed) effectively in a variety of settings and for an enduring period of time. As such, the program takes time.

Although the full curriculum includes 60 skills, not all will be taught to any given Skillstreaming group. Because the goal is to teach those skills in which students are weak or deficient and those that will be most helpful in their daily lives, a full curriculum for some groups may be only a few skills—for other groups, several skills. In a few cases in which Skillstreaming is used on a schoolwide basis, with the entire school working on a given skill at the same time, students may be exposed to a greater number of skills, though not all 60.

Whether a few skills or several are included, teachers should not move on to a second skill until the first is both well learned (as evidenced by successful role-play within the group) and regularly performed (as evidenced by successful homework outside the group). This teaching goal usually requires that the same skill be taught during more than two sessions. In fact, even at the price of student boredom, skills should be taught until they are nearly automatic, or "overlearned."

Materials

Other than the substantial cost of staff time, Skillstreaming is not an expensive program to implement. Necessary checklists and other program forms are provided in Appendix A and may be reproduced as needed. These materials may also be printed from the CD that accompanies this book.

A whiteboard or easel pad, skill cards listing the skill steps, and skill-step posters to hang in the classroom and school are also needed. Skill cards may be of the preprinted variety available from Research Press (see the example in Figure 1), or group leaders or students may make these cards themselves. (Skill posters are also available from Research Press.)

Other materials to enhance the effectiveness of Skillstreaming instruction already exist in most classrooms. For example, if a game or classroom item is an important part of a modeling display or role-play, the actual object should be used whenever possible. The use of such real-life materials is based on the important principle of identical elements, mentioned previously.

INSTRUCTIONAL VARIATIONS

In general, applications of Skillstreaming have been directed toward children selected from a larger classroom group. There are advantages to doing so, as well as other gains to be achieved from providing instruction to the whole class.

Therefore, instruction may be carried out in large or small groups and occasionally, in special circumstances, with individual students.

Large-Group Instruction

General instruction and modeling displays can be successfully carried out in view of a group of 20 or more students. Role-plays, however, are better carried out in two or more smaller groups, preferably with an adult leader assigned to each group. With fewer children in a role-play group, more opportunity exists for each child to assume the role of the main actor and to receive constructive suggestions, encouragement, and reinforcement. The more practice a student has with a particular skill, the more likely he or she will be able to apply that skill over time and in other environments. Thus, the whole group would meet first to generate skill-relevant situations, present the skill steps, and discuss the skill and its modeling. It is important not to stop instruction at this point because Skillstreaming is an experiential activity and the rehearsal component (role-playing) is vital for learning. The role-plays, feedback, and homework are therefore done in smaller groups.

When working with large groups, teachers have elicited assistance from other adults in the school (e.g., volunteers, school administrators, even custodians). Others have found success by using several students as coactors in role-plays, by asking students who are not role-playing at the moment to watch for and provide feedback

Figure 1: Sample Skill Card

Skill 1

Listening

1. Look at the person who is talking.
2. Sit quietly.
3. Think about what is being said.
4. Say yes or nod your head.
5. Ask a question about the topic to find out more.

on particular skill steps, and by assigning other helper roles (e.g., pointing to steps on the poster as the role-play unfolds, helping arrange props to make the role-play more realistic).

Still others choose to teach Skillstreaming within the classroom in a fashion similar to traditional reading groups. In this variation, the group leader introduces the skill and presents the modeling display to the whole group but conducts role-plays, feedback sessions, and assignment of homework in small groups. Thus, the group leader is able to spend time with students who need extra practice role-playing to learn the skill.

Small-Group Instruction

Under certain circumstances, elementary students may be assigned to smaller groups according to common skill needs. This will likely mean that participating students will not be from the same classroom or even from the same age group. Because role-playing is more effective when the teaching setting closely resembles the real-life environment, it is useful to include children whose social environments and peer groups are similar. Selecting participants from a common peer group will not only make the role-play more realistic but also increase the likelihood that students will attempt the skill with peers in the classroom or neighborhood.

The ideal small group consists of six to eight students, depending on student needs. If students exhibit particularly problematic behaviors, a more appropriate group size may be three or four students, or even fewer. If a smaller number is necessary because of members' aggression or out-of-control behavior, additional students may be added (perhaps at the rate of one new member per week) once the smaller group is operating successfully.

Individual Instruction

Although Skillstreaming is designed primarily to be carried out in a group setting, in special cases, modifications can be made to include one-to-one instruction. The child who needs additional help in learning a specific skill, who withdraws from group involvement, or who is behaviorally out of control would benefit from this type of instruction. When carried out individually, the Skillstreaming procedures remain the same, but the adult—or the child's peer if this is feasible—serves as the coactor in each role-play, providing the feedback except for that elicited from the child. Although individual instruction is a useful way of providing skill instruction to some children, the main objective should be to include all children in a Skillstreaming group as soon as possible.

CHAPTER 2

Skillstreaming Teaching Procedures

More than 30 years of research support the individual components of modeling, role-play (behavioral rehearsal), feedback, and generalization, as well as the positive results when the four components are implemented together. These four core teaching procedures of Skillstreaming are described here, along with the sequence of steps illustrating how these procedures are incorporated into instruction. The importance for program integrity of closely following these procedures is discussed last.

CORE TEACHING PROCEDURES

Modeling

Modeling is defined as learning by imitation. Imitation has been examined in a great deal of research and under many names, among them copying, empathic learning, observational learning, identification, vicarious learning, and matched-dependent behavior. A wide variety of behaviors can be learned, strengthened, weakened, or facilitated through modeling. These include acting aggressively, helping others, behaving independently, planning careers, becoming emotionally aroused, interacting socially, displaying dependency, exhibiting certain speech patterns, behaving empathically, and self-disclosing, among others. It is clear that modeling can be an important tool in teaching new behaviors.

Three types of learning by modeling have been identified: *Observational learning* refers to the learning of new behaviors that a person has never performed before. Children are great imitators. *Inhibitory* and *disinhibitory effects* involve the strengthening or weakening of behaviors previously performed only rarely by a person due to a history of punishment or other negative reactions. Modeling offered by peers is, again, a major source of inhibitory and disinhibitory effects. Children who know how to be altruistic and caring may inhibit such behaviors in the presence of models who are behaving more egocentrically and being rewarded for their egocentric behavior. Aggressive models may also have a disinhibitory effect and cause observing children to engage in aggressive behavior. *Behavioral facilitation* refers to the performance of previously learned behaviors that are neither new nor a source of potential negative reactions from others. One person buys something he seems to enjoy, so a friend buys one, too. A child deals with a recurring household matter in an effective manner, so a sibling imitates her behavior. A classmate tries talking over a class problem with the teacher; when he succeeds, a second student decides to approach the teacher in a similar way. These are all examples of behavioral facilitation effects.

Although modeling is powerful, it is also true that most people observe dozens and perhaps hundreds of behaviors every day that they do not imitate. Television, radio, magazines and newspapers, and the Internet expose people to very polished, professional modeling displays of someone's buying one product or another, but these observers do not later buy the product. And many people observe expensively produced and expertly acted instructional films, but they remain uninstructed. Apparently, people learn by modeling under some circumstances but not under others.

Modeling Enhancers

Research on modeling has successfully identified modeling enhancers, or circumstances that increase the degree to which learning by imitation occurs. These modeling enhancers are characteristics of the model, the modeling display, or the observer (the learner). These variables affect learning, as does use of a coping model.

Model characteristics

More effective modeling will occur when the model (the person to be imitated) (a) seems to be highly skilled or expert; (b) is of high status; (c) controls rewards desired by the learner; (d) is of the same sex, approximate age, and social status as the learner; (e) is friendly and helpful; and, of particular importance, (f) is rewarded for the given behaviors. That is, we are all more likely to imitate expert or powerful yet pleasant people who receive rewards for what they are doing, especially when the particular rewards involved are something that we too desire.

Modeling display characteristics

More effective modeling will occur when the modeling display shows the behaviors to be imitated (a) in a clear and detailed manner, (b) in the order from least to most difficult behaviors, (c) with enough repetition to make overlearning likely, (d) with as little irrelevant detail as possible, and (e) performed by several different models rather than a single model.

Observer (learner) characteristics

More effective modeling will occur when the person observing the model is (a) told to imitate the model; (b) similar to the model in background or in attitude toward the skill; (c) friendly toward or likes the model; and, most important, (d) rewarded for performing the modeled behaviors.

Coping model

Further, modeling is more effective when a coping model, or one who struggles a little to achieve the goal of competent skill performance, is presented. If learners perceive that the skill is "easy" and that it can be performed without any feeling, they may be less likely to try the skill when caught up in the emotion of a real-life event. When demonstrating Responding to Teasing (Skill 38) or Using Self-Control (Skill 36), for example, it is important to struggle a bit when performing the behavioral steps. This coping model must be demonstrated in a low-key manner and in an acceptable way so the struggle does not detract from the modeling display. Depicting coping models will further enhance students' ability to identify with the model and will likely give them more courage to try the skill themselves.

Stages of Modeling

The effects of these modeling enhancers, as well as of modeling itself, can be better understood by examining the three stages of learning by modeling.

Attention

Learners cannot learn from watching a model unless they pay attention to the modeling display and, in particular, to the specific behaviors being modeled. Attention is maximized by eliminating irrelevant detail in the modeling display, minimizing the complexity of the modeled material, making the display vivid, and implementing the modeling enhancers previously described.

Retention

To later reproduce the behaviors he or she has observed, the learner must remember or retain them. Because the behaviors of the modeling display itself are no longer present, retention must occur by memory. Memory is aided if the behaviors displayed are classified or coded by the observer. Another name for such coding is *covert rehearsal* (i.e., reviewing in one's mind the performance of the displayed behaviors). Research has shown, however, that an even more important aid to retention is *overt rehearsal.* Such overt practice of the specific behavioral steps is critical for learning and, indeed, is the second major procedure of Skillstreaming—role-playing. It should be noted at this point that the likelihood of retention via either covert or overt rehearsal is greatly aided by rewards provided to both the model and the learner.

Reproduction

Researchers interested in human learning have typically distinguished between learning (acquiring or gaining knowledge about how to do something) and performance (doing it). If a person has paid attention and remembered the behaviors shown during the modeling display, it may be said that the person has learned. The main interest, however, is not so much in whether the person can reproduce the behaviors that have been seen but in whether he or she does produce them. As for retention, the likelihood that a person will actually perform a behavior that has been learned will depend mostly on the expectation of a reward for doing so (e.g., the behavior will bring the desired outcome).

Verbal Mediation

Verbal mediation, or saying aloud what would normally be thought to oneself silently, is a valuable and necessary part of both modeling and role-playing. Saying the steps aloud as the model enacts the behavioral steps demonstrates the cognitive processes underlying skill performance and facilitates learning. For example, in Dealing with an Accusation (Skill 43), the model might say something like "The first step is to stop and say I have to calm down. I need to think of the rest of the steps. OK, I need to think about what the person accused me of. He said I knocked his

stuff off the table on purpose . . ." This type of accompanying narration increases the effectiveness of the modeling display (Bandura, 1977), draws attention to the specific skill steps as they are being portrayed, and helps to reduce behaviors or emotions that may compete with skill performance. Self-talk further enhances the effectiveness of the coping model.

Role-Playing

Role-playing has been defined as when an individual is asked to demonstrate specific behaviors not typical for him or her or to respond to certain situations with behaviors within his or her repertoire (Mann, 1956). Learning appears to be improved when the learner has the opportunity and is encouraged to practice, rehearse, or role-play the behaviors and is rewarded for doing so. The use of role-playing to help a person change behavior or attitudes has been a popular and useful approach for many years. However, as for modeling, behavior or attitude change through role-playing will occur and be more lasting only if certain conditions are met. If the role-player has enough information about the content of the role-play to enact it and if sufficient attention is paid to the factors that enhance role-play effectiveness, it is more likely that behavior or attitude change will occur. Specific role-play enhancers include (a) choice on the part of the group member regarding whether to take part in the role-play; (b) public commitment to the behavior; (c) improvisation in enacting the role-played behaviors; and (d) reward, approval, or reinforcement for performing the behaviors.

Seeing the modeling display teaches students what to do, but repeated practice in a variety of contexts is needed to increase skill fluency. However, in most attempts to help a person change behavior, neither modeling nor role-playing alone is enough. Combining the two is an improvement, for then the learner knows both what to do and how to do it. But even this combination is insufficient, for the learner still needs to know why he or she should behave in new ways. That is, a motivational or incentive component must be added. Performance feedback provides this incentive.

Performance Feedback

Performance feedback is defined as providing the learner with information on how well he or she has done during role-playing. It may take such forms as constructive suggestions for improvement, coaching, reteaching, material rewards, and, especially, social reinforcement such as praise and approval. Social reinforcement has been shown to be an especially potent influence on behavior change. In addition, positive feedback from peers has been shown to increase peer acceptance, as well as appropriate behavior (Jones, Young, & Friman, 2000; Moroz & Jones, 2002; Skinner, Cashwell, & Skinner, 2000).

Peer feedback has been shown to have positive effects on prosocial behavior. For example, Moroz and Jones (2002) implemented a positive peer reporting program that taught students to describe and provide praise to socially isolated classmates during structured sessions. Results showed a decrease in negative behaviors and an increase in positive social interactions in the classroom. Jones et al. (2000) also instructed peers in giving positive feedback to delinquent, socially rejected adolescents. This protocol included looking at the learner, smiling, saying a positive thing the learner did or said, and giving verbal praise. Their results indicated improved peer acceptance for the target youth. Younger children have also been successfully taught how to recognize socially appropriate behavior and to tell teachers when peers behaved in socially appropriate ways (to "tootle" versus "tattle"; Skinner et al., 2000). Results of these studies suggest involving peers in the endeavor to improve the social behaviors of skill-deficient children.

Because peer feedback has been found to be instrumental in improving the behavior of target youngsters, this is an important element in Skillstreaming. To be most effective, group leaders should follow these guidelines:

1. Provide reinforcement only after role-plays that follow the behavioral steps.

2. Provide reinforcement at the earliest appropriate opportunity after role-plays that follow the behavioral steps.

3. Always provide reinforcement to the coactor for being helpful, cooperative, and so forth.

4. Vary the specific content of the reinforcements offered (e.g., praise particular aspects of the performance, such as tone of voice, posture, phrasing).

5. Provide enough role-playing activity for each group member to have sufficient opportunity to be reinforced.

6. Provide reinforcement in an amount consistent with the quality of the given role-play.

7. Provide no reinforcement when the role-play departs significantly from the behavioral steps (except for "trying" in the first session or two; instead, coach the learner in following the skill steps).

8. Provide reinforcement for an individual learner's improvement over previous performance.

Generalization

As noted previously, the main interest of any intervention program and where most programs fail is not student performance during the instruction but, instead, to what degree the student uses newly learned skills in natural settings and contexts and experiences improved quality of life. The goal of Skillstreaming is successful social functioning in school, at home, or in other places. Generalization training assists the learner in identifying where and when skill use is desired or necessary. Chapter 5 includes a variety of generalization strategies.

STEPS IN THE SKILLSTREAMING SESSION

Carrying out the core Skillstreaming teaching procedures—modeling, role-playing, performance feedback, and generalization—involves leading the group through the following nine steps:

▶ Step 1: Define the skill

▶ Step 2: Model the skill

▶ Step 3: Establish student skill need

▶ Step 4: Select the first role-player

▶ Step 5: Set up the role-play

▶ Step 6: Conduct the role-play

▶ Step 7: Provide performance feedback

▶ Step 8: Select the next role-player

▶ Step 9: Assign skill homework

The following text describes these steps and illustrates the Skillstreaming procedure in operation. Table 2 provides a detailed summary of the steps for ongoing reference.

Step 1: Define the Skill

In this brief activity, the teacher leads a discussion of the skill to be taught. Whether the skill has been selected by the teacher or is a result of the recommended periodic skill negotiation between teacher and group members, this activity is a necessary beginning. The goal is to help students understand the skill to be taught in the session. This goal can typically be achieved in a few minutes of discussion; a long lecture is not required. The following dialogue shows a teacher briefly defining Skill 43, Dealing with an Accusation.

Teacher: Thank you for getting ready for the group so quickly. Today's skill is quite an important one, one that lots of people have trouble doing well—or even at all. It's called Dealing with an Accusation. Can anyone tell me what an accusation is? Margie? Yes, what do you think?

Margie: When somebody says you did something, like hitting somebody.

Teacher: That's one good way to explain it. Thank you. Anyone else? Devin, you had your hand up.

Devin: You do something that gets you in trouble, and somebody finds out. Then you get in trouble for it.

Teacher: That's a good part of it, Devin. Can someone make an accusation if you didn't really do something wrong, like hitting someone? Yes, Jeff?

Jeff: Somebody can say you did something, but you really didn't. Like my little brother told my mom I messed up his room, but I didn't.

Teacher: Thank you, Jeff. That's another good way of explaining what an accusation is. Someone may believe that you did something and may accuse you. You may have done it, or you may not have. Most times, it is upsetting to be accused of doing something whether or not you actually did it. So the skill we are going to learn today is how to handle these types of situations—how to deal with an accusation. Russ [co-leader], would you please hand out the skill cards? *(To the group)* You may look for the steps on the skill card or on the poster where these are listed.

Step 2: Model the Skill

Before the session, leaders should plan their modeling displays. Displays that relate to the group's real-world concerns will always be most effective so long as they incorporate the following guidelines:

1. Use at least two examples for each skill demonstration. If a skill is used in more than one group session, develop two new modeling displays.

2. Select situations relevant to students' real-life circumstances.

3. The model (i.e., the person enacting the behavioral steps of the skill) should be portrayed as a child reasonably similar to the group members in age, socioeconomic background, verbal ability, and other characteristics.

4. A coping model should be portrayed with skills that typically elicit strong emotion.

Table 2: Skillstreaming Session Outline

Step 1: Define the skill

1. Choose skills relevant to the needs of the students as they perceive them.

2. Discuss each skill step and any other relevant information pertaining to each step.

3. Use skill cards and/or poster or whiteboard or easel pad on which the skill and steps are written so all group members can easily see the steps and illustrations.

Step 2: Model the skill

1. Use at least two examples for each skill demonstration.

2. Select situations relevant to the students' real-life circumstances.

3. Use modeling displays that demonstrate all the behavioral steps of the skill in the correct sequence.

4. Use modeling displays that depict only one skill at a time. (All extraneous content should be eliminated.)

5. Show the use of a coping model.

6. Have the model "think aloud" steps that ordinarily would be thought silently.

7. Depict only positive outcomes.

8. Reinforce the model who has used the skill correctly by using praise or encouraging self-reward.

Step 3: Establish student skill need

1. Elicit from the students specific situations in which the skill could be used or is needed.

2. List the names of the group members. The co-leader may then list the situations identified by each student and record the theme of the role-plays.

Step 4: Select the first role-player

1. Select as the main actor a student who describes a situation in his or her own life in which skill use is needed or will be helpful.

2. Provide encouragement and reinforcement for the student's willingness to participate as the main actor.

Step 5: Set up the role-play

1. Have the main actor choose a coactor who most reminds him or her of the other person involved in the problem.

2. Present relevant information surrounding the real event (i.e., describe the physical setting and events preceding the problem).

3. Use props when appropriate.

4. Review skill steps and direct the main actor to look at the skill card or the skill steps on display.

5. Assign the other group participants to watch for specific skill steps.

Step 6: Conduct the role-play

1. Instruct the main actor to "think out loud."

2. As needed, assist the main actor (e.g., point to each behavioral step as the role-play is carried out; have the co-leader sit among the group members, directing their attention to the role-play).

Step 7: Provide performance feedback

1. Seek feedback from the coactor, observers, leader(s), and main actor, in turn.

2. Provide reinforcement for successful role-plays at the earliest appropriate opportunity.

3. Provide reinforcement to the coactor for being helpful and cooperative.

4. Praise particular aspects of performance (e.g., "You used a brave voice to say that").

5. Provide reinforcement in an amount consistent with the quality of the role-play.

Step 8: Select the next role-player

Ask, "Who would like to go next?"

Step 9: Assign skill homework

1. Assign homework to the main actors who have successfully role-played the skill.

2. Provide the main actors with the appropriate Homework Report.

3. Discuss with each main actor when, where, and with whom he or she will use the skill in real life.

From *Skillstreaming the Elementary School Child: Teaching Prosocial Skills* (3rd ed.), © 2012 by E. McGinnis, Champaign, IL: Research Press (www.researchpress.com, 800-519-2707).

5. The model should "think aloud" what would normally be thought to oneself as the modeling display unfolds.

6. Modeling displays should depict positive outcomes. In addition, the model who is using the skill well should always be reinforced.

7. Modeling displays should depict all the behavioral steps of the skill in the correct sequence without extraneous or distracting content.

8. Modeling displays should depict only one skill at a time.

Students are asked to watch and listen closely as the modeling unfolds. Particular care should be given to helping students identify the behavioral steps as they are being modeled. The leader can do this by pointing to the steps in the course of the modeling. As the model follows the behavioral steps, he or she "thinks out loud" what would normally be thought silently. At the conclusion of each modeling vignette, leaders ask, "Did I follow the first step?" "How do you know I did this?" The model may also provide self-reinforcement, such as "Yes, I followed all of the steps. I think I did a good job!"

Step 3: Establish Student Skill Need

Behavioral rehearsal is the purpose of the role-play. Before group members begin role-playing, it is important to identify each student's current and future need for the skill. Reenactment of a past problem or circumstances is less relevant unless the student predicts that such circumstances are likely to reoccur in the future. Such current student needs will likely have been established earlier as part of the selection and grouping process through use of the skill checklists. Nonetheless, an open discussion within the group is needed to establish relevant and realistic role-plays. Each student is in turn asked to describe briefly where, when, and with whom he or she would find it useful to use the skill just mod-

eled. Instruction with a large group requires that those children who will be role-playing give such information during each session. More than one or two sessions will be needed for all students to offer this information and be the main actor in a role-play of the target skill.

To make effective use of such information, it is often valuable to list the names of the group members on the whiteboard or easel pad at the front of the room and to record next to each name the theme of the role-play and the name (or role) of the person with whom the skill will be used.

Step 4: Select the First Role-Player

Because all members of the Skillstreaming group will be expected to role-play each skill taught, in most instances, it is not of great concern who does so first. Typically, teachers ask for volunteers to begin the role-play series. If for any reason there are group members who appear to be reluctant to role-play a particular skill on a particular day, it is helpful not to ask them to role-play first or second. Observing other students do so first can be reassuring and may help ease their way into the activity. For a few students, reluctance may turn into resistance and refusal. Refusal occurs infrequently with elementary-age students. However, because it does occur at times and is a significant roadblock to that student's learning, strategies for dealing with such problems are described at length in chapter 6. In general, students should be encouraged, reassured, and reminded to use the skill to meet their own needs rather than penalized, threatened, or otherwise coerced into participation.

Step 5: Set Up the Role-Play

Once a student has described a situation in which skill use may be useful, that student is designated the main actor. The main actor chooses a second person (the coactor) to play the role of the other person (e.g., teacher, peer, parent) with whom he or she will use the skill in real life. The main actor should be encouraged to select as the coactor someone who resembles the significant other in as many ways as possible—in other words, someone who most reminds the main actor of the actual person.

The group leader then elicits from the main actor any additional information needed to set the stage for the role-play. In order to make role-playing as realistic as possible, the leader should obtain a description of the physical setting, the events immediately preceding the situation, and the mood or manner the coactor should portray, along with any other information that would enhance realism. Props may be used if available and appropriate.

Step 6: Conduct the Role-Play

At this point the group leader should remind group members of their roles and responsibilities:

▶ Main actor: Follow the behavioral steps and "think aloud" what would normally be thought silently.

▶ Coactor: Stay in the role of the other person.

▶ Other students: Watch carefully for the enactment of the behavioral steps.

It is useful to assign separate behavioral steps to the observers, have them watch for the display of these steps, and then report on step use during the subsequent feedback session. For the first several role-plays, observers can be coached as to what kinds of cues to observe (e.g., posture, words chosen, tone of voice, facial expression).

Then the role-players are instructed to begin. At this point, it is the group leader's responsibility to provide the main actor with any help or coaching needed in order to keep the role-play going according to the behavioral steps. Students who "break role" to offer other information should be urged to get back into the role and explain later. If the role-play is clearly going astray from the behavioral steps, the scene can be stopped, needed instruction provided, and the role-play resumed. One group leader should be positioned near the skill poster and point to each of the behavioral steps as they are enacted. This will help the main actor, as well as the observers and coactor, follow each of the steps in order.

Role-playing should be continued until all group members have had an opportunity to participate in the role of the main actor. Sometimes this will require two or three sessions for a given skill. As noted, each session should begin with two modeling vignettes for the selected skill, even if the skill is not new to the group. It is important to note that, although the framework (behavioral steps) of each role-play remains the same, the content can and should change from role-play to role-play. When the role-plays have been completed, each student will be better equipped to act appropriately in a real-life situation.

Other strategies may be used to increase the effectiveness of role-plays. For example, role reversal is often useful. If a main actor has a difficult time perceiving the coactor's point of view, having the two exchange roles and resume the role-play can be most helpful. On occasion, the group leader can also assume the coactor role in an effort to give students the opportunity to handle types of reactions not otherwise role-played during the session. It may be critical to have a difficult adult role realistically portrayed, for instance. The leader as a coactor may also be particularly helpful when dealing with less verbal or more hesitant students. Finally, the leader as coactor may also be indicated with particular skills (e.g., Dealing with Another's Anger, Skill 32), which otherwise would require the student coactor to engage in inappropriate or attention-getting behaviors.

Step 7: Provide Performance Feedback

A brief period of feedback follows each role-play. Such feedback lets the main actor find out how well he or she followed the behavioral steps, evaluates the impact of the enactment on the coactor, and gives the main actor encouragement to try out the behavior in real life. Feedback is presented in the following order:

1. The coactor is asked to react first. Asking questions such as "How did you feel when she said that to you?" and "What do you think about the way she talked to you?" may be needed to prompt the coactor's feedback.

2. Next, the observers comment on whether or not the skill steps they were assigned to watch for were followed and on other relevant aspects of the role-play. When asking for this feedback, it is helpful to ask questions such as "Did he follow the first step, did he think about what he was asked to do?" and "How do you know he did this?" Many group members will likely explain that they heard the main actor talk about his thinking (think aloud).

3. Then the group leaders comment in particular on how well the behavioral steps were followed and provide social reinforcement (praise, approval, encouragement) for close following of the skill steps.

4. After listening to the feedback from the coactor, observers, and group leaders, the main actor is asked to make comments regarding the role-play and, if appropriate, to respond to the comments of others. In this way, the main actor can learn to evaluate the effectiveness of his or her skill performance in light of others' viewpoints.

Leaders should provide enough role-playing activity for each group member to have sufficient opportunity to be reinforced. The teacher should not provide reinforcement when the role-play departs significantly from the behavioral steps (except for "trying"). However, he or she may provide reinforcement for an individual student's improvement over previous performances and reteach the skill, if necessary.

In all aspects of feedback, group leaders must maintain the behavioral focus of Skillstreaming. Leader comments must point to the presence or absence of specific, concrete behaviors and not take the form of general evaluative comments or generalizations. Feedback may be positive or negative in content. Positive feedback should always be given first; otherwise the student may be concentrating on the negative comment and not hear other feedback. Negative feedback should be constructive in nature, offering suggestions for what might improve skill enactment. Group leaders will very likely need to model constructive comments before allowing students to give this type of feedback to a peer.

Whenever possible, children failing to follow the behavioral steps in the role-play should be given the opportunity to repeat the same behavioral steps after receiving corrective, constructive criticism. At times, as a further feedback procedure, we have videorecorded entire role-plays. Giving students the opportunity to observe themselves can be an effective aid, enabling them to reflect on their own verbal and nonverbal behavior.

Because a primary goal of Skillstreaming is skill flexibility, role-play enactment that departs somewhat from the behavioral steps may not be "wrong." That is, a different approach to the skill may actually work in some situations. Group leaders should stress that they are trying to teach effective alternatives and that learning the behavioral steps as presented will increase the number of behavioral choices group members have.

Step 8: Select the Next Role-Player

The next student is selected to serve as main actor, and the sequence just described is repeated until all members of the Skillstreaming group are reliably demonstrating in-group and out-of-group proficiency in using the skill.

Step 9: Assign Skill Homework

Skill homework constitutes the generalization component of Skillstreaming. Following each successful role-play, students are instructed to try in their own real-life settings the behaviors practiced during the session. It is useful to begin with relatively simple homework assignments (e.g., situations that occur in the school environment, situations without a high level of stress) and, as mastery is achieved, work up to more complex assignments. This sequence provides the teacher with an opportunity to reinforce each approximation toward proficiency. The student should not be expected to perform the skill perfectly when first using it in real-life contexts. Reinforcement should be given as the student's performance becomes closer to the ideal. Successful experiences when beginning to use the skill in the real world (homework assignments) and rewards received for doing so are critical in encouraging the student to attempt further skill use.

Homework assignments begin with the teacher and student together deciding when, how, and with whom the student will use the skill and progress to the stage where the student independently records the skills he or she has used. One of three stages of homework can be assigned, depending on the student's level of skill mastery. It is best to begin with Homework Report 1 for each skill and gradually progress to more independent levels. Part 2 of this book provides reports for the first two levels; the third level is a card made by teacher or student, as explained.

Homework Report 1

When using Homework Report 1, the student thinks of a situation (either at home, at school, or with peers) in which he or she feels the need to practice the skill. It is especially useful if the student selects the same situation he or she has role-played; having prior practice will likely increase the student's comfort level in trying the skill in real life. On the sample shown in Figure 2, the student or the teacher lists the student's name and the date the assignment is made. Together, teacher and student decide on and enter the name of the person with whom the skill will be tried and the time the student will make the attempt (e.g., during science class, on the playground, at home after school). After using the skill, the student writes down what happened, then evaluates his or her skill use by circling one of the faces on the report (☺ = I did great! ☺ = I did OK but could have done bet-

ter; or ☹ = I had trouble following the steps) and gives a reason for this self-evaluation (e.g., "I used all of the steps" or "I forgot a step"). It is important to convey to students that this evaluation pertains to how well they performed the skill steps, rather than how well the skill actually worked. If desired, the teacher may use the blank Homework Report 1 form in Appendix A. Having the child list the skill steps on the blank form is a good way to enhance skill learning.

Homework Report 2

The student who has nearly achieved mastery of a particular skill (i.e., who knows the steps well and shows success with the assignments on Homework Report 1) is ready to attempt self-recording or monitoring skill use independently. Following a Skillstreaming session, the student is given Homework Report 2 (see sample in Figure 3). Then, throughout the course of the day or week, the student lists the times of skill practice and completes the self-evaluation portion of the homework report according to the same criteria used in earlier homework assignments. He or she hands in the completed report periodically, at the group leader's request. After writing comments, giving verbal praise, or providing other reinforcement, the group leader returns the form to the student.

As appropriate, the teacher may use the blank Homework Report 2 form included in Appendix A.

Homework Report 3

In this final stage of structured homework, more than one skill is listed on a 3×5–inch index card. The student then tallies each skill practiced throughout the school week in school, home, or with peers. This method of self-recording gives the older student an inconspicuous way to chart skills used outside the group.

Using the Homework Reports

The first part of each Skillstreaming session after the first is devoted to presenting and discussing the homework reports. When students have

Skill 32: Dealing with Another's Anger

Name ___Chloe_____ Date ___November 15_____

SKILL STEPS

1. Listen to what the person has to say.

2. Think about your choices:

   a. Keep listening.

   b. Ask why the person is angry.

   c. Give the person an idea to fix the problem.

   d. Walk away for now.

3. Act out your best choice.

FILL IN NOW

With whom will I try this? _____My brother._____

When? ___After school._____

FILL IN AFTER YOU PRACTICE THE SKILL

What happened? ___He was mad cause he was grounded. I listened. I asked him

___if he wanted to watch TV with me. He didn't hit me._____

How did I do?

Why did I circle this? _____I listened. I made a good choice._____

Skill 54: Accepting No

Name _____ *Bobby* _____ Date _____ *January 10* _____

SKILL STEPS

1. Decide why you were told no.

2. Think about your choices:

   a. Do something else.

   b. Say how you feel in a friendly way.

   c. Write about how you feel.

3. Act out your best choice.

When did I practice?   How did I do?

I got grounded.   ☺   😐(circled)   ☹

Asked Jacob to come over. ☺   😐   ☹(circled)

I wanted a new video game. ☺(circled)   😐   ☹

Had to do work at recess. ☺(circled)   😐   ☹

made an effort to complete their homework reports, teachers should provide social reinforcement. Failure to do homework should be met with the teacher's disappointment and followed by reteaching. It cannot be stressed too strongly that without these or similar attempts to maximize generalization, the value of the entire teaching session is in jeopardy.

The majority of elementary school children will be able to progress through all stages of homework. If, however, particular students (those in the lower elementary grades or students with disabilities, for example) are unsuccessful with the more independent levels of homework (Homework Reports 2 and 3), these may be simplified or eliminated. For example, instead of requesting that a second grader complete a Homework Report 3, the self-recording assignment, the child may be asked to inform the teacher immediately after he or she has used a skill in the school setting. The teacher may then place a sticker or a star on a chart to record the student's skill performance.

Group Self-Report Chart

Group self-recording is a valuable additional component of the homework process used successfully by some schools. In this method, the teacher uses the Group Self-Report Chart (see sample in Figure 4) and asks each child to make a tally mark (or place a sticker or a star) next to each skill he or she practiced that day. Initially, time should be allowed for this reporting, most often the last 10 minutes or so of the school day. Appendix A includes a blank Group Self-Report Chart.

As time permits, several students might be asked to describe the specific situations in which they used a skill or skills. Again, teachers should praise these self-reports. As students become used to this self-reporting method, they may be allowed to record their skill use on the chart independently. If students do record their own skill use, it is important for the teacher to comment on the self-reporting, thus providing reinforcement. Although the primary purpose of this chart

is to encourage the continued use of skills taught in earlier Skillstreaming sessions, the chart also provides a record of the skills students are continuing to practice. If students do not report using specific skills, teachers will know which areas need review or reteaching.

Skill Contracts, Self-Recording Forms, and Awards

Skill contracts like the sample shown in Figure 5 can help students follow through with skill practice, as can self-recording forms (see sample in Figure 6). Skill awards like the example given in Figure 7 can likewise motivate continued skill use. Appendix A includes a variety of skill contracts, self-recording forms, and awards. (Suggestions for using such materials to enhance skill generalization are given in chapter 5.)

IMPLEMENTATION INTEGRITY

Recently, increased attention has been drawn to implementing interventions with integrity. Implementation integrity—also called implementation fidelity, treatment integrity, and procedural reliability—is defined by Lane et al. (2005) as "the extent to which the intervention plan is implemented as originally designed" (p. 22) and is concerned with both the consistency and accuracy of implementation (Gresham, Sugai, & Horner, 2001). Sanetti and Kratochwill (2009) go beyond this standard definition, stating, "Treatment integrity is the extent to which essential intervention components are delivered in a comprehensive and consistent manner by an interventionist trained to deliver the intervention" (p. 448).

This concept involves the following matters (Gresham, 2009; Sanetti & Kratochwill, 2009):

► Competence of the interventionist: What is the skill level of the interventionist? Does the interventionist believe in the strategy, or is he or she required by another to do this?

► Quality of intervention delivery: How well was the intervention implemented?

Figure 4: Sample Group Self-Report Chart

Skills	Mario	Lakeesha	Rita	Darwin	Joe	Brenda	Gabe	Aretha						
Responding to Teasing	X	X			X	X								
Asking for Help	X	X	X	X	X	X	X							
Accepting No		X	X		X		X	X						
Dealing with Another's Anger	X		X		X		X							

▶ Quantity of the intervention: How much of the intervention was delivered?

▶ Process of intervention delivery: For example, were all components of the intervention included?

Although acknowledged as a critical factor in assessing the usefulness of interventions, implementation integrity is rarely measured (Gresham, 2009; Gresham, MacMillan, Beebe-Frankenberger, & Bocian, 2000) and instead is often just assumed (Cochrane & Laux, 2007). We expect that the intervention will be implemented as originally planned; when change occurs, we assume the changes were due to the intervention. When there is no change, we assume this was due to an inappropriate or ineffective intervention (Gresham & Gansle, 1993). Instead of drawing one of these faulty conclusions, it is quite probable that the intervention in applied settings (e.g., school, clinic) was changed in some way (Gresham, 2005). Therefore, it is important that this concept be addressed when implementing Skillstreaming as an intervention to change the problem behavior of students.

Measuring implementation integrity is necessary in order to derive accurate conclusions regarding the effectiveness of the intervention and to help understand outcomes such as the behavior change of the target individuals (Lane et al., 2005; Wood, Umbreit, Liaupsin, & Gresham, 2007). Stated another way, "Intervention is effective only to the degree to which it is reliably measured" (Kulli, 2008, p. 145). In order to know whether Skillstreaming or any other intervention is producing the desired behavior change, monitoring the quality and quantity of the instruction, as well as the motivation of the interventionist, must occur.

Sanetti and Kratochwill (2009) offer several observations helpful in addressing treatment integrity:

▶ Typically, most intervention components are not equally important.

▶ Rigid implementation may not be most desirable, and flexibility may be needed.

▶ Evaluation and documentation are needed to assess the successfulness of multi-tiered models.

I will practice _____Accepting No (#54)_____

_____Darwin_____
Student

If I do, then _I will earn an extra 10 minutes_

recess for the class.

_____Ms. Barbour_____
Teacher

_____11/7_____
Date

To be reevaluated on or before

_____11/14_____
Date

Student _Lakeesha_

Date _3/19_

Color in a space each time you use the skill of

Listening (#1)

Classroom Survival Award

to

_____
Mario

for using the skill of

_____
Asking a Question (#9)

Date _____
3/28

► For some interventions, there may be a threshold beyond which increased use does not provide a meaningful impact.

► As requirements change for research proposals and publications, attention to treatment integrity may increase.

Ways to measure implementation integrity include both direct and indirect methods. Direct methods include direct observation and video observation. Indirect methods include self-reports, permanent products, interviews, and component checklists, with component checklists being the most common strategy. A process recommended by Jung, Gomez, Baird, and Keramidas (2008) is most useful for Skillstreaming purposes. Their instructions state:

> (a) provide a short checklist identifying the critical features of the strategy; (b) provide concrete examples of how this objective is addressed using the strategy; (c) model use of the selected strategy; and (d) offer to watch other team members using the selected strategy and provide feedback. (p. 31)

In addition to implementing the intervention with integrity, it is important that the intervention be appropriate to meet the needs of the youth. Therefore, some flexibility in implementation may be required (Maag, 2006; Sanetti & Kratochwill, 2009). Relative to Skillstreaming, this flexibility includes selecting modeling and role-play scenarios to address the needs of group members and changing the language of the skill steps to reflect cultural factors and in-dividual needs of the participants. For example, Sanetti and Kratochwill (2009) emphasize that "deviations may add effective strategies or make the intervention contextually relevant" (p. 451). These authors suggest that we emphasize "flexibility with fidelity" and distinguish between intervention adaptation (intentional adaptation of the intervention to meet individual needs of the recipient, such as context and culture) and intervention drift (unplanned, gradual changing of the intervention).

Both the Leader's Checklist and the Observer's Checklist, included in Appendix B, are used to ensure implementation integrity. The Leader's Checklist is completed by leaders at the completion of each session when first beginning groups. When leaders are consistently implementing all of the steps, this checklist may then be used every two or three weeks. This checklist may also serve as a planning guide to coach leaders through a Skillstreaming session. The Observer's Checklist is designed for use by a highly skilled trainer of group leaders, who observes newly trained group leaders to provide feedback to improve performance in implementing Skillstreaming instruction. This observation form should be used frequently when the trainer first begins his or her instruction. This feedback is most valuable to leaders early on to ensure procedures are being implemented as intended. This form also has been used by leaders to observe one another, thereby providing feedback to enhance their own skills.

CHAPTER 3

Sample Skillstreaming Session

This chapter presents an edited transcript of a Skillstreaming group session with students in a fourth-grade regular education classroom. The group consists of two leaders and ten students. This transcript depicts the leaders introducing students to what will happen in the group and follows the Skillstreaming teaching procedures discussed in chapter 2. The skill used for instruction is Responding to Teasing (Skill 38).

The goal of the introductory session for elementary students is to remind them of the concept of social skills, illustrate the activities that will be performed, and emphasize that in this group they will learn the things they want and need to learn. The following text suggests a typical format for this session. The teacher uses a whiteboard or easel pad to illustrate the Skillstreaming procedure and record students' homework situations, as well as a skill-step poster and skill cards on which steps are written.

INTRODUCTION TO SKILLSTREAMING

Introductions

Teachers introduce themselves if the students do not already know them, then ask students to introduce themselves if they do not know one another.

Explanation of Prosocial Skills and Group Purpose

Teacher: I want to welcome you to the Skillstreaming group. I've talked with each of you individually, so I know you have some idea of what we will be learning in this group. Let's review what the goal of this group is. All of us, at certain times, have difficulty getting along with others. So we will be learning "people skills," ways we can get along better with others—our friends, parents, and teachers, too. In this group, you'll need to let me know the skills you think you need and want to learn. First, let's talk about skills. What are examples of skills that people learn?

Mario: Playing a video game.

Lakeesha: Playing basketball.

Rita: Roller-blading.

Darwin: Keeping your temper.

Joe: Playing the guitar.

Overview of Skillstreaming Procedures

The teacher illustrates the four-step process by discussing learning another type of skill (in this case, an athletic skill).

Teacher: Those are all very good examples of skills. Darwin's skill is also a good example of a people skill. There are many others, like how to make a complaint if something happens that you don't think is fair, how to handle being teased by someone, or how to handle being left out of an activity with your friends. But whether it's people skills, or sports skills, or music skills, all skills are learned the same way. Let's take Lakeesha's example of basketball. Let's say that Mr. Staton here *(the co-leader)* has never played basketball, but he would like to learn. What's the first thing that has to happen? Let's say he wanted to learn the skill of shooting a lay-up.

Aretha: He would need to watch somebody shooting a lay-up.

Gabe: He would need a coach to tell him what to do.

Teacher: You're both right. The coach is the expert, and Mr. Staton needs to watch someone doing a good job shooting the ball. So the coach would need to show him how. *(Modeling)* After the coach shows him, what would Mr. Staton need to do next?

Brenda: Well, then he would do it.

Teacher: Exactly. After the coach shows Mr. Staton how to shoot a lay-up, he needs to try it. *(Role-playing)* But what if he has trouble and can't get the ball in the basket? What does the coach do then?

Joe: Mr. Staton needs help . . . to know how to do better.

Teacher: Yes, Joe. The coach needs to tell Mr. Staton what he did that was right and what he needs to do better. *(Performance feedback)* When an expert or coach tells someone what's good about his or her skill and what needs work, that's called *feedback*. So the coach gives Mr. Staton feedback on how well he did the lay-up. Now, is Mr. Staton ready to go out and play with the team?

Joe: He'd better shoot a lot more first!

Teacher: I agree. He would need to practice the skill first. *(Generalization)* So, that's how you learn the skill of shooting a lay-up. First, someone who knows how to do the skill well, like a coach, *shows* you. Then you *try* it. You get *feedback* on how you did, and then you *practice* what you've learned. These steps—show, try, feedback, practice—are how you learn any skill. Shooting a lay-up, playing the guitar, playing a video game, roller-blading, or controlling your temper.

Explanation of Reinforcement System and Discussion of Group Rules

Teacher: *(Showing the group a packet of paper tokens)* I have something to show you. These are special tickets we call "skill tickets." When you take part in the Skillstreaming group in the ways we just discussed—by trying the skill, giving your feedback or accepting feedback from others, and practicing the skill—you may earn a ticket. When I hand out a ticket, I'll also say why you earned it.

Aretha: Will we get a ticket for each thing we do?

Teacher: Good question. At first, when a new skill is being learned, you may earn several tickets in the group. Later on, though, as you perform the skill better and better, you won't need quite as many tickets to know that you are performing the skill well. When you return to your desks after the group, you'll write your name on the back of each ticket and keep your tickets in an envelope I'll give to you. There is also another way you will earn tickets. You'll earn tickets for following our guidelines, or rules, for our group.

Mario: What are the rules?

Teacher: What is a rule you think we should have? What behaviors should be shown in the group so everyone has the opportunity to learn?

Students: *(No response.)*

Teacher: What if everyone talked at once? Could we hear what people are saying?

Rita: I know! Don't talk when it's someone else's turn.

Teacher: That's a great rule. Let's see if we can phrase this in a positive way, in a way that tells us what to do instead of what not to do.

Rita: Listen when someone else is talking.

Teacher: Bravo! Can we all agree on "Listen to the person who is talking" as one of our group rules?

The dialogue continues until the group has defined the following rules: 1. Listen to the person who is talking; 2. Only one person talks at a time; 3. Keep hands and feet to self; 4. Leave objects at your desk. The co-leader lists these rules on chart paper as each rule is developed.

Teacher: So, you may also earn tickets for following these rules. What do you think you can do with these tickets?

Darwin: Can we buy things?

Teacher: Is this what you'd like to do with your tickets? *(Students nod and clap.)*

Teacher: Purchasing privileges seems like a good use of the tickets to me also.

The teacher shows the students a chart listing privileges, such as computer time, first in line for lunch, eating lunch with a friend, eating lunch with the teacher, and so on, along with the number of tickets needed to earn each privilege.

Do you see something on the list you'd like to earn?

Gabe: Yeah! I want to play a game with Jake instead of going out to recess. I don't like recess . . . too many problems.

Teacher: OK, then. I'll add this to our privilege chart. Twenty-five points to earn this seems reasonable to me. If you earn five tickets during each group, then you'll have enough to earn this privilege by the end of the week. Do you think this is reasonable, Gabe?

Gabe: OK. *(He smiles.)*

Teacher: Who else sees something on the chart they want to work for?

Amanda: I like computer time.

Teacher: Great! Then this is something you may work for. Each of you may turn in your tickets for privileges on Fridays. Be thinking about which privilege you'll choose, and you're free to change your mind and choose a different privilege or even save your tickets for a larger privilege later on.

Conclusion

Teacher: Thank you all for listening so well! I'm excited to start our group tomorrow. This will be a helpful group to learn different choices you have when you're dealing with difficult situations.

Subsequent sessions begin with review of students' Homework Reports.

SKILL INSTRUCTION

Step 1: Define the Skill

Teacher: Today we're going to learn a really important people skill. It's one that most of you told me that you would like to learn. It's called Responding to Teasing. What do you think that means?

Aretha: When somebody calls you a name and you get mad at them.

Rita: Like when my brother tells me my mom grounded me, but he lied.

Mario: This kid across the street calls me a nasty name all the time when I walk by his house.

Teacher: Those are all good examples of teasing. And as Aretha said, it's hard not to get mad when you are teased. But if you get mad and fight with the person who is teasing you, then you are the one who ends up getting in trouble. Is that right?

Gabe: Yeah. I get in trouble a lot for fighting.

Teacher: OK, then. Let's talk about how you can respond to teasing without getting into a fight and getting in trouble. Here are the steps that make up the skill of Responding to Teasing. Brenda, will you give everyone one of these cards, please.

Brenda hands out the skill cards while the teacher directs the group's attention to the skill-step poster in front of the group.

Thank you, Brenda. I'd like to read you the steps to the skill of Responding to Teasing.

Skill 38: Responding to Teasing

1. Stop and count to five.

2. Think about your choices:

    a. Ignore the teasing.

    b. Say how you feel.

    c. Give a reason for the person to stop.

3. Act out your best choice.

Step 2: Model the Skill

Teacher: These three steps, in this order, make up a good way to respond to teasing. Mr. Staton and I are going to model the skill for you—we're going to show you how to follow these steps. Just like the basketball coach, we'll show you the skill being done well. Try to pick out the steps as we model the skill. Later, you'll all have a chance to go through these same steps. Here's the situation: There's a student in my class who keeps saying mean things to me when we're outside at recess. I'll just be talking with my friends, and he'll come up to me and say things like my mother is ugly and make faces. What should I do first? What's the first step *(pointing to the step)?*

Darwin: You stop and count to five.

Teacher: Good. Now the second thing I do?

Brenda: Think about your choices.

Teacher: Yes. And I could ignore the teasing. I could say how I feel in a friendly way. Or I could give a reason to stop. And the third step?

Mario: You act out your best choice.

Teacher: Thank you. Now, I'm out here at recess, standing here talking with my friends. The kid who usually teases me is walking up to me—he's probably going to tap me on the shoulder to get my attention.

Mr. Staton: Hey, you, did you know that your mother is one ugly dude?

Teacher: OK, I need to calm down, so I'll stop and count to five. 1 . . . 2 . . . 3 . . . 4 . . . 5. Now I need to think of my choices. I could ignore him, but I've ignored him before. I could say how I feel. Or I could give him a reason to stop. I need to act out my best choice. I think it's best to keep ignoring him. Eventually he'll stop when he knows he can't get me mad.

Turns away and acts as if she's listening to friends talk.

Did I follow all of the skill steps? Did I follow the first step? Did I stop and count to five? *(Students respond.)* Did I think of my choices? *(Students respond.)* And what choice did I make?

Joe: You ignored him and kept talking with your friends.

Teacher: Yes, that's the choice I made. And how do you think I did on this skill?

Students respond with positive comments.

Yes, I think I did a good job, too.

Step 3: Establish Student Skill Need

Teacher: That's our modeling of the skill. Let's think of some times in your real lives when you are teased and it's difficult for you to deal with this teasing. I'll write your names on the board and your situation beside it so that we can remember the situations. Who can think of a time when you're being teased and it bothers you?

Lakeesha: When I go roller-blading, my brother always laughs at me. He says I'm really bad at it.

Mario: That kid across the street, he's always sayin' somethin'.

Rita: There's this kid who keeps calling me. My mom calls me to the phone, and then the kid hangs up!

The list continues as each student identifies a situation for skill use.

Step 4: Select the First Role-Player

Teacher: You all came up with really good examples of situations when you are teased that are difficult for you. Who would like to try the skill first? Who would like to role-play? OK, Mario. That kid across the street seems to really be bothering you.

Step 5: Set Up the Role-Play

Teacher: All right, Mario. Could you tell us a little more about the situation so that we can help you feel that you are in that situation?

Mario: Well, I go that way to get to Juan's house. I walk by after school. He's there, kinda by this big tree, in his yard, you know. I go by. I don't see him, but then he kinda comes out and starts talkin' to me.

Teacher: What kinds of things does he say, Mario?

Mario: He says he's got proof that I'm into bad stuff and he's gonna tell. I know there's nothin' he's got to tell anybody.

Teacher: All right. I think that gives us a pretty good idea of the situation. Is there anything else?

Mario: *(Shakes his head no.)*

Teacher: Mario, who in the group reminds you most of the boy who is teasing you?

Mario: I guess Gabe.

Teacher: Gabe, would you be willing to help us out with this? Will you be the coactor in the role-play? We'll help you with what to say to Mario. Will you come on up in front? Gabe will be the kid across the street, and when Mario walks by, Gabe will step out and say that he knows Mario is into bad stuff and he's going to tell. Is that right, Mario?

Mario: Yeah. He says he'll tell the cops.

Teacher: OK, then. *(To the group)* Before we get started with the actual role-play, I'm going to ask each of you to watch the role-play carefully. I want you each to watch for a certain step. Darwin and Brenda, will you watch to see if Mario does the first step, see if he stops and counts to five? Lakeesha and Aretha, will you watch to see if he thinks of his choices? And Rita and Joe, will you watch to see if he acts out his choice? When the role-play is over, I need you to tell Mario and the rest of us just what he did and how well you think he did.

Step 6: Conduct the Role-Play

Teacher: Mario, you will need to talk aloud what you are thinking so that we know you are following the steps. Are you all ready?

Gabe: Hey, you. I'm talkin' to you. I tell you, I'm gonna tell on you, man. I'm gonna tell the cops you're into some pretty bad stuff.

Teacher: Good, Gabe. Now Mario, look at the skill steps. Go ahead and talk out loud what you are thinking. What's the first thing you need to do?

Mario: Stop and count to five.

Teacher: OK. Go ahead.

Mario: 1 . . . 2 . . . 3 . . . 4 . . . 5.

The teacher points to the second skill step on the skill poster.

Mario: I think of my choices.

Teacher: You could ignore, say how you feel, or give a reason to stop.

Mario: I'll ignore. It doesn't matter anyway 'cause there's nothin' he's gonna tell. *(Walks away.)*

Teacher: OK, Mario!

Step 7: Provide Performance Feedback

Order of feedback is coactor, observers, main actor, teacher.

Teacher: Let's get some feedback for Mario. Gabe, if you were the real kid across the street, how do you think you'd react to what Mario did?

Gabe: I'd feel pretty stupid. I couldn't get him goin'. Maybe I'd do it to somebody different.

Teacher: So you felt Mario did a good job ignoring, that you wouldn't keep teasing him?

Gabe: Yeah. He did a good job.

Teacher: Thank you, Gabe. Thanks for helping out, too. Who watched to see if Mario followed the first step? Did he stop and count to five?

Observers: Yeah.

Teacher: For the second step, did Mario think of his choices?

Observers: Yeah.

Teacher: How do you know that he was thinking of his choices?

Aretha: He talked it out loud. I heard him say it.

Teacher: Good watching, Aretha. What choice did he decide on?

Lakeesha: To ignore.

Teacher: Did he follow the third step? Did he act out his best choice?

Observers: Yeah. He ignored.

Teacher: How did he ignore?

Rita: He walked away from the kid.

Teacher: Nice job, everyone! Mario, how did it feel? Was it easy to do?

Mario: It wasn't easy. But OK, it was OK.

Teacher: Was there something you would like to have done better?

Mario: No. But sometimes it gets to me.

Teacher: You certainly did a nice job in this role-play. You followed each of the skill steps. I also knew what you were thinking because you talked aloud your thinking. And, you made the choice to calmly walk away.

Teacher: Mario, are you saying that in real life, when the kid across the street really says those things to you, that you might have some trouble?

Mario: Maybe. I can try it.

Teacher: Good for you, Mario. Let's plan out your homework assignment together when the group is finished.

Step 8: Select the Next Role-Player

Teacher: Who would like to role-play the skill next?

The process continues until all have had a chance to role-play the skill.

Step 9: Assign Skill Homework

The teacher hands out the Homework Reports, helps group members identify a time to try out the skill, and coaches them through the process next described for Mario.

Teacher: Mario, let's plan your homework assignment. Are you ready?

Mario: I guess.

Teacher: You seem a bit unsure. I know Responding to Teasing is a difficult skill. Let's go ahead and plan your homework, and if you want to role-play this skill again before you try

it in real life, we can do this during group tomorrow, OK?

Mario: Yeah, I want to practice again.

Teacher: OK. After another practice. Write your name and the date here. The name of the skill and the skill steps are listed for you. Now, with whom will you try this skill? Here you can write the name of the person who teases you. *(Mario writes the name.)* Good. Then, let's decide when you'll try the skill.

Mario: After school, when I'm walkin' to Juan's.

Teacher: OK, go ahead and write "after school" on the next line. Then, after you try out the skill, you'll write what happened. They'll decide how you did by circling one of the faces. You'll choose a happy face if you followed all of the steps. You'll choose the happy face even if the skill didn't work out the way you wanted but you still followed all of the steps. Choose the straight-line face if you followed most of the steps and an unhappy face if you didn't use the skill at all. Then, on the last line, you'll explain why you circled the face you chose.

Mario: I got it.

Teacher: Good. Feel free to ask me any questions about this later, OK?

Mario: OK.

To increase the likelihood that Mario will be successful in using the skill with the real-life provocation, the teacher will coach Mario again before he actually tries the skill.

CHAPTER 4

Refining Skill Use

Although Skillstreaming is a psychoeducational intervention derived primarily from social learning theory, cognitive-behavioral interventions such as problem solving, anger control, and verbal mediation are embedded in its instructional format and can enhance its effectiveness. This chapter briefly examines the role of these approaches in Skillstreaming, as well as that of strategies to increase a student's social performance, including reducing competing problem behaviors, supportive modeling, empathy, nonverbal behaviors, and skill shifting/skill combinations.

COGNITIVE-BEHAVIORAL STRATEGIES

Kaplan and Carter (2005) explain the concept of cognition relative to behavioral intervention strategies to include cognitive processes, cognitive structures, and inner speech. Cognitive structures relate to our beliefs and ideas and involve "more the way we think as opposed to what we think" (p. 381). Gresham (2005) further explains this concept:

> Cognitive-behavioral theory is based on the premise that thoughts, emotions and actions are inextricably linked and that changing one of these necessarily produces changes in the others. These reciprocal relationships between thoughts, emotions, and actions serve as the fundamental basis of all cognitive-behavioral intervention strategies. (p. 213)

Therefore, cognitive structures can be modified through strategies such as teaching problem solving, impulse control, and self-mediation.

Smith, Lochman, and Daunic (2005) further cite support for using these strategies to prevent and remediate patterns of aggressive and disruptive behavior. For example, many aggressive youth perceive negative intentions of others, even when actions clearly appear accidental in nature, whereas more socially competent youth do not. Incorporating elements of the cognitive-behavioral approach will promote the self-control needed by many students to change their typical manner of reacting, recall skill steps, and generalize the skills they learn. Knowledge of the following areas—problem solving, anger/impulse control, and verbal mediation—will guide group leaders in enhancing Skillstreaming instruction.

Problem Solving

As Ladd and Mize (1983) point out, children and adolescents may be deficient in such problem-solving competencies as knowledge of appropriate goals for social interaction, knowledge of appropriate strategies for reaching a social goal, and knowledge of the contexts in which specific strategies may be appropriately applied. A major goal of providing instruction in problem solving, as stated by Cartledge and Feng (1996), is "to teach people how to think through and resolve interpersonal conflicts using a four-step process: (a) identifying and defining the problem, (b) generating a variety of solutions, (c) identifying potential consequences, and (d) implementing and evaluating a solution" (p. 62). Older students will also need to learn to evaluate the quality of solutions generated (e.g., assertiveness and effectiveness) (Maag & Swearer, 2005). Problem Solving (Skill 41) presents the specific steps for using this process in a social context. However, the cognitive aspect suggests that the general skill of problem solving is useful in conjunction with other skills. Therefore, problem solving may be applied broadly, as well as taught as one skill of many.

Anger/Impulse Control

Many students may know the desired and expected behavior and may, in fact, be likely to behave in this manner in many situations. However, when angry, anxious, or otherwise upset, they are unable to see beyond the emotion-producing event. Before many students will be able to recall the steps of a specific skill, they must use strategies to stop themselves from reacting in a perhaps well-established pattern of aggression or other unproductive behavior.

In contrast to the direct facilitation of prosocial behavior in Skillstreaming, anger control training, developed by Feindler (Feindler, 1979, 1995; Feindler & Ecton, 1986) facilitates such skill behavior indirectly by teaching ways to inhibit anger and loss of self-control. In this method, youngsters are taught how to respond to provocations to anger by (a) identifying their external and internal anger triggers; (b) identifying their own physiological/kinesthetic cues signifying anger; (c) using anger reducers to lower arousal via deep breathing, counting backwards, imagining a peaceful scene, or contemplating the long-term consequences of anger-associated behavior; (d) using reminders, or self-statements, that are in opposition to triggers; and (e) self-evaluating, or judging, how adequately anger control worked and rewarding oneself when it has worked well.

Two programs that pair Skillstreaming with an anger control component include Aggression Replacement Training and the EQUIP Program. Aggression Replacement Training (Glick & Gibbs, 2010; Goldstein, Glick, & Gibbs, 1998) includes Skillstreaming, anger control training, and a moral reasoning component. The EQUIP Program (Gibbs, Potter, & Goldstein, 1995) employs these three components within the context of a positive peer-helping milieu. The Prepare Curriculum (Goldstein, 1989, 1999b) combines Skillstreaming with anger control training, empathy training, problem-solving training, and other competencies.

The majority of Skillstreaming skills used under stressful conditions include an anger or impulse control strategy—counting to five or taking three deep breaths, for example. Emphasizing these methods, taking additional time to teach them and reinforce their use, or using the anger control training process just described will increase the likelihood of success in students' real-life skill use.

Verbal Mediation

As discussed in chapter 2, verbal mediation, or saying aloud what would normally be thought to oneself silently, is an important part of both modeling and role-playing. Saying the steps aloud as the models or role-players enact the behaviors demonstrates the cognitive processes underlying skill performance and facilitates learning. For example, in Joining In (Skill 17), the model might say, "I want to ask if I can play, but I'm afraid they might say no. But I'm going to take the chance. OK, the first step is to watch."

This type of accompanying narration increases the effectiveness of the modeling display (Bandura, 1977), draws observers' attention to specific skill steps, and may facilitate skill generalization (Stokes & Baer, 1977). Verbal mediation may also be employed to demonstrate a coping model. For example, "They are all going to the party. I really want to go, but I can't—I wasn't invited. But feeling hurt won't get me invited. I need to think of my choices" (Skill 51, Dealing with Being Left Out).

Verbal mediation has been used to teach impulse control in hyperactive children (Kendall & Braswell, 1985), anger control in adolescents (Goldstein & Glick, 1987), impulse control in aggressive youngsters (Camp & Bash, 1981), academic behaviors through self-instruction training (Meichenbaum, 1977), and strategies for coping with depression in students with emotional and behavioral disorders (Maag & Swearer, 2005). By practicing talking themselves through a skill or saying aloud ways to control the impulse to react in an undesirable way, students learn to regulate their actions until these actions become nearly automatic. As stated by Camp and Bash (1985):

> A good deal of evidence suggests that adequate development of verbal mediation activity is associated with (1) internalization of the inhibitory function of language, which serves to block impulsive and associative responding in both cognitive and social situations, and (2) utilization of linguistic tools in learning, problem-solving, and forethought. (p. 7)

Many elementary-age children will need to be taught the process of thinking aloud by having them practice while they are engaged in other types of activities (e.g., completing academic tasks, doing a classroom chore). Maag and Swearer (2005) offer factors to increase the effectiveness of verbal mediation, including the following:

1. Initially, self-instruction should be limited to three words or a short phrase or sentence.
2. The student should verbalize the exact wording of the phrase.
3. The phrase should refer to increasing or decreasing a specific behavior (rather than being a vague statement).
4. The student should be reinforced for using self-instruction.

FACTORS IN SUCCESSFUL SKILL USE

In addition to strategies relating to the cognitive-behavioral approach, factors that impact successful skill use include skill fluency, social perceptions, reduction of competing behaviors, nonverbal behaviors, empathy, and supportive modeling.

Skill Fluency

Fluency in performing selected social skills is largely achieved through the generalization principle of overlearning. As is the case for other skills, such as learning to read or playing a sport, prosocial skill performance is often somewhat artificial and rote in the initial stages of learning. The more practice students have in using the skill in a variety of different situations and settings and with different coactors, the more fluent and natural the performance will become. A positive relationship between the amount of social skills training and successful performance has been found (Gresham et al., 2006; McIntosh, Vaughn, & Zaragoza, 1991). When skill fluency is at issue, more intense and frequent skill training is called for.

Perceptions of Social Situations

Processing Social Information

A model for processing social information useful in refining the skill use of elementary school children is presented by Dodge (1983) and his colleagues. This model includes (a) encoding relevant information, (b) applying meanings, (c) accessing a response, (d) evaluating a response, and (e) enacting a response.

Encoding relevant information

Relative to a social interaction, children must first attend to cues that are appropriate to the interaction. Some children may focus on all of the cues in an interaction, thus having difficulty determining which cues to single out for response. Aggressive children often focus on the cues that appear to them to be aggressive ones. Others may ignore salient social cues—for example, failing to recognize boredom in one's listener when dominating a conversation (Gresham & Elliott, 1990). Further noted by Gresham and Elliott, "Some children are deficient in a social skill because certain social cues which would prompt socially appropriate behavior are absent" (p. 29). Typical social cues may be absent, for example, when a child is playing with a group of familiar peers.

Applying meanings

One's perception of intent influences one's behavior (Dodge, Murphy, & Birchsbaum, 1984). Meaning is given to the social cue in relation to the individual child's emotional needs or goals. For example, children who often act aggressively may interpret the intent of an action as hostile.

Accessing a response

Children typically do what they know or what is familiar to them. It is far easier for children to access a behavior and follow through on its performance when they have mastery of that behavior. Aggressive children, for instance, access more aggressive and less effective ways to solve problems with others (Guerra & Slaby, 1989). The focus of social skills training is to increase these children's repertoire of choices.

Evaluating a response

The capacity to evaluate the potential consequences of an action is associated with social competence. Aggressive youth, for example, identify fewer negative consequences for aggression and view their aggressive choices more positively than do others (Cartledge & Milburn, 1995). In addition, children who are aggressive often believe that their aggression will bring rewards, not negative consequences, including being treated less aversively by others (Perry, Perry, & Rasmussen, 1986).

Enacting a response

The performance of a behavior or skill is relative to the child's proficiency in performing that skill, as well as to his or her motivation to do so. Social performance, then, involves the enactment of a sequence of behaviors in relevant and appropriate ways within a context.

Social Perceptions and Behavioral Flexibility

Even if a student becomes proficient in a given skill, the student may misread the context in which the prosocial skill is desirable or acceptable. Although the procedures to teach social skills are the same as those in teaching academics, the teaching of social skills is more complex due to the reciprocal nature of social interactions. With academic instruction, it is often the case that there is one, and only one, correct response. Furthermore, that correct response is always correct. Social skills performance, on the other hand, is influenced by culture, setting, and group dynamics (Scott & Nelson, 1998).

A major emphasis in psychology concerns the importance of the situation or setting, as perceived by the individual, in determining behavior. Morrison and Bellack (1981), for example, state that individuals must not only possess the ability to enact given behavioral skills, they must also know when and how these responses should be applied. These authors further state that in order to use this knowledge, individuals must have the "ability to accurately 'read' the social environment" (p. 70). This ability, they suggest, includes awareness of the norms and conventions in operation at a given time, as well as understanding of the message given by the other person.

Students can be taught to read the context (situation and setting) of the social situation accurately and adjust their behavior accordingly. Therefore, emphasis must be placed not only on skill performance but also on such questions as the following: "What is the behavior expected in this setting?" "Which skill should I use with this person, considering his or her role?" and "What signs are there that this is a good time to use the skill?" Attending to such questions while teaching behavioral skills will likely result in more successful skill use and guide students in developing the flexibility needed to adjust skill use across settings, situations, and people.

The work of Dodge (1985) and Spivack and Shure (1974) suggests that children should be able to respond to the following questions throughout their skill performance:

▶ Why should I use the skill?

▶ With whom should I use the skill?

▶ Where should I use the skill?

▶ When should I use the skill?

▶ How should I perform the skill?

Although many of these issues are addressed in the skills themselves as particular behavioral steps and in the four components of Skillstreaming (modeling, role-playing, performance feedback, and generalization), additional emphasis can be achieved through group discussion, supplementary role-play practice, and related activities.

Why should I use the skill?

Children will be more likely to learn a new behavior or skill if they are motivated to do so. Understanding how prosocial skill performance will help them meet their needs—get the favor they want or need, stay out of trouble, and so forth—is valuable in enhancing motivation. Therefore, as teachers and other group leaders introduce each skill, they must point out the specific and direct benefits to be gained.

With whom should I use the skill?

To perform the skill competently, the child must learn to assess and interpret the verbal and nonverbal cues of the person or persons to whom the skill performance is directed. For example, it is sometimes the case that a child who is learning Joining In (Skill 17) fails to assess the receptivity of the target peer group. If the group appears to be avoiding the skill-deficient child (e.g., continuing to move the activity away, refusing to make eye contact, or even shouting at the child to go away), the child will need to learn how to attend to such cues and interpret their meaning. The teacher can help by guiding the child in selecting another person or group to approach or by urging the child to use a related backup skill with the first group. Likewise, although Saying No (Skill 55) may help avoid trouble when directed toward a friend, the outcome may be quite different if the skill is tried with a parent who is directing the child to get ready for school. Such parameters of skill use may not be easily identi-

fied by many children, and discussions and perhaps role-plays of this issue will need to be an integral part of instruction.

Where should I use the skill?

The skill-deficient child will need help in evaluating the setting in which he or she intends to use the skill. A child's using Suggesting an Activity (Skill 23), for instance, may be desirable during classroom free play or during outside recess but would not be desirable while grocery shopping with a parent. Although adults may assume that most children automatically make this type of determination, this has not proven to be the case. Instead, varied settings in which the skill will likely be successful or unsuccessful should be addressed through group discussion and multiple role-plays.

When should I use the skill?

When a skill should be used is often a question for elementary-age students. It is not unusual, for example, for the child to use Asking a Question (Skill 9) while the teacher is giving directions or while a parent is involved in an interaction with another person. Therefore, discussions related to the timing of skill use need to be included with each skill.

How should I perform the skill?

The manner in which a child performs a skill can determine its effectiveness. For example, a child who uses Asking a Favor (Skill 19) in an angry manner will likely find that the favor is not granted. Likewise, the child who employs the steps of Responding to Teasing (Skill 38) but who is obviously upset at being provoked may not find that the skill yields a positive outcome.

Reduction of Competing Problem Behaviors

Gresham (1998a) explains that the problem behavior may be more efficient for the child than a more socially acceptable behavior. In other words, the outcome the child desires is easier to obtain through using the problem behavior than through using an alternative, more socially acceptable behavior or skill. The problem behavior is also likely to be reliable as well, consistently leading to reinforcement for the individual. A goal, then, is to reduce the reliability and efficiency of the problem behavior.

For example, when Lana wants to use the colored markers, she typically just grabs them away from whoever may be using the color she wants. By the time the peer complains and a teacher intervenes, Lana is finished using the marker. Grabbing the marker works for her. Grabbing is reliable (it works most of the time), and it's efficient (it works quickly and she doesn't have to wait to use the marker). A goal, then, is to reduce the reliability and efficiency of the problem behavior—in other words, to make sure the problem behavior doesn't work for the child. For children whose emotional responses (e.g., anger, fear, frustration) inhibit or prevent skill performance, Elliott and Gresham (1991) suggest that instruction in the prosocial skill be paired with strategies to reduce the interfering problem behavior. Therefore, in the example above, the function of Lana's behavior is to gain the marker. Lana's plan includes positive reinforcement for asking for help in obtaining an item (using a skill) but also consequences (loss of the privilege of using the classroom markers) if she grabs the item from a peer. Students whose problem behavior is more intense or resistant to such change procedures will benefit from more-comprehensive behavior change strategies such as those described in chapter 6.

Nonverbal Behaviors

Nonverbal communicators such as body posture and movements, facial expressions, and voice tone and volume give others messages either consistent with or contradictory to verbal content. Consider, for example, a student who is told to leave the playground for breaking the rules. Often it is not the breaking of the rule per se that results in the playground supervisor's ac-

tion. Rather, one hears comments like "She was defiant" or "He didn't seem sorry for what he did." When the playground supervisor is further questioned regarding the student's defiance or failure to apologize, nonverbal evidence may be called upon (e.g., "She just stood there" or "He didn't look sorry!"). Understanding the influence of nonverbal language is an important factor in learning prosocial behaviors. Fox and Boulton (2003), for example, researched the behaviors that discriminated between victims and nonvictims of bullying. They found that 50 percent of the behaviors that best predicted victimization were nonverbal behaviors, including looking scared, standing in a way that suggests weakness, and looking like an unhappy person.

Nowicki and Duke (1992) illustrate six areas of nonverbal communication:

1. Paralanguage (voice tone, speech rate, variation of speech, nonverbal sounds)

2. Facial expressions

3. Postures and gestures

4. Interpersonal distance (space) and touch (intimate, personal, social, and public zones)

5. Rhythm and time (e.g., being on time, spending time with friends)

6. Objectics (hygiene, style of dress)

In brief, skill-deficient students will need to be made more aware of the ways in which nonverbal communicators send clear and definite messages.

Empathy

Even very young children possess the capacity to show empathy. Denham (1998), citing the work of Zahn-Waxler and Radke-Yarrow (1982, 1990), states that "children as young as two years of age are able to broadly interpret others' emotional states, to experience these feeling states in response to others' predicament, and attempt to alleviate discomfort in others" (p. 34). Chronically aggressive or other skill-deficient youth have been shown to display a pattern of personality traits high in egocentricity and low in concern for others (Slavin, 1980).

Expression of empathic understanding can serve both as an inhibitor of negative behaviors and as a facilitator of positive actions. Results of a number of studies inquiring into the interpersonal consequences of empathic responding show that empathy is a consistently potent promoter of interpersonal attraction, dyadic openness, conflict resolution, and individual growth (Goldstein & Michaels, 1985). In addition, Grizenko et al. (2000) found more lasting improvement from social skills instruction when social perspective taking was added. In other words, students who are able to show empathy are far less likely to act out aggressively toward others, are more accepted and sought after in social situations, are more able to participate in resolving interpersonal disputes, and are more satisfied with themselves.

Some helpful methods of encouraging empathy include (a) instructing students in skills such as Expressing Concern for Another (Skill 30) and Expressing Your Feelings (Skill 27); (b) providing opportunities for role reversal during role-plays, followed by actors' expression of feelings; (c) providing opportunities for observers to take the perspective of others (e.g., the main actor) during feedback sessions; and (d) encouraging empathy toward others through the modeling and discussion of appreciation for individual differences.

Supportive Modeling

Typically, aggressive youth are regularly exposed to highly aggressive models. Parents, siblings, and peers are often frequently chronically aggressive individuals themselves (Knight & West, 1975; Loeber & Dishion, 1983; Robins, West, & Herjanic, 1975). At the same time, relatively few prosocial models that might help counteract the effects of aggressive modeling exist for these youth to observe and imitate. When prosocial models are available, they apparently can make a tremendous difference in social development.

Werner and Smith (1982), in their longitudinal study of aggressive and nonaggressive youth *Vulnerable but Invincible,* clearly demonstrated that youth growing up in a community characterized by high crime, high unemployment, high secondary school dropout rates, and high levels of aggressive models were able to develop into effective, satisfied, prosocially oriented individuals if they had sustained exposure to at least one significant prosocial model—be it parent, relative, teacher, coach, neighbor, or peer.

The classroom teacher can be a powerful model for students. Needless to say, a powerful negative effect can be exerted on students if the teacher models prosocial skill deficiencies. Throughout the course of the school day, the teacher should make a sustained effort to model desirable, prosocial behaviors and to use the behavioral steps for selected skills when it is appropriate to do so. When frustrated or angry with an individual student's behavior, for example, the teacher can greatly affect student learning if he or she models the steps of Dealing with Your Anger (Skill 31) in a clear and deliberate manner.

SKILL SHIFTING, COMBINATIONS, ADAPTATION, AND DEVELOPMENT

Skill Shifting

Sometimes during the course of a Skillstreaming session devoted to a given skill, the need may arise for instruction in a different skill. When this is the case, the group leader should either shift to teaching the new skill on the spot or make note of the need to do so in the near future. For example, in a session devoted to Dealing with Your Anger (Skill 31), one student developed a role-play related to having difficulty with an academic assignment. Although this student often did become angry during such situations, instruction in the skill of Asking for Help (Skill 2) was also necessary to teach her to deal effectively with this type of event.

Students will often find it valuable if they become proficient in knowing when and how to shift from one skill to another. Thus, group instruction should help students discern when a skill is unsuccessful, when an alternative skill should be attempted, and which specific skill to try. In one group, for example, students were attending a schoolwide assembly. Joe used the skill Asking a Favor (Skill 19) with Paul by asking him to move over so that Joe could see better. Paul not only refused to move, he also began to tease Joe. Joe needed to shift to Responding to Teasing (Skill 38) to deal with his immediate problem, but he also needed to think of another skill to use so he would be able to see the assembly. Problem Solving (Skill 41) or Making a Complaint (Skill 47) might have been useful for Joe to try.

Skill Combinations

For many youngsters, relationships with adults and peers may present difficult interpersonal challenges—challenges that draw heavily upon their repertoire of interpersonal skills for solutions. Often competence in single skills is insufficient. For example, Hannah feels left out and is isolated from her classmates. She uses the skill of Joining In (Skill 17), but they continue to leave her out and refuse her friendly overtures. Darwin continues to be made fun of by his peers, and despite his efforts to ignore them (Responding to Teasing, Skill 38), they continue to taunt him. Despite her efforts and effective use of Ignoring Distractions (Skill 10), Lakeesha is still unable to complete her work on time. When Gabe uses Negotiating (Skill 44) to convince his mother to reduce his chores so he will have more time to practice basketball, his mother refuses. Yet another student successfully uses Introducing Yourself (Skill 14) but then doesn't know what to say next to the person she just met (Beginning a Conversation, Skill 15).

Many children experience these reactions when challenged with complex social situations. Single-skill responses, even when performed correctly, prove inadequate. The target of skill use (parent, teacher, peer, etc.) does not respond in a manner that helps the student resolve the conflict or otherwise get his or her needs met. At other times, the student may use a skill profi-

ciently but attempt it with a person not in a position to accept this skill (e.g., starting a conversation with an adult in a manner more appropriate for use with a peer). In still other cases, a student may correctly use a skill but choose a poor time or misperceive the appropriateness of the social context in selecting one skill when another may have been more helpful. Instruction must therefore involve both individual skill competency and mastery of skill combinations.

The following edited transcript presents one example of instruction in skill combinations. Three skills—Saying No (Skill 55), Dealing with Another's Anger (Skill 32), and Using Self-Control (Skill 36)—are first modeled by the group leaders and then role-played by two group members. The steps in these three skills are presented in Table 3.

Leader: During the last several group meetings, we have worked on only one skill at a time. Today we're going to do things a little differently. Sometimes using only one skill to deal with a problem isn't enough. Sometimes more than one skill is needed. We have worked on all of these skills: Saying No, Dealing with Another's Anger, and Using Self-Control. John, last week, when you did your homework assignment on Saying No, you told the rest of us that the skill didn't work too well for you—that when you used the skill with a friend who wanted you to steal money from your parents, it didn't work too well.

John: Emanuel won't take no. He kept on. We got in a fight.

Leader: And from what you told me, that wasn't what you wanted to have happen. I'm going to do a modeling display with Libby. She is going to try to get me to take something from the convenience store after school. I'm going to say no, but Libby is go-

Table 3: Sample Skill Sequence

Skill 55: Saying No

1. Decide whether or not you want to do what is being asked.

2. Think about why you don't want to do this.

3. Tell the person no in a friendly way.

4. Give your reason.

Skill 32: Dealing with Another's Anger

1. Listen to what the person has to say.

2. Think about your choices:

   a. Keep listening.

   b. Ask why the person is angry.

   c. Give the person an idea to fix the problem.

   d. Walk away for now.

3. Act out your best choice.

Skill 36: Using Self-Control

1. Stop and count to 10.

2. Think of how your body feels.

3. Think about your choices:

   a. Walk away for now.

   b. Do a relaxation exercise.

   c. Write about how you feel.

   d. Talk to someone about it.

4. Act out your best choice.

---

ing to keep pressuring me to steal. In fact, she's going to get really angry with me, so I'll not only have to say no, but I'll have to deal with Libby's anger, too. But Libby will keep on, and then I'll have to use self-control to keep from getting so angry myself so I don't do something I'm sorry for later. That's the sequence of skills we're going to model. Then some of you will have the chance to try it, too. *(To Libby)* Are you ready? We're in the convenience store, over by the candy aisle.

Libby: Hey, the guy who is supposed to be at the counter isn't there. I'm hungry. Let's take some of this stuff. I'll go by the counter and watch, and you take some.

Leader: *(Thinking aloud while looking at the steps in the skill of Saying No)*

"Step 1: Decide whether or not you want to do what is being asked." I don't want to do this.

"Step 2: Think about why you don't want to do this." I know if I steal I'll get caught and get into big trouble.

"Step 3: Tell the person no in a friendly way." *(To Libby)* I'm not going to take anything.

(To herself) "Step 4: Give your reason." *(To Libby)* It's wrong, and we would get into big trouble. Let's get out of here.

Libby: Come on! It's only candy. It's not like they would put us in jail even if we were caught. But we won't be. Just put it in your backpack. The guy is busy over there. Now, take some!

Leader: Libby, I won't steal. Let's leave.

Libby: Are you a chicken? Who would even know? No one. Now I'm telling you to take some. Do it! Do it now, or I'll tell everyone at school what a dork you are. And then you'll be in big trouble. You know what happens to dorks, don't you?

Leader: *(Thinking aloud while looking at the skill steps to Dealing with Another's Anger)* I can tell she's really angry. "Step 1: Listen to what the person has to say." I have listened to what she had to say. I don't think continuing to listen would help, and I know she's angry because I won't do what she wants me to do—to steal.

"Step 2: Think about your choices." I could use my allowance and just buy the candy for her. Or I could walk away. I'm going to walk out of the store and wait for Libby outside.

"Step 3: Act out your best choice." *(Walks off to the side.)*

Libby: And where do you think you are going? I told you what I would do, and I'll do it. You're a joke! Nothing but a joke!

Leader: *(Thinking aloud and looking at the skill steps in Using Self-Control)*

Now I'm getting angry. "Step 1: Stop and count to 10." 1 . . . 2 . . . 3 . . . 4 . . . 5 . . . 6 . . . 7 . . . 8 . . . 9 . . . 10.

"Step 2: Think of how your body feels." I feel like I could explode.

"Step 3: Think about your choices." I could walk away, or I could try to find someone to talk to about this. I think I'll go home and talk to my sister. Maybe Libby will forget about it by tomorrow.

"Step 4: Act out your best choice." Libby, I'm going home. See you tomorrow.

(To the group) How did I do with this combination of skills? *(Students respond positively.)* Yes, I followed the steps of Saying No. When that didn't work and Libby got really angry, I switched to the skill of Dealing with Another's Anger. Then when I started to get angry, too, I switched to the skill of Using Self-Control. And I ended up not losing control. There are other ways I could have done this, with other combinations of skills. What would be a situation that each of you has that's pretty complicated, starting with the skill of Saying No? *(Group members identify situations.)* John, would you like to go first? You told us about the problem, and this would be a good situation. John, who in the group reminds you most of Emanuel?

John: Logan does.

Leader: All right. John and Logan, why don't you come up here. Logan, you are trying to convince John to steal money from his parents so that the two of you can go to the concert.

When he says no, you're going to get angry with him, and we want to see a little bit of anger. John, you'll have to deal with his anger. Then when you start to get angry or upset yourself, you'll need to use self-control. The skills and steps are up here on the chart to help you. We'll watch John go through all three of these skills. Are you ready? OK. Logan, you start to encourage John to steal from his parents when he doesn't have the money to go to the concert.

Logan: So, you don't have the money. You can take it from your mom. Just take it from her purse. She'll never know.

John: *(Thinking aloud and looking at the skill steps to Saying No)*

"Step 1: Decide whether or not you want to do what is being asked." He wants me to steal from my mom. I can't do it.

"Step 2: Think about why you don't want to do this." She'll know it's gone, and she needs the money for other stuff.

"Step 3: Tell the person no in a friendly way." *(To Logan)* I want to go to the concert. But I can't steal from my mom.

(To himself) "Step 4: Give your reason." *(To Logan)* She'd know the money was gone.

Logan: Come on. How would she know you took it? Just say you didn't do it. No problem.

John: I won't steal.

Logan: It's not really stealing. It's your mom. Come on. Take the money. Oh, yeah, I know you just don't want to go. You're just makin' up excuses.

Leader: John, Logan seems to be getting angry now.

John: *(Thinking aloud and looking at the skill steps for Dealing with Another's Anger)*

"Step 1: Listen to what the person has to say." I guess I'll listen to what he says.

Logan: I thought you were my best friend, but you won't go. And this is a great concert. Man, you're off my list. You acted like you were my best bud. You liar.

John: *(To himself)* "Step 2: Think about your choices." I could keep listening. I could ask why, or I could give him an idea. I'll try that.

"Step 3: Act out your best choice." *(To Logan)* I am your best friend, and I do want to go. I just don't have the money. Maybe I could ask my mom, maybe do some of her chores.

Logan: The concert's on Saturday, jerk. And your mom won't give it to you . . . you already said. You're a mama's boy, won't steal from her!

John: *(Thinking aloud and looking at the skill steps for Using Self-Control)*

"Step 1: Stop and count to 10." 1 . . . 2 . . . 3 . . . 4 . . . 5 . . . 6 . . . 7 . . . 8 . . . 9 . . . 10.

"Step 2: Think of how your body feels." My stomach is all jumpy.

"Step 3: Think about your choices." I could just walk. Or I could talk to someone.

"Step 4: Act out your best choice." *(To Logan)* It's not fair to say stuff about my mom. I'm going to leave. *(Walks away.)*

Leader: Let's get some feedback.

Other skill combinations may also be helpful. Hannah, for example, who tried Joining In

(Skill 17) but continued to be rejected by her peers, might need to use Expressing Your Feelings (Skill 27) following the group's rejection and then perhaps Suggesting an Activity (Skill 23) with a peer outside of the original group. Darwin, who continued to be made fun of despite his proficient use of Responding to Teasing (Skill 38), may have been more effective using the combination of Dealing with Fear (Skill 34) and Making a Complaint (Skill 47). Likewise, Lekeesha may find that if Ignoring Distractions (Skill 10) doesn't help her complete her work, she might use the skills of Completing Assignments (Skill 6) or Asking for Help (Skill 2). Gabe, whose use of Negotiating (Skill 44) failed with his mother, may need to use the skill combination of Reacting to Failure (Skill 53) and Problem Solving (Skill 41).

Other useful skill combinations include the following:

▶ Joining In (Skill 17) and Dealing with Being Left Out (Skill 51)

▶ Dealing with an Accusation (Skill 43) and Accepting Consequences (Skill 42)

▶ Deciding What Caused a Problem (Skill 46) and Negotiating (Skill 44)

▶ Asking Permission (Skill 37), Accepting No (Skill 54), and Dealing with Boredom (Skill 45)

▶ Knowing Your Feelings (Skill 26) and Expressing Your Feelings (Skill 27)

▶ Setting a Goal (Skill 13), Dealing with Fear (Skill 34), and Contributing to Discussions (Skill 7)

Skill Adaptation and Development

As students express concerns and difficulties, and as teachers observe problems, new skills can and should be developed. Consider the situation, for example, in which a group of students are continually disruptive when moving into the group setting. The perceptive teacher, recognizing that transitions are difficult for this particular group of students, develops the following skill:

Coming to Group

1. Put materials away.

2. Look up to show the teacher you are ready.

3. Wait quietly until your table is called.

4. Walk to the group area.

In a different situation, a student may have difficulty when not picked to be first for a game. Steps for a new skill, titled "Dealing with Not Being First" might be as follows:

Dealing with Not Being First

1. Take a deep breath.

2. Say, "Everybody can't be first. Maybe I'll be first next time."

3. Say, "I knew I could handle this!"

Melisa Genaux, a behavioral expert in the area of autism, developed a specific skill for students with Asperger's syndrome. Because so many of the students with whom she works have behavior difficulty when their routines change, she developed the following skill:

Changes in Routine/It's Not What I Thought Would Happen Skill

1. Stop.

2. Take a deep breath.

3. Count to five.

4. Say, "OK."

5. Follow the direction.

In some circumstances it may be appropriate to retain a given skill but alter one or more of its behavioral steps. Steps may be simplified as the skills and needs of the students suggest. For example, a child who repeatedly becomes out of control when losing may learn only two of the behavioral steps constituting Skill 49, Dealing with Losing.

> 1. Say, "Everybody can't win."
> 2. Say, "Maybe I'll win next time."

Group leaders should use their experience and judgment in adjusting the content of these skills.

CHAPTER 5

Teaching for Skill Generalization

Historically, therapeutic interventions have reflected a core belief in personality change as both the target and outcome of effective intervention; thus, environmental influences on behavior were largely ignored. It has been assumed that the positive changes believed to have taken place within the individual's personality would enable the individual to deal effectively with problematic events wherever and whenever they might occur. That is, transfer and maintenance would occur automatically.

Research on psychotherapy initiated in the 1950s and expanded in the 1960s and 1970s sought to ascertain whether gains at the end of the formal intervention had in fact generalized across settings and/or time. Stokes and Baer (1977) described this time as one in which transfer and maintenance were hoped for and noted if they did occur ("train and hope"). The overwhelming result of these investigations was that, much more often than not, transfer and maintenance of intervention gains did not occur. Treatment and training did not persist automatically, nor did learning necessarily transfer (Goldstein & Kanfer, 1979; Keeley, Shemberg, & Carbonell, 1976). This failure, revealed by evidence accumulated during the train-and-hope phase, led to a third phase—the development, evaluation, and use of procedures explicitly designed to enhance transfer and maintenance of intervention gains.

As the social skills movement in general and Skillstreaming in particular have matured and

evidence regarding effectiveness has accumulated, it has become clear that skill acquisition is a reliable finding across both training methods and populations. However, generalization is another matter. Both generalization to new settings (transfer) and over time (maintenance) have been reported to occur in only a minority of cases. The main concern of any teaching effort is not how students perform in the teaching setting, but how well they perform in their real lives. Therefore, generalization is often considered the most important goal in social skills instruction (Gresham, 1998a, 1998b). Approaches to enhance transfer and maintenance are listed in Table 4 and discussed in the following pages.

Beyond these strategies, many concerned with the social development of children and adolescents hypothesize that social skills often fail to generalize due to the presence of stronger, competing problem behaviors. Children may fail to use a newly learned skill not just because reinforcement in their real lives does not occur or because the Skillstreaming instructor has not attended to the generalization principles adequately during the instruction. As Gresham, Sugai, and Horner (2001) state, "One reason . . . that socially skilled behaviors may fail to generalize is because the newly taught behavior is masked or overpowered by older and stronger competing behaviors" (p. 340). Although failure of generalization is surely to occur if generalization strategies are

Table 4: Transfer- and Maintenance-Enhancing Procedures

Transfer

Before Instruction

Entrapment (including relevant peers in the instruction)

During Instruction

1. Provision of general principles (general case programming)

2. Overlearning (maximizing response availability)

3. Stimulus variability (training sufficient exemplars, training loosely)

4. Identical elements (programming common stimuli)

After Instruction

5. Instructed generalization

6. Mediated generalization (self-recording, self-reinforcement, self-punishment, self-instruction

Maintenance

During the Skillstreaming Intervention

1. Thinning reinforcement (increase intermittency, unpredictability)

2. Delaying reinforcement

3. Fading prompts

4. Providing booster sessions

5. Preparing for real-life nonreinforcement

Beyond the Skillstreaming Intervention

6. Programming for reinforcement in the natural environment

7. Using natural reinforcers

---

not put in place, some students may experience intense emotions such as anger or anxiety or in other ways have difficulties in regulating their emotions or behaviors. For these youth, Skillstreaming efforts must include additional strategies to refine skill use (chapter 4) and reduce problem behaviors (chapter 6).

The Generalization Integrity Checklist, included in Appendix B, guides Skillstreaming instructors in the use of generalization principles and strategies and helps ensure that the fidelity of Skillstreaming generalization is addressed. This tool is for use by group leaders to evaluate how they incorporate generalization into their training before, during, and after carrying out Skillstreaming instructional procedures. The checklist may also be used by Skillstreaming master trainers as they work with and observe novice group leaders.

TRANSFER-ENHANCING PROCEDURES

Efforts to develop means of maximizing transfer have resulted in considerable success. A va-

riety of useful techniques have been developed, evaluated, and put into practice. As suggested by Kame'enui and Simmons (1990), these are separated into procedures to implement before, during, and after instruction.

Before Instruction

Skillstreaming employs the principle of transfer enhancement by including as group members the same people the youth interacts with on a regular basis outside of the group (McIntosh & MacKay, 2008; Walker et al., 2004). Including the peer group allows peers to reward the target student for skill use (Maag, 2006). This concept is referred to as *entrapment*, or providing natural reinforcement by peers for the student's performance of a desirable social behavior (McConnell, 1987). Thus, if possible, in the school setting all members of a Skillstreaming group should be from one class. For the same reason, in residential, agency, or institutional settings, teaching groups are most often constructed to directly parallel the facility's unit, crew, cottage, or ward structure. Participation in the same group affords an excellent opportunity to teach participants positive alternatives for dealing with their real-life difficulties.

During Instruction

Provision of General Principles

Generalization may be facilitated by providing the student with the general mediating principles that govern satisfactory performance on both the original and transfer task. The student can be given the rules, strategies, or organizing principles that lead to successful performance. The general finding that understanding the principles underlying successful performance can enhance transfer to new tasks and contexts has been reported in a number of domains of psychological research, including studies of labeling, rules, advance organizers, and learning sets. It is a robust finding, with empirical support in both laboratory and psychoeducational settings.

No matter how competently Skillstreaming leaders seek to create in the role-play setting the "feel" of the real-life setting in which the student will need to use the skill and no matter how well the coactor in a given role-play matches the actual qualities the real target person possesses, there will always be differences between role-play and real world. Even when the student has role-played the skill a number of times, the demands of the actual situation will depart in some respects from the demands portrayed in the role-play. And the real parent, real peer, or real teacher is likely to respond at least somewhat differently than the student's role-play partner. When the student has a good grasp of the principles underlying a situation (demands, expected behaviors, norms, purposes, rules) and the principles underlying the skill (why these steps, in this order, toward which ends), successful transfer of skill performance becomes more likely.

Overlearning

Transfer of training is enhanced by procedures that maximize overlearning or response availability: The likelihood that a response will be available is clearly a function of its prior use. We repeat and repeat foreign language phrases we are trying to learn, we insist that our child spend an hour per day in piano practice, and we devote considerable time practicing to make a golf swing smooth and automatic. These are simply expressions of the response-availability notion—that is, the more we have practiced responses (especially correct ones), the easier it will be to use them in other contexts or at later times. It has been well established that, other things being equal, the response emitted most frequently in the past is more likely to be emitted on subsequent occasions. However, it is not sheer practice of attempts at effective behaviors that is of most benefit to transfer but practice of successful attempts. Overlearning involves extending learning over more trials than would be necessary merely to produce initial changes in the individual's behavior. In all too many instances, one or two successes at a given task are taken as evidence to move on to the next task or the next level of the original task. This is an error in terms of transfer via overlearning. To maximize transfer, the guiding rule should not be "practice makes perfect" (implying that one simply practices until one gets it right and then moves on) but "practice of perfect" (implying numerous overlearning trials of correct responses after the initial success).

Some students who have just received good feedback from group members and leaders about their role-play (all steps followed and well portrayed) may object to the request that they role-play the skill a second or third time. Although valid concerns exist about the consequences of boredom when teaching a group of often restless students, the value of skill repetition cannot be overstressed. Often, leaders, not students, are more bored by the repetition. To assuage student concerns, leaders can point to the value for professional athletes of warm-ups, shoot-arounds, batting practice, and other repetitive practice. Such practice makes core skills nearly automatic and frees the player to concentrate on strategy.

In many real-life contexts, people and events actually work against the student's use of prosocial behaviors. It is therefore appropriate for a Skillstreaming group to spend two, three, or even more sessions role-playing a single skill. To reduce the possible interference of new learning on previously learned materials, a second skill should be introduced only when a student can recall the steps of the first skill, has had opportunities to role-play it, and has shown some initial transfer outside of the group teaching setting (e.g., has successfully completed a homework assignment).

Stimulus Variability

The previous section addressed enhancement of transfer by means of practice and repetition—that is, by the sheer number of correct skill responses the student makes. Transfer is also enhanced by the variability or range of situations to which the individual responds. Teaching related to even two situations is better than teaching related to one. As Kazdin (1975) comments:

> One way to program response maintenance and transfer of training is to develop the target behavior in a variety of situations and in the presence of several individuals. If the response is associated with a range of settings, individuals, and other cues, it is less likely to be lost when the situations change. (p. 21)

Epps, Thompson, and Lane (1985) discuss stimulus variability for transfer enhancement as it might operate in school contexts under the rubrics "train sufficient examples" and "train loosely." They observe that generalization of new skills or behaviors can also be facilitated by training students under a wide variety of conditions. Manipulating the numbers of leaders, settings, and response classes involved in the intervention promotes generalization by exposing students to a variety of situations. If, for example, students

are asked to role-play a given skill correctly three times, each attempt should involve a different co-actor, a different setting, and, especially, a different need for the same skill.

Identical Elements

In perhaps the earliest experimental work dealing with transfer enhancement, Thorndike and Woodworth (1901) concluded that, when one habit had a facilitative effect on another, it was to the degree that the habits shared identical elements. Ellis (1965) and Osgood (1953) later emphasized the importance for transfer of similarity between characteristics of the training and application tasks. As Osgood (1953) noted: "The greater the similarity between practice and test stimuli, the greater the amount of positive transfer" (p. 213).

In Skillstreaming, the principle of identical elements is implemented by procedures that increase the "real-lifeness" of the stimuli (places, people, events, etc.) to which the leader is helping the student learn to respond with effective, satisfying behaviors. Two broad strategies exist for attaining such high levels of correspondence between in-group and extra-group stimuli. The first concerns the place in which Skillstreaming occurs. Typically, groups remain in the school or institution and by use of props and imagination recreate the feel of the real-world context in which the student plans to use the skill. Because skills learned in context are more likely to generalize (Gresham, Sugai, & Horner, 2001), whenever possible, the Skillstreaming group leaves the formal teaching setting and meets in the actual locations in which the problem behaviors occur: "Fight on the playground? Let's have our session there"; "Sitting alone at lunch? Let's move to the lunchroom"; "Argument with a teacher in the hallway? Today's group will meet out there."

After Instruction

Instructed Generalization

One of the group leaders should be the person with whom the students regularly interact (e.g., a classroom teacher). This group leader's experience with group members aids in identifying needed skills and allows for prompting and coaching of student skill use as situations arise during the day (Pelco & Reed-Victor, 2007). McIntosh and MacKay (2008) state, "The person teaching the [social skills] lessons should be the person who supervises the generalization setting" (p. 19). The Skillstreaming group leader may additionally imbed instruction within naturally occurring events, such as academic skill classes (Smith & Gilles, 2003). This powerful strategy, termed *instructed generalization* or *capturing teachable moments,* greatly enhances both skill learning and generalization.

Mediated Generalization

The one certain commonality present in both teaching and real-life settings is the target student. Mediated generalization—mediated by the student, not by others—is an approach to transfer enhancement that relies on instructing the student in a series of self-regulation competencies (Neilans & Israel, 1981). Operationally, it consists of instructing the student in self-recording, self-reinforcement, self-punishment, and self-instruction. Epps et al. (1985), working in a special education setting, have structured these generalization-mediating steps as follows.

Self-recording

1. The teacher sets up the data collection system—that is, selects a target behavior, defines it in measurable terms, and decides on an appropriate recording technique.

2. The teacher tries out the data collection system.

3. The teacher teaches the student how to use the data collection system.

4. The teacher reinforces the student for taking accurate data.

This technique is helpful for several reasons: First, the group leader can become aware of the student's functioning in all settings. In other words, implementing self-recording procedures may give the teacher an indication of the frequency with which the student actually attempts the skill. Second, skill performance may not always result in positive reinforcement from others, but having the student record performance lets the student know that the teacher will later reinforce these efforts. Finally, many students are far more motivated to use newly learned skills when they, rather than an outside observer, monitor and record their performance. Figure 6, in chapter 2, presents a sample Self-Recording Form; additional self-recording forms are provided in Appendix A.

Self-reinforcement

Steps in self-reinforcement are summarized by Epps et al. (1985) as follows:

1. The teacher determines how many points a student has earned, and the student simply records these.

2. The teacher tells the student to decide how many points should be awarded for appropriate behavior.

3. The student practices self-reinforcement under teacher supervision.

4. The student employs self-reinforcement without teacher supervision.

Frequently, environmental support is insufficient to maintain newly learned skills. In fact, as mentioned earlier, many real-life environments actually discourage children's efforts at prosocial behavior. For this reason, teaching of self-reinforcement procedures is especially valuable.

Self-recording forms provide a reinforcing function. Self-reinforcement may also consist of verbal praise, in addition to (and later in lieu of) earning points. For example, if the student follows all the steps of a particular skill especially well, self-reinforcement might take the form of saying something positive (e.g., "Good for me" or "I did a good job"). Teachers can help encourage students by having them rehearse self-rewarding statements following completion of homework assignments or after spontaneous skill use. Video-recording role-play efforts can also be very reinforcing; in addition, being able to review performance helps students assess their skill proficiency.

Self-punishment

Self-punishment is taught in a manner directly parallel to that just described for self-reinforcement. As described here, self-punishment refers to the student's failure to earn points if he or she does not display a desired behavior. It is important to note that, when self-punishment is used with elementary-age children, the language needs to stress the child's accountability—for example, "You didn't earn your points" as opposed to "I am taking points away." Some practitioners may condone taking away points that the student has already earned; however, at this age level, removing previously earned points may result in behaviors even more problematic than the one leaders hope to remediate.

Self-instruction

According to Epps et al. (1985), self-instruction involves the following steps:

1. The teacher models the appropriate behavior while talking through the task aloud so that the student can hear.

2. The student performs the task with overt instructions from the teacher.

3. The student performs the task while talking aloud the self-instructions (overt instructions).

4. The student performs the task with silent (covert) self-instructions.

   Cognitive behavior modification strategies, especially those relying heavily on verbal mediation or self-instructional processes, have grown in popularity. Verbal mediation, or "thinking aloud," is further emphasized during the modeling and role-play portions of the Skillstreaming groups.

MAINTENANCE-ENHANCING PROCEDURES

Maintenance of behaviors developed through skills training approaches is primarily a matter of reinforcement during the original teaching and in the child's natural environment. The strategies first discussed can be accomplished during the Skillstreaming intervention; the last two apply to generalization after the intervention is over.

During the Skillstreaming Intervention

Thinning Reinforcement

A rich, continuous reinforcement schedule is optimal for the establishment of new behaviors. Maintenance of learned behaviors will be enhanced if the reinforcement is gradually thinned. Thinning of reinforcement proceeds best by moving from a continuous (every trial) schedule, to some form of intermittent schedule, to the level of sparse and infrequent reinforcement characteristic of the natural environment. In fact, the maintenance-enhancing goal of such a thinning process is to make the reinforcement schedule indistinguishable from that typically found in real-world contexts. For example, a student would initially receive a reward for each time he or she uses a skill (as recorded on Homework Report 1), then the reinforcement would gradually be thinned and the student would receive the reward (perhaps a larger or more desirable reward) for two or more skill performances (as recorded on Homework Report 2).

Delaying Reinforcement

Resistance to extinction is also enhanced by delay of reinforcement. During the early stages of learning a new skill, immediate reinforcement contingent upon display of the behavior or skill is necessary. Once the skill has become a part of the child's behavioral repertoire, reinforcement should be delayed, more closely approximating the reinforcing conditions in the natural environment.

Delay of reinforcement may be implemented by (a) increasing the size or complexity of the responses required before reinforcement is provided; (b) adding a time delay between the response and the delivery of reinforcement; and (c) in token systems, increasing the interval between the receipt of tokens and the opportunity to spend them and/or requiring more tokens in exchange for a given reinforcer (Sulzer-Azaroff & Mayer, 1991). For example, the student may initially receive a reward (e.g., tokens) for performing the skill in real life as soon as the skill is observed, then later receive a token for self-report of skill use at the end of the day.

Fading Prompts

Prompting may involve describing the specific types of situations in the real world in which students should use a given skill (i.e., instructed generalization). Students can be encouraged to use a particular skill, or verbally prompted, in a variety of real-life settings. Historically, teachers have used this principle of generalization by prompting students during "teachable moments," or times the skill is actually needed. When potential problems arise in the classroom, the teacher can elicit a prosocial response by suggesting a particular skill. For example, Todd, who often became disruptive in the classroom, had completed all of his academic assignments and was sitting quietly at his desk. Rather than waiting for Todd to become disruptive, the teacher suggested that he use Deciding on Something to Do (Skill 12). This proactive approach turns naturally occurring problem situations into realistic learning opportunities, thus providing more opportunities for practice. Furthermore, it helps create a positive environment for learning ways to deal with interpersonal problems.

Another way of prompting skill use is to provide written prompts in the form of leader-created cue cards or cue sheets. Cue cards and sheets list the behavioral steps of a skill, along with a space for the student to check each step, either as each is enacted or after all steps are completed. The card may also include a place for self-evaluation. The student may tape the card to his or her desk if it is a skill that is to be used in the classroom or keep it in a pocket or folder if it is for use in another setting (e.g., on the school bus, on the playground, in another classroom, at home). For example, Michelle needed to practice Staying Out of Fights (Skill 40) on the playground and in the school hallways. Her cue card is shown in Figure 8.

Displaying a poster of a given skill will help students remember to practice it. Placed wherever it is most appropriate, the cue poster presents the title of the skill and its behavioral steps. If students have been instructed in the skills of Playing

Figure 8: Michelle's Cue Card

Staying Out of Fights

☑ 1. Stop and count to 10.
☑ 2. Decide what your problem is.
☑ 3. Think about your choices:
   Walk away.
   Talk to the person.
   Ask someone for help.
☑ 4. Act out your best choice.
How did I do? _____ *Great!* _____

a Game (Skill 18) and Dealing with Losing (Skill 49), for example, displaying cue posters for these skills in the area of the classroom used for free-time activities may remind the students of these particular skills and skill steps.

Maintenance may be enhanced by the gradual removal of such suggestions, reminders, coaching, or instruction. Fading of prompts is a means of moving away from artificial control (the leader's) to more natural self-control of desirable behaviors. As is true for all the enhancement techniques examined here, fading of prompts should be carefully planned and systematically implemented.

Providing Booster Sessions

Periodically, it may be necessary to reinstate instruction for certain prosocial behaviors to continue in the natural environment. Booster sessions between teacher and student (behavioral coaching), either on a preplanned schedule or as needed, have proven valuable (Feindler & Ecton, 1986; Karoly & Steffen, 1980; Walker et al., 2004). When the teacher notices that skills previously taught are not used on a consistent basis, these sessions may also be carried out with the group as a whole. In such cases, the skill is retaught via the same methods as initially presented (modeling, role-playing, performance feedback, and generalization). Because the instruction is a review of the skill, the session will likely move more quickly than initial skill instruction.

Preparing for Real-Life Nonreinforcement

Both teacher and student may take energetic steps to maximize the likelihood that reinforcement for appropriate behaviors will occur in the natural environment. Nevertheless, on a number of occasions, reinforcement will not be forthcoming. Thus, it is important for the student to be prepared for this eventuality. As described previously in this chapter, self-reinforcement is one option when desirable behaviors are per-

formed correctly but are unrewarded by external sources.

Graduated homework assignments

The student may also be prepared for nonreinforcement in the natural environment by completing graduated homework assignments. It may become clear at times as Skillstreaming homework is discussed that the real-life figure is too difficult a target—too harsh, too unresponsive, or simply too unlikely to provide reinforcement. When this is the case, with the newly learned skill still fragile, leaders may redirect the homework assignment toward two or three more benevolent target figures. When the student finally does use the skill correctly with the original target figure and receives no reinforcement, these previously reinforced trials help minimize the likelihood that the behavior will be extinguished.

Group reward plans

Using plans in which all group members work together to achieve a common goal helps to create a cooperative spirit in the classroom and will often result in children's reminding one another to use the skill when a situation suggests its use. An example of a group reward plan is the "Skill of the Week" bulletin board. In this procedure, the teacher or the students decide on a target skill. Most often, this skill will be one recently taught in the Skillstreaming group or one that the students need an extra reminder to use throughout the day. The class may want to draw pictures or write descriptions of times when they can use the skill and display these along with the title of the skill. Any awards students receive may be displayed on this board. A large picture may be drawn and divided into 20 or so "puzzle pieces." When any student uses the skill, he or she may color in one section of the puzzle. When the puzzle is completely colored in, the class may have a "Skill of the Week" party. This strategy emphasizes the use of prosocial skills, reminds students to use selected skills, and publicly reinforces skill use.

Contingency contracting

Contingency contracting, an additional type of homework, is an agreement between the teacher and student stating a behavioral goal the student will work to achieve and the reward that will be earned for achieving that goal. The goal and reward are negotiated by the teacher and student. Typically, both parties agree to carry out an action—the student to perform a selected behavior or skill (for a given length of time or a predetermined number of times) and the teacher to provide the mutually agreed upon reinforcement (e.g., a class popcorn party). Contingency contracting has been found to both enhance generalization of learned skills in addition to reducing the problem behavior. For example, Mruzek, Cohen, and Smith (2007) found that contingency contracting, along with Skillstreaming, decreased problem behavior for students on the autism spectrum.

Homme, Csanyi, Gonzales, and Rechs (1969) present several rules to follow when implementing contingency contracts. These include the following:

1. Initial contracts should require a small amount of behavior change.
2. The payoff (reward) should be given immediately after the performance of the task.
3. Frequent rewards should be provided.
4. Contracts should reward accomplishments rather than obedience.
5. The terms should be clearly stated.
6. Contracts should be fair.
7. Contracts should be reviewed regularly.
8. Contracts should be phrased in a positive manner.
9. Contracting should be carried out consistently.

Further, contracts should be in writing, not merely verbal; signed by both teacher and student; have beginning and ending dates; and, if appropriate, specify a reward for a particular behavior or skill performance and a bonus reward for extraordinary performance. (Figure 6, in chapter 2, presents a sample skill contract.)

Social skills games

A variety of games can be developed and used to enhance skill learning. Group games require students to practice a variety of social skills (e.g., joining in, sharing, being a good sport). Types of games that lend themselves well to Skillstreaming include board games and role-playing games.

Cartledge and Milburn (1980) make several points worth considering when using social skills games:

1. The connection between performing a skill in the game setting and in real life needs to be made explicit.
2. The winner (if there is one) should be determined on the basis of performance rather than solely on the basis of chance.
3. If rewards are used, they should be given for appropriate (skilled) participation rather than for winning.
4. Participants should not be "out" in a game without provisions for being allowed to participate again within a short period of time.
5. If teaming is required, skill-deficient children should be included on the same team as skill-competent children.

Skill folders

All students in the Skillstreaming group should keep a prosocial skills folder. This is simply a way of organizing materials—cue cards, homework assignments, skill contracts, awards, self-monitoring forms, lists of appropriate alternative activities for use with particular skills, and the like. Students will then have an easy record of the behavioral steps to the skills they have practiced in the past.

Beyond the Skillstreaming Intervention

The generalization-enhancing techniques examined thus far are directed toward the student. But maintenance of appropriate behaviors also may be enhanced by efforts directed toward others, especially those in the student's natural environment who function as the main providers of reinforcement.

Programming for Reinforcement in the Natural Environment

The student's larger interpersonal world includes a variety of people—parents, siblings, peers, teachers, neighbors, classmates, and others. By their responsiveness or unresponsiveness to the student's newly learned skills, to a large extent they control the destiny of these behaviors. We all react to what the important people in our lives think or feel about our behavior. What they reward we are more likely to continue doing. What they are indifferent or hostile to will tend to fall into disuse.

During the past several years, Skillstreaming efforts have included increased involvement of educators, agency and institutional staff, parents, and peers in students' acquisition and maintenance of skills. The suggestion that support staff be trained as "transfer coaches" is one reflection of this goal (see chapter 1). Parents have been a second target for procedures designed to enhance the likelihood that prosocial skills, once learned, will be maintained. Forms helpful in communicating with parents are discussed in chapter 7 and included in Appendix A. Other ways of involving parents in social skills generalization efforts are described in Slim, Whiteside, Dittner, and Mellon (2006); Brannon (2008); and Adams, Womack, Shatzer, and Caldarella (2010).

Using Natural Reinforcers

An especially valuable approach to maintenance enhancement is the use of reinforcers that occur naturally in the student's real-world environment. Galassi and Galassi (1984) offer the following comment:

> We need to target those behaviors for changes that are most likely to be seen as acceptable, desirable, and positive by others. Ayllon and Azrin (1968) refer to this as the "Relevance of Behavior Rule." "Teach only those behaviors that will continue to be reinforced after training." (p. 10)

Alberto and Troutman (2006) suggest a four-step process to facilitate the use of natural reinforcers:

1. Observe which specific behaviors are regularly reinforced and how they are reinforced in the major settings that constitute the student's natural environment.

2. Instruct the student in a selected number of naturally reinforced behaviors (e.g., certain social skills, grooming behaviors).

3. Teach the student how to recruit or request reinforcement (e.g., by tactfully asking peers or others for approval or recognition).

4. Because its presence in certain gestures or facial expressions may be quite subtle for many students, teach the student how to recognize reinforcement when it is offered.

CHAPTER 6

Managing Behavior Problems

Problems can and do occur in the Skillstreaming group, just as they may in any group teaching endeavor. Students may be unmotivated to participate as requested, actively resist meaningful group involvement, or fail to see the relevance of the skills to their everyday lives. Their resistive behavior may interfere not only with their own skill acquisition but also with the learning of others in the group.

Just as one type of reinforcer may be rewarding for one child but not for another, a particular management strategy is likely to be more effective for one child than for another. Therefore, this chapter describes a range of strategies according to three tiers or levels of intervention: Universal strategies (to be used with managing the group as a whole), targeted strategies (for some students exhibiting moderate behavior problems), and individual strategies (for students with significant problem behaviors). Teachers and other group leaders should individualize these methods, using the least intrusive techniques first.

UNIVERSAL STRATEGIES

Learning Climate

The atmosphere of the Skillstreaming group should be positive. The teacher should openly notice the children following group rules, making prosocial choices, and "being good" rather than catching them breaking rules. A benefit of this approach is the fact that when a teacher sees a child behaving appropriately and states approval of that behavior publicly, children engaging in unacceptable behavior are likely to stop that behavior and engage in the behavior that received approval (Kounin, 1970).

Sarason, Glaser, and Fargo (1972) urge teachers to present positive reinforcement openly to specific youngsters in such a manner that the entire class is aware of it. As they comment:

> Positive reinforcement for productive activity for the whole group is a powerful preventive technique. It can eliminate or reduce the great majority of behavior problems in classrooms. Try to praise the children who are paying attention. Attend to those who are sitting in their seats, doing their work in a nondisruptive manner. "That's right, John, you're doing a good job." "You watched the board all the time I was presenting the problem. That's paying attention." . . . These responses not only reinforce the child to whom they are directed, but they also help to provide the rest of the class with an explicit idea of what you mean by paying attention and working hard.

Such open attempts to "catch them being good" are highly effective in the Skillstreaming group.

Physical Structure

The physical environment can structure the learning setting. To minimize potential behavior problems during teaching, the area in which

Skillstreaming instruction is carried out needs to be large enough so students can participate in role-plays without disrupting other group participants. Positioning student chairs an arm's length away from one another is useful to help create physical distance. To reduce distractions, enticing activities such as games should be moved out of the group's view. Visuals are useful to assist learning; therefore, the group rules or behavioral guidelines should be posted and reviewed prior to each instructional session as a reminder for the entire group to use positive behavior. In the classroom in general, allowing space for traffic can minimize disruption of ongoing activities as students move from one area to another. Enhancing the physical structure of the group setting or classroom with strategies like those just described can minimize and avert many behavior problems; the structure can then be gradually lessened as the children become more familiar with working together.

Rules and Procedures

As discussed in chapter 1, it is important to establish student expectations and rules for the Skillstreaming group. Typically, four to eight rules at the elementary level are recommended (Evertson, Emmer, & Worsham, 2003). Most group leaders will need to use some type of reinforcement system (e.g., social and token) to positively reinforce rule following.

A number of effective "rules for the use of rules" exist in the behavior management literature (Greenwood, Hops, Delquadri, & Guild, 1974; Sarason et al., 1972; Walker, 1979), including the following:

1. Define and communicate rules for student behavior in clear, specific, and, especially, behavioral terms. It is better to say, "Raise your hand before asking a question" than "Be considerate of others." A statement such as "Be kind or considerate of others" is a good goal, but it is too abstract. Instead, student behaviors should be clearly defined and phrased in a manner that students will un-

derstand, such as "Wait until another person has finished talking before you begin" and "Leave toys and other objects at your desk."

2. It is more effective to tell students what to do than what not to do. For example, if it is necessary to address aggression, instead of "No pushing or shoving," the rule should be phrased as "Keep hands and feet to yourself." Other positive examples include "Talk over disagreements" instead of "No fighting" and "Work quietly" instead of "Don't talk out of turn."

3. Rules should be communicated in a manner that will help students remember them. Depending on the age group and rule difficulty, memorization aids may include keeping rules short and few in number, repeating the rules several times, and posting the rules in written form in the classroom, as well as sending them home to parents. Rules should be reviewed at the beginning of each Skillstreaming session until all children remember them. Periodic review of rules may also be needed.

4. Following the rules is more likely when students have had a role in rule development, modification, and implementation. However, often school and classroom rules are established by a committee of adults without student participation. Allowing the group to participate encourages the children's commitment to abide by the rules. Students can be asked to think of behaviors they feel they need to work together. Often students will state many rules that group leaders themselves would have identified. At times, more specific guidance may be needed, ideally in the form of leading questions, such as "Would everyone have a chance to be heard if everyone talked at once?" or "How might you let the leader know that you have something you want to say?"

In addition to the preceding ideas, further effective rules for rules are that (a) they be developed before group instruction begins; (b) they be fair, reasonable, and within students' capacity to follow; (c) that all members of the group understand them; and (d) they be applied consistently and fairly to all group members.

Rules are guidelines governing appropriate and inappropriate student behaviors; procedures are what students need to know and follow to meet their own personal needs and perform routine instructional and classroom housekeeping activities. As is the case for rules, classroom procedures need to be explicitly taught; one cannot assume that students will know them without instruction. Unlike rules, which need to be taught "up front," procedures (e.g., for obtaining help, leaving the room, using rest room passes, sharpening pencils, handing in class work) usually can be explained as the need arises. However, procedures also will need to be clearly stated, closely monitored, consistently followed, retaught when necessary, and consequated when not followed.

Supportive Interventions

Students will more readily learn the Skillstreaming curriculum when it is presented in an encouraging and supportive environment. The previous section described considerations related to planning and structuring such a learning environment. The following interventions are designed to support children's desirable behaviors in an unobtrusive manner within the actual teaching sequence. These interventions include group teaching techniques, enhancing motivation, precorrection and specific praise, behavioral redirection, prompting, simplifying surface management techniques, and relationship-based techniques.

Group Teaching Techniques

What do teachers actually do to support positive behaviors in the learning setting? According to Kounin (1970), first, the teacher knows what is going on. Such *with-it-ness* is communicated to the class in a number of ways, including swift and consistent recognition and, when necessary, con-

sequating of low-level behaviors likely to grow into disruptiveness or more serious aggression. Closely connected to such attentiveness is *overlapping,* the ability to manage simultaneously two or more classroom events, whether instructional or disciplinary. *Smoothness,* the ability to transition from one activity to another without "downtime," is a third facilitative teacher behavior. Downtime is a time for students to become bored and act out; avoiding or minimizing downtime significantly deters such behaviors.

Another way to minimize boredom is by instructing with *momentum,* maintaining a steady progress or movement throughout a particular lesson, class, or school day. A *group focus,* the ability to keep the entire class involved in a given instructional activity, also diminishes the likelihood of student aggression. Finally, an especially significant contributor to a supportive learning environment is the teacher's communication of *optimistic expectations.* Students live up to (and, unfortunately, also down to) what important people in their lives expect of them. The teacher who expects a child to be a "slow learner" or a "behavior problem" because of his or her past record, a sibling's past poor performance, or the neighborhood the student comes from will likely be rewarded with low performance or behavior problems. By contrast, the teacher who lets the student know he or she can achieve and will have the teacher's help along the way is likely to motivate the student to be more successful and less disruptive. The message is, expect the best of your students—you may well get it!

Consistent application of rules and procedures provides clear expectations for student behavior and establishes that the teacher is in charge of the classroom. Yet such consistency is difficult to maintain over time. Teachers become tired, overworked, and distracted. When this occurs, students are quick to get the message that perhaps "just this once" can become more than once. Then the boundary between what is and is not acceptable is no longer clear. Students of all ages test the limits to reestablish the boundary, and, as this happens, the foundation for a supportive learning environment begins to erode.

Supportive environments are predictable environments. As noted previously, a well thought out and fairly and consistently enforced set of school rules or guidelines strongly helps establish such predictability. Consistent enforcement means that all staff are aware of and enforce rules in agreed-upon ways. But the demands of fairness and consistency may be contradictory at times. Consistency requires rule enforcement for all applicable occasions; fairness may require taking special circumstances into account and not enforcing a given rule in some instances.

Enhancing Motivation

Motivation is not an easy task. Many of the youth offered the opportunity to learn from Skillstreaming are highly competent in the regular use of antisocial behavior. Furthermore, these behaviors may be frequently encouraged and rewarded by significant people in these students' lives—family, peers, and others. Two types of motivators are at the teacher's disposal: extrinsic and intrinsic. *Extrinsic motivators* are tangible rewards provided contingent upon performance of desired behaviors. Tangible motivators are, in fact, widely used in schools and other institutions serving children and youth. The stars and stickers of the preschool and primary years take the form of points, pizza and popcorn parties, and special privileges and activities in the later grades. Extrinsic rewards appear to be especially useful in eliciting initial involvement in learning unfamiliar skills.

Many teachers of Skillstreaming report that using only external rewards—whether in the form of tangible reinforcers, a token economy, a levels system, or other incentives—is insufficient on a sustained basis. Substantial intrinsic motivators also must be present.

In Skillstreaming, one *intrinsic motivator* resides in the skills themselves, especially those that students select themselves and use successfully in their real-world settings. As discussed in

chapter 1, negotiating the skill curriculum is central. Allowing youth to select the skills they feel *they* need is a major step toward participation motivation. When student-selected (or, to perhaps a somewhat lesser degree, teacher-selected) skills yield positive outcomes in interactions with family, peers, or significant others, motivation is further enhanced.

In addition to regular negotiation of the skill curriculum, a second tactic augments intrinsic motivation: communicating to the students, both during the initial structuring of the Skillstreaming group and periodically afterward, that the goal of Skillstreaming is to teach choices or alternatives, not substitutes. Many students who participate have been reprimanded and punished literally hundreds of times for behaviors their parents, teachers, or others deem inappropriate. In one way or another, they have been told, "Stop doing that, and do this instead (e.g., "Stop talking and listen"; "Stop hitting and talk out the problem").

Although it is certainly desirable to decrease inappropriate behavior, a more successful means of reaching this goal is to expand the child's behavioral repertoire, or range of possible responses. If, for example, someone wrongly accuses the student of stealing something and the only response to accusations he or she has learned, practiced, and been rewarded for is fighting, the student will fight again. The student has, in effect, no choices. If Skillstreaming teaches the student that accusations may also be responded to by explanation, investigation, negotiation, walking away, and other means, at least some of the time he or she may use one of these more desirable options.

Precorrection and Specific Praise

Precorrective statements attend to both the demands of the setting and the desired behavior. The goal with precorrection is for the teacher to anticipate problems that may occur in the instructional environment, in this case the Skillstreaming setting. For example, if students typically have difficulty transitioning to a group activity, it is likely they will have similar difficulty moving to the area where Skillstreaming instruction occurs. Precorrective statements tell the students what is expected. In other words, the teacher tells the students, and perhaps models for them, the exact behavioral expectations. For transition, a precorrective statement might be something like "When it's time for Skillstreaming group, close your math folders and look at me so I know you're ready to come to the group. When I call your table, please walk slowly and sit in a circle chair. Now watch me and see what I do. What did I do first?" and so on. When the students follow the expectations, specific praise (e.g., "Thank you for walking quietly") will be necessary to reinforce the expectation. Both precorrective statements and behavior-specific praise have been shown to decrease problem behaviors in the classroom (Stormont & Reinke, 2009). Fullerton, Conroy, and Correa (2009), for example, trained teachers interacting with young students with behavior problems to use specific praise during transitions. As the teachers increased their use of specific praise statements, children's engagement in the activity increased, as well as their compliance with expectations. Using these strategies also makes the environment more predictable for students.

Behavioral Redirection

One way to encourage a student's appropriate behavior while preventing the occurrence of negative actions is to employ behavioral redirection. For example, a student who frequently disrupts the Skillstreaming group by standing up and walking around may be asked to assist the teacher in pointing out the skill steps as they are being role-played. Another example would be asking a student who inappropriately brings a toy to the group to take other classroom materials and put them on the teacher's desk, replacing the toy on the way. Still another student who feels the need to dominate conversation in the group may be asked to write his or her ideas on the computer.

Behavioral redirection allows the teacher to emphasize the student's positive, helping actions without having to ignore the student's negative behaviors or deal with them in a manner disruptive to the learning of others.

Prompting

Prompting, or telling a student what to do in a given situation, can minimize behavior problems and also provides a positive, encouraging environment in which to foster learning. One of the teacher's main functions is to anticipate student difficulties during the group and be ready to prompt a desirable response. During role-plays, for example, students practicing a new skill may forget a step or several steps, or they may not know how to behave to carry out a particular step. The teacher may give instructional comments (e.g., "You're now ready to . . ."), offer hints to elicit the behavior, or coach the student from start to finish. An important function of role-playing is to practice the proficient display of the behavioral steps. If students are allowed to fail, they have had only more practice at failing.

> **EXAMPLE.** Todd stood up in front of the group to role-play the skill of Joining In (Skill 17). He continued to stand there while the two coactors played the game Todd had planned to join. The teacher then said, "Todd, do you remember what to do first?" Todd shook his head and replied no. The teacher responded: "Look up at the chart. Decide if you want to join in."

To provide for a successful role-play, in this case the teacher found it necessary to give Todd a verbal prompt for each skill step while pointing to the step on the chart.

Simplifying

Simplifying, or asking less at one time, is another way to increase the likelihood that students will experience success in the Skillstreaming group. Students' abilities to handle particular group tasks will vary. Some may have difficulty following a series of instructions, understanding instructions, or knowing what to say during feedback. Methods of simplifying include the following:

▸ Have the student role-play one behavioral step at a time.

▸ Reward minimal student accomplishment.

▸ Shorten the role-play.

▸ Have the student read a prepared script portraying the behavioral steps.

▸ Ask the student to take the role of coactor before that of main actor.

> **EXAMPLE.** When it was Alisha's turn to role-play Setting a Goal (Skill 13), she began to talk in a silly, high-pitched voice, digressing from the steps. When prompted by the teacher to look at the first step and try it out, she continued to act the clown. Instead of requesting that Alisha return to her seat and try this another day, the teacher restated the first behavioral step by saying to Alisha, "Is there something, one thing, you would like to do better with in math? You do a terrific job with the skills we have worked on so far, and now we're getting into multiplication. Would learning how to multiply be a goal you might want to set?" Alisha responded that this would be OK, she guessed. "Great. Then you've done the first step. You've decided on a goal. We'll work on the second step, the steps to achieve this goal, during another session." Alisha calmly returned to her seat.

Surface Management Techniques

Several techniques for managing mild and commonly occurring misbehaviors have been suggested by Redl and Wineman (1957). These methods, termed *surface management techniques,* have been used successfully to deal with problem behaviors in Skillstreaming groups.

Planned ignoring

Mild misbehaviors can best be dealt with by simply ignoring them. Many times, drawing attention to such behaviors is more distracting to the learning process than the occurrence of the behaviors themselves. Positively reinforcing concurrent appropriate behavior adds to the elimination of the inappropriate action. This strategy is most effective when the group leader plans in advance which mild behaviors will be ignored.

> **EXAMPLE.** Paul frequently played with his clothing, rolling up his shirt or picking at his shoes during the sessions despite the teacher's requests for him to stop. Because Paul's behavior did not appear to distract others, the teacher decided to ignore it to see whether, with lack of attention, the behavior would diminish.

Proximity control

In proximity control, the teacher moves closer to (stands near, sits next to) the student who is misbehaving. Often, simply moving closer to the student who is engaging in distracting behavior will draw the student's attention back to the learning situation. For students who do not mind being touched, a hand on the shoulder is an effective way of drawing the student back to task.

> **EXAMPLE.** While the group was providing feedback to the role-players, Tommy began making noises. The leader quietly moved away from the front of the group, stood next to Tommy, and touched his shoulder while continuing to elicit feedback about the role-play.

Signal interference

Signal interference includes nonverbal communicators that let the student know a behavior is unacceptable. This may include eye contact, hand gestures, clearing one's throat, or frowning. Some students who engage in mildly disruptive behavior may not even realize they are doing something distracting to others. In such cases, prearranging with the child a specific signal (e.g., a word or gesture) to cue the student that the behavior is occurring has been a useful strategy.

EXAMPLE. While the group leaders modeled the skill, Michelle started tapping her foot against Tommy's chair. Tommy then hit his foot against Michelle's chair. The group leader caught Michelle's eye and shook her head no.

Interest boosting

When a student's attention appears to be drifting away from an activity, it is often helpful to redirect the student's interest. This can be done by involving the student more directly in the activity, asking for the student's input, or directing a high-interest question to the group.

EXAMPLE. Brian was getting restless—moving his chair, turning around—while a student was reporting performance on a homework assignment. The teacher quickly summarized the student's performance, provided positive feedback, and involved Brian by asking him in what other situations the skill could be used.

Humor

At times, a student may say something very clever or humorous in the Skillstreaming group. Such a humorous moment can quickly ease a tense situation. As long as the humor is not at the expense of a specific individual or group or the student is not being rewarded for being a class clown, it is fine to go ahead and laugh with the group.

EXAMPLE. The group had been through a difficult lesson the day before. While the group was getting ready to begin the next day, one student told a silly knock-knock joke, and all the other group members laughed. Instead of reprimanding the student, the teacher laughed along with the others for a few moments and then began the instruction.

Restructuring the program/capturing teachable moments

Sometimes the classroom schedule must be abandoned in favor of dealing with a problem that has just occurred. If the class appears tense and upset due to a playground problem, for example, requiring the students to participate in practice of Beginning a Conversation (Skill 15) clearly will not meet their immediate needs. Instead, the teacher should abandon the preplanned lesson and restructure the lesson by changing the skill to be taught.

EXAMPLE. The students came to the Skillstreaming group very agitated and loudly complaining that the playground supervisor was unfair in taking a certain disciplinary action. Even though the teacher's plan for the day was to work on a different skill, he abandoned this plan and introduced the more timely skill of Making a Complaint (Skill 47).

Capturing such teachable moments employs Skillstreaming to better manage the Skillstreaming group. Many problem behaviors—including withdrawal, disruptiveness, threatening, and so forth—may be viewed as behavioral excess: too much talking, too much bullying, and so on. Each such behavior, however, may equally well be construed as behavioral deficiency—too little listening to others, too little empathy, and so on. As stated by Greene (2010), "In the past 30 years, research has told us that challenging kids are challenging because they lack the skills *not* to be challenging" (p. 29). Thus, an additional way to reduce problem behaviors is to replace them with desirable ones. Skills may be taught as previously scheduled (as part of regular sessions) or at spontaneous times that help students reduce behavior problems (i.e., teachable moments).

EXAMPLE. In one group session, Leroy, who was angry because of an incident that had occurred on the playground during noon recess, verbally began to attack Justin. While the teacher first needed to clarify that Leroy would not be allowed to physically harm Justin and take steps to make certain the learning setting remained safe for all group members, the incident created the opportunity to learn. Here was the chance to teach Leroy an alternative, more prosocially skilled way of handling the same situation. In this situation, the teacher reminded Leroy of a previously practiced skill (Making a Complaint, Skill 47), handed him the skill card listing the steps, encouraged him to try out the skill, and prompted him through skill use. The teacher gave Justin a skill card for Dealing with an Accusation (Skill 43) and asked him to respond to Leroy by using the skill steps.

Removing seductive objects

It is natural for students to be distracted by interesting objects and toys. Including the rule of leaving toys and other objects at one's desk may prevent such distractions from occurring during Skillstreaming groups.

> **EXAMPLE.** Troy brought a flashlight to the group and began showing it to others before instruction started. The teacher asked Troy to finish showing the flashlight and then directed him to put it either in his desk or in the teacher's desk for safekeeping.

Taking a break

When a student's behavior is not easily controlled within the instructional setting, it may be best for the student to take a break. Redl and Wineman (1957) have described this approach as "antiseptic bouncing." It is not intended as a punitive measure but as a strategy for removing the student from a situation before he or she loses control. With this technique, the student is asked to leave the room to get a drink of water, run an errand, and so forth.

> **EXAMPLE.** Randa couldn't seem to settle down in the group. She continually moved about in her chair, talking to the students sitting next to her. The teacher called Randa away from the group and requested that she take a book back to the library right away.

In some cases, a student may know he or she is emotionally unable to handle the classroom or group setting and may request a time-out or cooling-off period. Referred to by Grayson, Kiraly, and McKinnon (1996) as the *cooling-off ap-*

proach, this method allows the student to spend time alone in a nonstressful setting or time with an adult to discuss the student's concerns. This form of therapeutic crisis intervention may avert more serious behavioral difficulties. The teacher needs to monitor the student's use of cooling-off periods carefully to judge that the student does not employ it to avoid a particular classroom activity, subject, or Skillstreaming task.

> **EXAMPLE.** Billy became gradually more agitated in the group. When the teacher inquired whether he was having a problem, Billy asked to sit on a rug in the reading area for two or three minutes. After that, he calmly returned to the group.

Reality appraisal

This technique involves giving students an explanation of why a behavior is not acceptable, or "telling it like it is." The approach also helps students understand the consequences of their behavior.

> **EXAMPLE.** During feedback, most of the students began talking all at once. The group leader responded, "If everyone is going to talk at once, we can't hear anyone's ideas."

Relationship-Based Techniques

Psychologists and educators have long known that the better the relationship between the helper and client (or teacher and student), the more positive and productive the outcome of their interaction. In fact, it has been demonstrated that a positive relationship is a potent factor in effecting academic achievement (Jones & Jones, 2008) in addition to long-term behavior change. The techniques next described draw primarily on the relationship between teacher and student and can often be combined with other management techniques for maximum effect. Specifically, these include empathic encouragement and threat reduction.

Empathic encouragement

Empathic encouragement is a strategy in which the teacher first shows understanding of the difficulty the student is experiencing and then urges the student to participate as instructed. Often this additional one-to-one attention will motivate the child to participate and follow the teacher's guidance. In applying this technique, the teacher first listens to the student's explanation of the problem and expresses an understanding of the student's feelings and behavior (e.g., "I know it's difficult. Learning something new can be frustrating"). If appropriate, the teacher responds that the child's view is a valid alternative for dealing with the problem. The teacher then restates his or her own view with supporting reasons and probable outcomes and urges the student to try out the suggestion (e.g., "But if you don't try the skill, you won't know if you can do it. Let's give it a try").

> **EXAMPLE.** While two students were role-playing Responding to Teasing (Skill 38), Michelle leaned back in her chair and began to sneer in an angry manner. After several minutes of being ignored, Michelle became even more restless and began muttering loudly enough to be quite distracting to the group. The leader began by taking Michelle aside and saying, "You appear quite angry. What's the problem?" Michelle responded by stating that it was stupid to ignore someone who was teasing her because that wouldn't make the person stop. The only thing that would get the others to stop was to beat them up. The teacher expressed understanding of how horrible it can feel to be teased but pointed out that fighting seems to result in being physically hurt and getting into trouble as well: "Sometimes kids tease so that they can get someone into trouble. The goal we talked about is to deal with teasing in a way where you won't get hurt and you'll also stay out of trouble." Michelle stood quietly, but her anger appeared to lessen. "Well, let's not decide if this is a useful skill for you until you try it out in a role-play. Is that reasonable?" Michelle replied that this would be OK, and she and the teacher rejoined the group.

Threat reduction

This technique is helpful in dealing with students' anxiety. Children who find role-playing or other types of participation threatening may react with inappropriate or disruptive behaviors or withdraw from the learning process. To deal with this problem, the teacher should provide reassurance or even physical contact (e.g., an arm around the student, a pat on the back). The teacher should also encourage group members to express support for role-players and others who participate.

> **EXAMPLE.** Sam experienced anxiety because he couldn't think of a role-play situation. The teacher responded by asking the group, "Let's think of some situations in which Sam could use the skill. Then, Sam, you may choose one of these situations to role-play."

Other strategies for threat reduction include postponing the student's role-playing until last and clarifying and restructuring those aspects of the task that the student experiences as threatening.

TARGETED INTERVENTIONS

The universal interventions just described are designed to support students' desirable behaviors in an unobtrusive manner within the instructional setting while, in most cases, allowing instruction to continue. At times, however, more structured and directive interventions may be necessary. This section provides a brief review of behavior management techniques appropriate for this age group and describes a procedure for setting limits.

The first step in managing problem behavior is for group leaders to ask themselves, Why at this moment is the student engaging in this particular behavior? All behavior serves a purpose or a function. In order to intervene in useful ways, teachers must be able to assess that function. Typical functions of problem behavior include obtaining something (attention or object), escape of a task or expectation, avoidance of a person, or self-regulation (e.g., reducing anxiety). Questions that may be asked include the following: Is the student's goal to seek attention or to avoid a task or a person? To avoid participation? To reduce anxiety? Group leaders need to make a guess or a hypothesis. The teacher may ask the following types of questions to confirm the hypothesis: Could it be that you don't want to participate? Could it be that you want me to leave you alone? Or, could it be that this whole thing seems too complicated? Perhaps the hypothesis is that the student is displaying resistive behavior to avoid a task he or she perceives as too complicated (e.g., one that has too many steps). In this case, the teacher may need to simplify the task. Another student may be experiencing anxiety as she realizes that her turn to role-play is approaching. In this situation, the teacher will likely need to offer reassurance. Still another student may not be receiving the desired amount of attention from others. Another may have been engaging in undesirable behaviors to belong and to be perceived as "cool." In these last two examples, the teacher may need to restructure the lesson to allow students to gain attention or belonging by being a helper or participant in the next role-play.

Behavior Management Techniques

Behavior management techniques (i.e., behavior modification) both promote skill learning and inhibit problem behaviors. The effectiveness of behavior modification technology rests upon a firm, well-validated foundation. Beyond the repeated demonstration of their effectiveness, behavior modification techniques are relatively easy to learn and use; may be administered by the teacher, parent, peers, or the child; and have a long history of successful use. For these reasons, the techniques can maximize time and opportunity for student learning. A major way to substitute appropriate for inappropriate behaviors is to present positive reinforcement to the student following and contingent on the occurrence of appropriate behavior. Table 5 presents a variety

of material and social reinforcers appropriate for elementary-age students. A more detailed discussion of principles of behavior management is included as Appendix C in this book.

Setting Limits

As noted previously, youth who frequently behave in their everyday lives in an angry, aggressive, intimidating, bullying, and threatening manner may also do so in the Skillstreaming group. No matter how skilled the leader is in modeling, conducting role-playing, and so forth, if the group is not safe, learning cannot take place. If such behaviors are not dealt with immediately, swiftly, and successfully, other students will avoid the group.

Vigilance and responsiveness not only serve to protect the victim but also offer an additional teaching opportunity for the attacker. For example, suppose in the group Sue gives feedback in an offensive manner to Linda, who has just completed a role-play. The first problem is Sue, whose intimidating behavior is one of the things that brought her to the Skillstreaming group. The second problem is the role-play observers. Observers who have not yet role-played may be thinking that they will be treated similarly when it is their turn. The third problem is Linda, who is getting feedback that will discourage rather than encourage her to use the skill. So how can the leader serve as a protector for all of these students? One way to do so would be to prompt Sue to restate the feedback in a helpful way. If that response is not in her skill repertoire, the leader could whisper to Sue what to say and have Sue repeat it. This teaches Sue a little about giving constructive feedback and lets her know that intimidating comments are not acceptable. Linda gets more appropriate feedback, which will help encourage real-world skill use. The observers get the message that if Sue puts them down, the leader will come to their aid. In an active manner, the leader protects and instructs all of the group members.

The following five-step method, designed to deal with behavioral concerns while continuing

Table 5: Material and Social Reinforcers

Material Reinforcers

Objects

Food (peanuts, raisins, apples, cereal)

Stars/stickers

Pictures to color

Letters of praise to the principal or parent

Ribbons

Pencils, paper, colorful folders

Coupons for fast food restaurant

"Good Work" buttons

Comic books

Posters

A photograph of the student

Awards

Small toys or trinkets

Activities

Computer time

Reading comics

Using the teacher's equipment or materials

Having one-to-one time with an adult

Going to lunch early

Tutoring a younger child

Taking free time in the library

Completing duties for the teacher (e.g., running errands)

Social Reinforcers

Nonverbal

Smiling

Nearness to the student

Thumbs-up

Looking interested

Giving a hug

Applause

Nodding

Giving a pat on the back

Giving a "high five"

Arm around the student

Verbal

Thank you.

You really paid attention.

That's right.

Good thinking.

I'm pleased that you chose to do that.

Bravo.

I like the way you're being a good sport (or other behavior).

Wow!

Fantastic.

Terrific.

Good answer.

That was a very kind (friendly, caring) thing to do.

You did a great job.

I like that.

---

to support the student who is acting out, will protect the learning of others.

Step 1: Reward Positive Behavior

Foremost among behavior management techniques for dealing with behavior problems is positive reinforcement, discussed in detail in Appendix C. Many disruptions can be reduced or even eliminated by applying positive reinforcement to such desirable behaviors as listening, participating, and following the group guidelines. Positive reinforcement also has a powerful effect on a student who is behaving inappropriately if other children who are engaging in desirable behavior are rewarded. For example, if those who are listening are reinforced with verbal praise, a ripple effect is created, and the inattentive child will most likely begin to listen as well (Kounin, 1970). This strategy allows the teacher to control the group in a positive, helping way and decreases the impulse to nag children to pay attention.

Step 2: Offer Positive Consequences

Reminding students of the positive consequences of desirable behavior will often encourage them to stop an undesirable behavior and engage in a more desirable one. Offering positive consequences means the student is told that a specific desirable behavior will earn a given reward. Examples include the following: "When you listen, you may have a turn" and "When you put your materials away, you may join the group." Some behaviors may need a tangible positive consequence: "When you wait your turn, you'll earn a point (or token or ticket)." Reminding students to engage in a specific appropriate behavior to earn a privilege or reward lets them know that positive actions lead to good things—and it does so in an encouraging, helpful manner. It is important to present the positive consequences for stopping an undesirable action before informing the student of any negative consequences.

Step 3: Inform the Student of Negative Consequences

The majority of minor behavioral difficulties (e.g., inattention, noise making, etc.) will likely be remedied by employing Steps 1 and 2 of this plan. However, if a student's inappropriate behavior does not cease, it may be necessary to inform the student of the negative consequences if he or she chooses to continue the undesirable behavior. Examples of such negative consequences include sitting away from the group for a minute, not earning points or other rewards that have been structured within the plan, or not having a privilege, such as extra recess time. Such consequences should be as logically related to the misbehavior as possible. For example, if the student misuses classroom materials, he or she would then lose the privilege of using these materials for the rest of the day. Informing the student of a negative consequence thus provides a warning of what will happen if the student continues to engage in that behavior.

Step 4: Allow the Student to Make a Choice

After the student is informed of both positive and negative consequences, he or she is instructed to make a choice—either stop the behavior and earn the positive reinforcement or continue the behavior and accept the negative consequences. When students are given a choice, power struggles are eliminated. We cannot make students behave in the way we would like them to behave; however, we can structure the system of rewards and negative consequences to encourage students to make prosocial choices.

Often it is helpful to allow the student time to make the choice. Informing the student that he or she will have two minutes to make the choice to put materials away or one minute to make the choice of whether or not to stop disrupting the group allows the teacher to leave the student alone, lessens the potential for a power struggle, and allows the student to maintain dignity.

Step 5: Enforce Positive or Negative Consequences

Either the positive or negative consequences are next carried out. If the student chooses negative consequences by continuing the inappropriate behavior, these are delivered in a calm and firm manner. For example, if the student continues to disrupt the Skillstreaming group by making noises and the consequence for this behavior is to sit away from the group for two to three minutes, then the student is required to follow through. Once a negative consequence has been enforced and repeated if necessary, the teacher should reevaluate the structure of the learning environment, making accommodations for that student—for example, seating the student closer to a group leader or implementing an individual behavior management plan.

If the student makes the choice to stop the behavior as requested, then the student should receive the positive consequence (e.g., remaining with the group or continuing to use class materials). It is important to stress that once a student has earned a reward for a given positive behavior (e.g., points for listening), the reward should not be taken away as a negative consequence for another undesirable behavior. Loss of a reward previously earned may result in more severe maladaptive behavior, such as aggression or loss of motivation to earn the reward.

> **EXAMPLE.** When Deron began disrupting the group by making silly comments and laughing, the group leader rewarded those students who had been listening with both verbal praise and "participation tickets" (Step 1). Deron continued the behavior, and the leader responded, "Deron, when you show that you are listening, you may have a turn to role-play" (Step 2). Deron stopped the comments and laughter and was selected as the next role-player. If he had continued, the leader would have calmly walked over to Deron, saying, "Deron, you need to stop the silly comments. It's distracting all of us. If you stop, you will earn some participation tickets to use for extra recess time this afternoon" (Step 2). "If you continue, you will not earn your tickets for participating, and you'll need to sit away from the group" (Step 3). "You will need to decide what you are going to do. You have two minutes to make your choice" (Step 4). Depending on the choice Deron makes, the positive or negative consequences follow (Step 5).

INDIVIDUAL INTERVENTIONS

Students who do not increase positive behaviors when provided with universal interventions (consistent structure and routines, along with supportive interventions) or with targeted procedures may require an individual behavior plan. A student for whom it is frequently necessary to use time-out, for example, will likely benefit from such a plan. Individual plans are more likely to be

successful if they are based on consideration of the function of the student's problem behavior. Following is a brief summary of the processes of functional behavioral assessment and the corresponding development of a behavior intervention plan.

Functional Behavioral Assessment

Functional assessment is a method for identifying the variables that reliably predict and maintain problem behavior. The goal of the assessment is to better understand behavior and why the individual acts in this manner. Assessment includes evaluating the antecedents that prompt undesirable behavior to occur, the consequences that maintain the behavior, and the setting events or broad context in which it occurs.

It is important to distinguish between functional behavior analysis and functional behavioral assessment, or FBA, which is now widely used in schools and other application settings. Originally developed from the field of applied behavior analysis, functional behavior analysis has been used in highly controlled settings by manipulating variables to assess their impact on behavior (Gresham, Watson, & Skinner, 2001; Horner & Carr, 1997). Most frequently, it has been employed to assess the purpose of aberrant behavior, often self-abuse or severe aggression of individuals with developmental disabilities (Ingram, Lewis-Palmer, & Sugai, 2005).

The Individuals with Disabilities Education Act (IDEA, 1997, 2004) includes the requirement that an FBA be conducted in schools when a change to a more restrictive placement due to disciplinary action is considered, when IEP behavioral goals are not sufficient, when a student has been suspended for more than 10 days, and when the student's behavior impedes school functioning or others' ability to learn (Cook et al., 2007). This requirement brought FBA technology into the daily lives of teachers, administrators, and support personnel as they worked to transfer the strategy to students in the schools in meaningful ways.

FBA is the process recommended most frequently to address severe maladaptive behaviors (Blood & Neel, 2007) and has been successful in reducing behavior problems and increasing student engagement (Blair, Fox, & Lentini, 2010; Boyajian, DuPaul, Handler, Eckert, & McGoey, 2001; McLaren & Nelson, 2009).

The goal of completing an FBA is to design meaningful supports for individual students in need of intense interventions and support (Ingram et al., 2005). Outcomes of an FBA include operationally defining the problem behavior, identifying the antecedents that predict occurrence and nonoccurrence of the behavior, and identifying the consequences maintaining the behavior (McIntosh et al., 2008). In other words, questions to be answered through the FBA process include the following (Horner & Carr, 1997):

1. What maintains the problem behavior?

2. What is our prediction of when the problem will occur and when will it not occur?

3. How can we prevent the problem behavior?

4. What do we do when the problem behavior does occur?

FBA is a team-based process involving obtaining information about the student from multiple sources (peers, parents, teachers) and from multiple environments and contexts (e.g., group versus independent; different school settings, such as playground, various classrooms, cafeteria; Kulli, 2008). Information is gained through processes such as direct observations, rating scales, and record reviews (Gresham, Watson, & Skinner, 2001). Kern, Hilt, and Gresham (2004) found that, when assessing students with emotional-behavioral disorders and those at risk for these disorders, the most commonly applied methods for FBA in the schools were direct observation and teacher interviews. Once collected, the data are summarized in a way to make decisions regarding useful interventions (Gresham, Watson, & Skinner, 2001) and to describe the relationship among setting events, antecedents, behavior, and consequences (Ingram et al., 2005).

Behavior Intervention Plan

Typically, school behavior plans have been developed based on the disciplinary infraction rather than on individual student needs or the setting in which the challenging behavior occurs (Crone & Horner, 2003). Behavior intervention plans, or BIPs, include both instructional and environmental strategies. Based on the function of the student's problem behavior (what gains accrue for the student or how the behavior serves to avoid a task, person, or situation), BIPs structure interventions to discourage the student's undesirable behavior, teach acceptable alternative or replacement behaviors, and provide the opportunity and motivation for the student to engage in positive behaviors (Cook et al., 2007). It is important to note here that the focus of both the FBA and the following BIP development is not solely to change the student's behavior through teaching skills and changing consequences but also to change the environment and what adults or peers do to prevent the occurrence of the undesirable behavior.

Replacement behaviors may be either academic or social and are those that (a) are considered appropriate, (b) serve the same function (e.g., attention, escape), (c) are incompatible with the behavior of concern (e.g., cannot be performed at the same time as the behavior of concern), and (d) are stated positively (Scott, Anderson, & Spaulding, 2008). Further, the replacement behavior should also be meaningful to the student and serve the student's real-life need.

BIPs must also include changing setting events and antecedents to reduce the occurrences of the behavior or concern. As stated by Cook et al. (2007), "Altering the environmental events that precede and follow the problem behavior allows educators to act in a proactive manner to deter student problem behavior" (p. 193). Reducing the problem behavior allows the student to learn an alternative replacement behavior (e.g., a prosocial skill). As Carr and his colleagues (2002) observe, "The best time to intervene on problem behavior is when the behavior is not occurring. Intervention takes place in the absence of problem behavior so that such behavior can be prevented from occurring again" (p. 9). In addition, consequences and crisis management procedures are included in the plan. Following the development of the BIP, decisions must be made regarding who must be trained, who will provide the training, and how outcomes for the student will be measured (Scott et al., 2008).

Matching interventions to the function of the problem behavior improves the effectiveness and efficiency of the selected interventions (LaRue, Weiss, & Ferraioli, 2008). Function-based behavior intervention plans have better reduced the number of problem behaviors (Ingram et al., 2005; Trussell, Lewis, & Stichter, 2008) and increased academic engagement (Carter & Horner, 2007; Crone, Hawken, & Bergstrom, 2007).

Steps in the FBA/BIP Process

The FBA/BIP process follows these general steps:

1. Identify the behavior to be changed. To do this, list the student's problem behaviors in concrete, observable, and measurable terms. Then choose one behavior to decrease in frequency. This may be the behavior that bothers you the most or the one creating the greatest problem for the student.

2. Obtain baseline data to determine how frequently and under what conditions the undesirable behavior occurs. This process need not be complicated. For example, you may list the undesirable behavior and make a tally mark for each occurrence of the behavior on a given day, generally assessing whether the day has been "typical" for the child. Or you may find an A–B–C format useful (specifying *antecedent* conditions under which the behavior occurred, the specific *behavior* exhibited by the child, and the *consequenc-*

es that the child receives as a result of that behavior). The A–B–Cs can be written on a sheet of paper and quickly documented whenever the behavior of concern is observed.

3. On the basis of the preceding assessment and including other assessment data as appropriate, consider what setting events (characteristics of the environment) or antecedents (what happens right before the behavior occurs) seem to precipitate the behavior and what factors seem to maintain the problem behavior. Then hypothesize as to the function or purpose of the child's behavior (i.e., what that behavior achieves for the child). Instead of looking solely at the child's overt behavior (e.g., hitting, refusing, crying), ask what the child is accomplishing from this behavior. The answer to this question is a "best guess" about the function of the child's behavior: to gain attention (e.g., from peers or adults), to escape or avoid (e.g., a task or person), or to gain access to something (e.g., a desired item or activity; Jolivette, Scott, & Nelson, 2000). Is the child's goal to seek attention or to belong? To reduce anxiety? To avoid participation? Perhaps the student is displaying the particular resistive behavior to avoid a task he perceives as too complicated (e.g., one that has too many steps). Another student may be experiencing anxiety as she realizes that her turn to role-play is approaching. Still another child may not be receiving the desired amount of attention from others. Another may engage in undesirable behaviors to belong and gain friends.

4. When you have identified what is motivating the child's behavior (e.g., attention, escape, etc.), identify an alternative or replacement behavior. The replacement behavior serves the same function or purpose as the undesirable behavior. For example, if the undesirable behavior is aggression when the student wants to engage in a preferred task (e.g,

using the computer or playing a game), the replacement behavior would be Asking Permission (Skill 37).

5. Teach the replacement behavior.

6. Determine an effective reinforcer and deliver it consistently when the replacement behavior occurs. If the reward is given immediately following the replacement behavior, it is more likely that the behavior will be repeated. Some small reinforcer (e.g., verbal encouragement, a sticker) should be given immediately following the behavior. A larger reward (e.g., a special privilege) may be given later—for example, when the child's sticker card is full.

7. Once the individual plan has been implemented, monitor behavior change. A chart or graph of the replacement behavior and the initial behavior of concern will show the degree of progress. It is important to evaluate the child's progress. If the replacement behavior is not increasing (or the problem behavior is not decreasing), the plan must be altered. It could be that the hypothesis about the problem behavior was incorrect, that the replacement behavior selected did not serve the same function for the child as the problem behavior, and so forth. Effective individual interventions are ones that work; as such, monitoring the effectiveness of the plan and making needed changes as indicated by the data are important aspects of behavior change.

Case Example

The following example illustrates use of these steps to address aggression, a significant behavioral concern that occurred in a Skillstreaming group.

Sam joined the Skillstreaming group because of his aggressive behavior in a variety of school settings. The group leader successfully worked with the group to negotiate the skill curriculum, including Sam's skill needs: Dealing with Your Anger (Skill 31), Problem Solving (Skill 41), and Knowing Your Feelings (Skill 26). Expectations were generated from the group, and several rules were accepted and clearly defined, including keeping hands and feet to oneself. During Skillstreaming groups, when Sam appeared to become agitated, the group leader worked on coaching Sam through one of the prosocial skills that had previously been instructed (Knowing Your Feelings). Nonetheless, Sam continued to instigate fights with peers during the group instruction.

The teacher decided to increase the positive reinforcement, delivering more frequent tokens, which could then be exchanged for work on the computer, which Sam enjoyed. Yet his problem behavior continued. When the teacher asked Sam to remove himself to an office area within the classroom, he was often too agitated to go there successfully. The teacher thought about the function or purpose of Sam's aggression and didn't have any ready answers. Sam's behavior seemed to escalate so quickly; it was difficult to pinpoint the precipitating factors. So the teacher sought the advice of the school's intervention team.

A functional behavioral assessment was then conducted by the team, including Sam's parents. Through observation, checklists, and interviews with Sam, it was discovered that Sam had similar issues working in his math group, though he did well when he worked alone. The antecedent to his aggression was being asked to perform in front of a group in both math and Skillstreaming. The setting events seemed to be classes in which he was required to sit in close proximity with others. The team hypothesized that, when Sam was presented with a group activity where he must perform in front of others, he escaped the activity by throwing materials, saying mean things, or hitting a peer. The objective of Sam's behavior plan became to help him participate in group activities (Skillstreaming, math) without hitting, throwing materials, or saying mean things to instigate a fight.

The team designed a BIP for Sam in which a replacement behavior was defined. Because the function of Sam's aggression seemed to be escape, the team wanted to create a way for Sam to avoid the anxiety of being in close proximity with peers and being asked to perform in front of them without having to use aggression. It was decided that Sam would be instructed to use a "break card" when he felt agitated and that both the math teacher and the Skillstreaming group leader would allow Sam to leave their groups and go to the office area to draw until he had calmed down. This replacement behavior served the same function as the aggression (i.e., escape). The Skillstreaming leader even developed a new skill, "Taking a Break," and coached Sam in this skill.

Taking a Break

1. Decide if my body is telling me that I'm getting anxious.

2. Tell myself, "I can walk away from this."

3. Pick up my break card and hand it to the teacher.

4. Walk calmly to the office area.

Because Sam's behaviors of concern (hitting peers, saying mean things to peers, throwing materials) occurred in more than one setting, and because of the intensity of his aggression, additional interventions beyond Skillstreaming were indicated. In this case, Sam was instructed in anxiety-reducing relaxation strategies in ad-

dition to Skillstreaming. Sam also worked with both the math teacher and the Skillstreaming group leader to position his chair a bit away from these instructional groups so he would feel less anxiety (a modification of setting events) and was allowed to hold up a "pass" card if he was asked to participate but did not feel he could (a modification of antecedents). With the help of his parents, Sam's reinforcement for participating was increased (time with his video games at home), and a crisis management plan was designed in case he became aggressive. Consequences for aggression included not being allowed to play his video games at home and restriction of privileges at school (increased supervision during times at school when he would be in close proximity to peers). Sam's plan and data related to aggressive incidents were periodically reviewed by the school's intervention team.

Over time, data suggested Sam was learning to deal with his anxiety of performing a task when in close proximity to others. Incidents of aggression decreased, as well as the frequency of taking breaks. The intervention team then decided to reduce the frequency of reinforcement provided to Sam. It was further decided to discuss his progress graph with him and to involve him in planning a new goal. Together with his teachers, Sam decided he only needed to use a break card twice per day. A contract was then developed for Sam to earn a reward at the end of the week if he used his break card two times or fewer for three of five days.

CHAPTER 7

Building Positive Relationships with Parents

With very few exceptions, parents genuinely care about their children's academic and social progress as they enter the world of school and beyond. Often, cultural and socioeconomic differences impair the development of a common understanding between parents and teachers. Such misunderstandings are unfortunate and have the potential to put the social and emotional welfare of young children at risk. Although many teachers indicate that parent involvement is difficult to achieve, Skillstreaming is a productive and often nonemotional way to begin parent and school collaboration.

Traditionally, parent contact has taken the form of PTA/PTO meetings, parent-teacher conferences, or, as far too often has been the case with a child prone to behave aggressively or disruptively, the "bad news call." Teachers able to create positive relationships with parents often view and deal with parents quite differently. They demonstrate understanding of cultural and economic differences. They recognize and appreciate parents as the child's first (and continuing) teachers. They seek contact early and frequently, seeing this as an opportunity to collaborate in supportive, mutually reinforcing ways. Displaying such attitudes helps create the opportunity for the parent, teacher, and student to become a problem-solving team.

The role of parents and the family has gradually changed from being on the periphery to being a central focus in the child's education. It is more widely understood that establishing close working relationships with parents, especially in the early grades (i.e., kindergarten through third grade), can have a positive effect on the child's school adjustment (Adams et al., 2010; Bruder, 2010; Strain & Timm, 2001; Walker, Colvin, & Ramsey, 1995). For children with disabilities, as required by IDEA (1997, 2004), goals for family outcomes include that families know their rights, effectively communicate their children's needs, and help their children develop and learn (Bruder, 2010). Thus, parents are not only expected to be involved with their child's education but are expected to participate in their child's learning. Opportunities for the child to be successful in school, home, and peer group increase with a cooperative working relationship between parents and the school.

Although there is an increased emphasis on expanding the role of the family in the young child's school experience (e.g., involving parents to a greater degree in decision making, parent training), teachers and other professionals may not be sufficiently prepared for such collaboration (Friesen & Stephens, 1998). A model for the development of positive and productive relationships presented by Fialka and Mikus (1999) may be helpful to the teacher or other Skillstreaming leader. This model calls for a partnership between home and school that can be developed through specific phases of parent-teacher interaction.

The first phase of relationship development, which Fialka and Mikus call *colliding and campaigning,* involves fostering understanding and beginning to build trust between parent and teacher. During this initial phase of relationship building, each party typically has difficulty listening to the other. Instead, it is often the goal to state their own perspectives about the child, the problem, or the intervention, with the hope of persuading the other to see the issue from their vantage point and to accept their solution. During initial parent contacts, then, it is important for each party to have the goal of listening for understanding, asking for more information, and being willing to explore different possibilities in resolving concerns. With successful work at the first phase, parents and teachers move to the middle phase, *coordinating, cooperating, and compromising,* in which their interactions are based on more effective listening and cooperating. Being able to suspend their personal agendas to explore a common ground and asking each other to explain ideas will give rise to respect for the other and increased capacity for problem solving. *Collaborating and creative partnering,* the third phase of relationship building, continues to be based on listening and inquiring. During this phase, there is more open sharing of each party's needs, hopes, and fears. Differences of opinion are more easily understood and accepted, and decision making becomes more balanced between the parties. Although these phases are described as discrete, relationships will often move back and forth among the phases as parents and teachers engage in problem solving.

Emotional and behavioral problems affect the child in all life situations—home, neighborhood, school, church, and so forth. In addition, families experience significant stress when their child has emotional and behavioral problems. Collaboration between teacher and parent best addresses the child's behavioral and social needs. Communication with the student's family should,

therefore, be one of the most important components of any school program (Quinn et al., 2000).

PARENTING AND CHILDREN'S AGGRESSION

Aggression is a difficult behavior to change. It is primarily a learned behavior, and many children have learned it well. From their early years, they live with family and peers who repeatedly model, reward, and even overtly encourage hurtful actions toward others. In a real sense, aggression becomes for many children a behavior that "works"—both for them and for the significant people in their lives.

In school, agency, and other institutional settings, many chronically aggressive youths participate in interventions like Skillstreaming, designed to teach prosocial alternatives. They learn to maintain self-control or walk away from confrontations rather than incite, attack, or fight. They then use one of these prosocial alternatives in the presence of a family member or neighborhood peer and, rather than reward the constructive attempt, the other party responds critically. "No son of mine is going to be a punk. You hit him before he hits you!" says the parent. "Are you chicken?" says the peer.

Overall, parents do the best they can with what they know. However, parenting styles and practices significantly affect the young child's later school and social adjustment. Considerable research evidence suggests that children exhibiting aggression during the preschool years, for example, often have been exposed to harsh, punitive, rigid, and authoritarian discipline and parents who model aggression (Jewett, 1992). Conversely, parenting practices related to prosocial behavior include appropriate and fair discipline, sufficient supervision, involvement in the child's life (e.g., school and peer contacts), an attitude of support, and the ability to resolve conflicts and handle crises in the family (Walker et al., 1995). Reid, Webster-Stratton, and Hammond (2007) have summarized effective parent training strategies, which include reducing harsh and inconsistent parenting, increasing positive and responsive parenting, promoting parent skills in cognitive stimulation, and increasing home-school bonding.

A seven-year follow-up study of parents of kindergarten children found that four types of parenting behavior promoted young children's later adjustment in school (Pettit, Bates, & Dodge, 2000). These positive parenting behaviors included warmth, supportive discipline (e.g., calm discussions), interest and involvement in the child's life (e.g., peer contacts), and the proactive teaching of social skills. In addition to promoting positive adaptation across the elementary school years, these parenting skills may also serve as a protective factor, buffering the risks associated with family stressors (e.g., financial stress, divorce).

PARENT INVOLVEMENT IN SKILLSTREAMING

Parents can and should be involved in Skillstreaming for a variety of important reasons. First, parenting practices may be at cross purposes with what is taught in the school (Cartledge & Milburn, 1995). A specific skill taught in the Skillstreaming group may not be supported at home, and its use may actually be discouraged. For example, a young child's attempt to use the skill Saying No (Skill 55) may be met with the parent's response to "stop talking back." Such contradictions from important people in the child's life will be confusing and may discourage further use of the skill. When parents understand the goals of Skillstreaming, as well as the specific behaviors included, they are far more likely to be receptive to the child's skill initiations. Furthermore, because Skillstreaming provides a specific way of teaching children "what to do," the opportunity exists to alter how parents deal with the child's problems in the home and with peers and siblings. For example, when parents learn to reinforce and prompt prosocial skill use—and to change the consequences that maintain a child's aggression (Patterson, 1982)—more positive

and supportive parenting will likely result. In this way, parent involvement and cooperation in Skillstreaming have the potential to improve parenting skills. In addition, parents' ratings of their child's self-control and social skills have been shown to improve when parents are trained as coaches and involved in the social skills training (Slim et al., 2006).

Second, many social and behavioral problems originate in the home setting (Walker et al., 1995). Therefore, the more settings in which prosocial skill use is prompted and rewarded, the greater the likelihood that the skills taught will be maintained and will generalize. As discussed in chapter 5, children may easily learn the Skillstreaming skills, but they are unlikely to continue to use skills over time or in a variety of situations and environments unless specific procedures are implemented to facilitate their use. Reinforcement and prompting of skill use in the home setting is a way to enhance continued use of skills.

A third rationale for including parents in Skillstreaming concerns the profound effect of modeling on the young child's behavior. When parents and siblings model behaviors for dealing with stress and anger, for example, the young child follows these models.

LEVELS OF PARENT INVOLVEMENT

In a survey of teachers, Brannon (2008) found the most successful ways of involving parents include (a) involving the family in homework through discussion or activity, (b) informing parents what is occurring in class via newsletters or website, (c) informing parents of the class and school expectations so they understand and may be supportive, (d) asking parents to volunteer so they are exposed to behavioral expectations, and (e) holding events (such as breakfast or evening programs) to ease parents into the partnership and share what their children are learning.

In collaborating with parents on behalf of the young child, several goals are apparent. Cartledge and Milburn (1995) emphasize the value in conveying to parents the importance of social skills learning to the child's development, an awareness of the social skills needed to be successful outside the home, and actions parents may take to assist the child in skill learning. The level of involvement will vary according to the receptivity of both parents and professionals. The following levels should be prescriptively matched to the needs of the child targeted for skills training.

Orientation Level

The first level of parent involvement can best be described as an orientation to Skillstreaming skills and procedures. The purpose of this level is to promote parent awareness and understanding. An orientation meeting to describe Skillstreaming objectives and ways parents might help their child use the prosocial skills at home is very helpful. In such a meeting, leaders may present examples of skills, discuss the goals of Skillstreaming, and explain the learning process (modeling, role-playing, performance feedback, and generalization in the form of homework). Showing *The Skillstreaming Video* (Goldstein & McGinnis, 1988) and conducting a mock group are specific activities that will increase parent understanding. Allowing time for questions and input about skills for instruction will also increase parents' understanding and involvement.

An alternative to an orientation meeting is to send a letter home explaining the goals of Skillstreaming instruction and the activities in which the child will be participating (i.e., watching leaders act out a skill, trying out the skill steps in the group, giving and receiving feedback about skill performance, and completing skill homework assignments). The Parent Orientation Note is helpful in this regard (see sample in Figure 9). Orienting parents to the types of skills and procedures used is necessary because many of the skill-use situations occur in the family environment. If parents are uninformed about Skillstreaming goals, they may justifiably question the purpose of discussing home-related situations at school.

Other ways to promote parent involvement at the orientation level include the following:

1. Have parents assess their child's skill strengths and weaknesses by completing all or part of the Parent Checklist (in Appendix A) and talk with them about skills they value in the home. Conversations with parents about needed skills will help identify cultural aspects of the skills and permit better choices of where, when, and with whom individual skills will be most beneficial.

2. Frequently inform parents of the child's progress in the various skill areas, focusing on positive reports. (Parent Homework Notes, described in the following discussion, are a primary vehicle for communication.)

3. Videorecord the child in a role-play situation and share this video with the parents during a conference to encourage further understanding of Skillstreaming's goals and procedures.

4. Invite parents to participate in a mock Skillstreaming group in which parents learn a skill through modeling, role-playing, feedback, and generalization

5. Encourage parents to support skill learning by giving the child positive feedback for practicing skills he or she has successfully role-played in the school or other learning environment.

Support Level

Following successful parent involvement at the orientation level, the teacher or other group leader should seek to involve parents at the support level. The goal at this level is to gain more active parental support. Parent activities at this level are as follows:

1. Support the child's demonstration of the social skill by helping the child complete assigned homework in the home environment. Feedback to the teacher will be given

Figure 9: Sample Parent Orientation Note

Date _____12/20_____

Dear Parent or Guardian:

Your child and his or her classmates are learning to handle a variety of day-to-day concerns in positive ways. Sharing, taking turns, handling teasing and anger, and following directions are some of the concerns we are working on. We are all learning specific steps to social skills in order to handle these problems in acceptable ways.

The process we are using to learn these skills is called Skillstreaming. First, your child is watching someone else use the skill. Then he or she will try out the skill and receive feedback about how well he or she performed the skill from both peers and adults. Finally, your child will be asked to practice the skill in real-life situations.

Each week we will be sending home a note describing the skill and its steps. We hope that you review this note with your child and help your child practice the skill at home. Please feel free to call me or e-mail me if you have any questions.

Sincerely,

_____Teacher/Leader_____

Phone ____555-1234_____

E-mail ___teacherleader@anyschool.com_____

via the School-Home Note (see sample in Figure 10).

2. Notice and reward the child's specific skill use in the home and neighborhood environment and provide ongoing encouragement.

3. Observe a Skillstreaming group in progress and participate as coactors in the group.

4. Help assess the child's skill progress by judging skill performance at home and in neighborhood settings.

Cooperative Level

At the cooperative level, parents are involved in selecting skills needed in the home and neighborhood setting and regularly give feedback to the teacher or other group leader about the child's use of skills. Parents will also be involved in prompting the child's use of the skills at home and will provide encouragement and reinforcement for the child's performance. At the cooperative level, teachers and parents work together as a team to teach and support the child's skill development. The Parent/Staff Skill Rating Form is helpful in this regard (see sample in Figure 11). Staff in residential or other teaching settings may also use this form.

Family Skillstreaming Level

Program evaluations have suggested that children's prosocial responses are more likely to be rewarded, supported, and even reciprocated if significant others also participate in Skillstreaming training programs. Some of these joint efforts have involved teaching empathy skills to adolescents and their parents (Guzzetta, 1974), teaching delinquent youths and their families alternatives to aggression (Goldstein, Glick, Irwin, Pask-McCartney, & Rubama, 1989), and training adolescents and their peer groups in a variety of social skills (Gibbs et al., 1995; Goldstein, Glick, Carthan, & Blancero, 1994). The success of these programs strongly suggests the effectiveness of instruction for both skill-deficient youth and the significant people in their lives.

For students and their families, schools are increasingly community resources, offering a range of health-related and social service programming. Expansion of the purposes of schools is likely to continue, and family Skillstreaming, in which children participate in Skillstreaming along with their siblings and parents, holds promise as a regular offering in this context, as well as in mental health and other settings.

Figure 10: Sample School-Home Note

Student _Karina_   Date _11/30_

DESCRIPTION OF LESSON

Skill name: _Accepting No (#54)_

Skill steps:

1. Decide why you were told no.
2. Think about your choices.
   a. Do something else.
   b. Say how you feel in a friendly way.
   c. Write about how you feel.
3. Act out your best choice.

Skill purpose, use, value _Keep positive relationships by accepting being told no._

DESCRIPTION OF SKILL HOMEWORK

Karina will use this skill at home when she is told no by a parent.

REQUEST TO PARENTS

1. Provide skill homework recognition and reward.
2. Respond positively to your child's skill use.
3. Return this School-Home Note with your comments (on the back) about quality of homework done and questions/suggestions for the teacher.
4. Please sign and return this form to _Mr. Staton_

by _12/5_

Signature _[signature]_   Date _12/5_

Figure 12: Sample Parent/Staff Skill Rating Form

Date _____ 2/2 _____

_____ Darwin _____ is learning
(student's name)

the skill of _____ Being a Good Sport (#50) _____

The steps involved in this skill are:

1. Decide how you and the other person played the game.
2. Think of what you can honestly tell the other person.
   a. "Congratulations."
   b. "You played a good game."
   c. "You're getting a lot better at this game."
3. Act out your best choice.
4. Help the other person put equipment or materials away.

1. Did he or she demonstrate this skill in your presence?   ☑ yes   ☐ no

2. How would you rate his or her skill demonstration? *(check one)*

   ☐ poor   ☐ below average   ☐ average   ☑ above average   ☐ excellent

3. How sincere was he or she in performing the skill? *(check one)*

   ☐ not sincere   ☑ somewhat sincere   ☐ very sincere

Comments:

_____ Losing is hard for Darwin. He used the skill twice when playing video _____

_____ games with his brother. He is doing better! _____

_____

Please sign and return this form to _____ Mr. Staton _____

by _____ 2/10 _____

Signature _____ *(signature)* _____ Date _____ 2/10 _____

CHAPTER 8

Skillstreaming in the School Context

Teachers and school administrators continue to report their greatest challenge is to reduce classroom and school disruption, often occurring in the form of student aggression and violence. In a 2004 Gallup poll (Rose & Gallup, 2004), educators cited discipline as the most serious issue in today's schools, second only to the lack of financial support. It is further estimated that between two and seven percent of students have significant emotional or behavioral problems, which often include anger and aggression (Kauffman, 2005). This chapter reviews issues surrounding school violence and aggression and suggests how Skillstreaming can play a role in reducing them.

VIOLENCE PREVENTION

Although it may be true that students today come to school with many more significant concerns than in the past, certain factors related to the school itself have been found to contribute to violence. Experts generally advocate a multifaceted or combined program of school safety, including the development of school policies addressing weapons and crisis response, environmental factors such as school facilities and family and community resources, and prevention through education. Educational strategies, school climate, and disciplinary policy and methods play a central role.

Educational Strategies

Educational approaches to preventing violence and aggression include conflict management, social skills instruction, mentoring programs, behavioral programs, intensive academic instruction, drug prevention, student advocacy programs, peer helper programs, student assistance (counseling) programs, prejudice reduction / cultural sensitivity curricula, and community service. An important goal of such schoolwide approaches is "to give everyone involved in the school the same skills, language and terminology for handling stress and conflict—to create an environment that is consistently nonviolent and nurturing" (Ascher, 1994, p. 4).

To be effective in reducing discipline problems, improving school climate, and increasing students' self-esteem and ability to assume responsibility (Walker et al., 1995), such programs need to be instituted at an early age and should include many individuals in the child's environment (teachers, peers, and other school staff, such as custodians and paraprofessionals). Furthermore, teachers and other school personnel will need professional staff development in the areas of conflict resolution, how to respond to violence, and team building.

School Climate

The culture or climate of a school is reflected in the prevailing values and beliefs held by school staff, parents, and students. These values and beliefs define acceptable behavior and determine the manner in which the school should function. As stated by Modro (1995):

The most important factor that needs to be addressed even before policies that will support school safety is the atmosphere, or "feeling tone," in which education takes place. Does our educational system reflect a genuine belief in the essential dignity of each child? Do educators believe in the inherent value of the people they serve? The fear is that many mirror for our children what some of them already see reflected in society. (p. 11)

Johnson (2009) reviewed 25 studies published in 2007–2008 that addressed the relationship between the school environment and school violence and considered both the social and physical environments. Lower rates of school violence were associated with positive relationships with teachers, students' clear understanding of the rules and their perceptions that the rules were fair, students' feelings of ownership in their school, positive classrooms and other school environments that focused on student understanding, and safety interventions that increased the perception of physical order.

A positive school climate not only provides an environment for students to learn prosocial skills but also enhances academic achievement and teacher retention (Cohen, Pickeral, & Mc-Closkey, 2009; MacNeil, Prater, & Busch, 2009). In order to learn, students must believe their school is a safe environment, free from harassment and aggression (Goldstein, Young, & Boyd, 2008). Indeed, half of all students who take a weapon to school say they do so for their own protection (Sprague & Walker, 2000).

Learning environments need to create opportunities for children to participate in rule setting and to accept responsibility, and children must be taught the skills necessary for prosocial participation in these activities. Creating a better balance of positive to negative consequences is also necessary to foster a positive school climate. Some children, in particular those who have well-established patterns of undesirable behavior, are more likely to receive an overabundance of negative consequences. For these individuals, positive feelings about school and learning itself are unlikely. Such children need more instruction, not less.

Disciplinary Policy and Methods

Exclusionary practices remain the primary way the schools deal with student disruption, aggression, and violence. This fact also applies to students at the preschool level, with those in this age group being three times as likely to be expelled than students in grades K through 12 (Gilliam, 2005). The problem is that such practices fail to work in the long run. Suspension and other forms of traditional punishment do not prevent or deter future misconduct for students with chronic or intense behavior problems (Goldstein et al., 1998). Neither do such policies make schools safer; in fact, the opposite appears to be true (Brownstein, 2010). For example, Nickerson and Martens (2008) explored different approaches to school violence prevention through a survey of over 2,000 school principals. These authors found that a focus on security/enforcement and suspending students actually related to a higher incidence of disruption and crime.

In addition, suspension and other exclusionary practices often exacerbate the very behaviors they are designed to extinguish (Mendler & Curwin, 1999). Because we know that time spent in learning is the best predictor of increased academic achievement (Skiba & Sprague, 2008), suspensions often contribute to a student's academic failure. Such long-term negative outcomes include poor academic achievement, grade retention, negative feelings about school, truancy, and dropping out (Bock, Tapscott, & Savner, 1998; Dupper & Bosch, 1996; Hickman, Bartholomew, Mathwig, & Heinrichs, 2008). For example, Hickman et al. (2008) examined the histories of school dropouts and graduates. Students who dropped out showed higher rates of behavior problems in early grades, a history of absenteeism as early as first grade, more often repeated a grade, and showed lower grades and test scores than did graduates. Students themselves have reported that suspensions were "not at all" helpful (Costenbader & Markson, 1998). In addition, issues of equity exist: Minority students are more likely to be suspended than nonminority students and are disciplined more severely for minor disciplinary infractions (Advancement Project/Civil Rights Project, 2000; Applied Research Center, 1999; Brownstein, 2010; Cartledge, 2003; Costenbader & Markson, 1998; Skiba, Peterson, & Williams, 1997).

Furthermore, the positive relationship between school attendance and academic success has been well documented, encouraging the examination of the relationship of school suspension to academic achievement (Andrews, Taylor, Martin, & Slate, 1998; Zins, Bloodworth, Weissberg, & Walberg, 2004). The more students are excluded from school, the more likely they are to fall behind academically. And because it is more acceptable to act bad than it is to act stupid (Brendtro, Brokenleg, & Van Bockern, 2002), students are more likely to act disruptively and aggressively to avoid work that is not understood. It makes sense that students who are not in school will fail to learn what they need to learn.

Mayer (2001) summarizes what schools can do to create an environment that will facilitate the reduction of behavior problems:

1. Reduce punitive methods of control
2. Provide clear rules (expectations) for student conduct
3. Assure support to educators
4. Minimize academic failure experiences
5. Teach critical social skills
6. Use function-based behavior management
7. Respect, value, and understand ethnic and cultural differences
8. Support student involvement and participation

Johns, Carr, and Hoots (1995, p. 2-2) recommend that school discipline be evaluated by asking the following questions:

1. Does the disciplinary process allow students to accept responsibility for their actions?
2. Does the disciplinary process continually place importance on the value of academic participation and achievement?
3. Does the disciplinary action build positive self-image?
4. Does the disciplinary action teach students alternative methods of dealing with problems?

In other words, disciplinary programs in schools today and in the future need to be instructional in nature. Instructional alternatives may include assigning the student to a social skills class (dealing with specific alternatives to the conflict that resulted in suspension and where more desirable behaviors may be learned), requiring the student to complete community service (where he or she will be more likely to be exposed to appropriate models and receive the attention needed to foster a more positive self-image), and having the student complete an in-school intervention focusing on conflict resolution.

Bullying

One form of aggression that deserves closer scrutiny is bullying. Bullying is common in preschool and elementary school classrooms (Beane, 1999; Manning, Heron, & Marshall, 1978; Smith & Levan, 1995). Bullying often begins in preschool and presents significant behavioral issues not only for the young child who is the target but for the bully and observers as well.

It is important to distinguish between bullying and other types of aggression that may occur in the preschool and kindergarten setting. The most common form of bullying is teasing; however, occasional teasing does not constitute bullying. Neither is bullying considered rough play or accidentally hurtful events. Instead, in bullying, there is a physical or psychological imbalance of power (Newman, Horne, & Bartolomucci, 2000). The most accepted definition of bullying is presented by Olweus (1991), who states, "A person is being bullied or victimized when he or she is exposed, repeatedly and over time, to negative actions on the part of one or more persons" (p. 413).

This type of aggression can be either direct or indirect (Olweus, 1993). Direct, or overt, bullying typically is observable verbal or physical aggression. Direct bullying includes hitting, pushing, kicking, and tripping, as well as the verbal behaviors of yelling, threatening, and cursing (Ahmad & Smith, 1994). Indirect bullying includes behaviors such as spreading rumors, backbiting or scapegoating, and convincing others to ignore or isolate the victim. Both types can be very harmful.

Bullying also may be a precursor to more severe and dangerous violence (Greenbaum, Turner, & Stephens, 1989; Hoover & Oliver, 1996; Olweus, 1991). Kauffman, Mostert, Trent, and Hallahan (1998) note that "engaging in aggressive antisocial acts is not good for children; it does not help them develop appropriate behavior, but increases the likelihood of further aggression, maladjustment, and academic and social failure" (p. 14). When ignored, bullying often escalates in intensity and continues in frequency (Goldstein, 1999a).

Young children often engage in bullying or other aggressive acts to exert their power over others or to control a situation—for example, to get what they want, whether it is a toy, candy, a peer's lunch, or attention from peers. Bullying often is unreported because it typically occurs in places without sufficient adult supervision (e.g., playground, lunchroom, hallways, neighborhood park, to and from school). Many children do not report bullying for fear that they will receive even more aggression from the bully. Based on what adults often teach children, children are likely to question whether anything will be done about the provocation. After all, haven't adults reinforced the belief that children shouldn't tattle? Sometimes the target is even reprimanded by the adult, further rewarding the bully for the aggression.

The goal of Skillstreaming is to teach prosocial alternatives. By experiencing direct teaching of behavioral skill steps, children who are targets or observers of bullying can learn assertiveness skills to deal effectively with being teased and with other peer provocation (Using Brave Talk, Skill 3; Dealing with Teasing, Skill 27), to tell an adult about a problem (Knowing When to Tell, Skill 35), to problem solve (Solving a Problem, Skill 30), and to say no (Saying No, Skill 38). Other skills from the Skillstreaming curriculum also may be effectively used in bullying contexts.

The bully also deserves our attention and instructional efforts. The bully, although often maintaining a level of social status with peers (Hoover & Oliver, 1996), often feels isolated from others. It is important to expand this child's repertoire of choices by teaching friendship-making skills (Group II) as well as ways to deal with anger (Dealing with Your Anger, Skill 31) and skills for dealing with feelings (Group III). In addition, because the bully seeks power or control, he or she can be given influence in a prosocial, positive way by helping to teach the skills to peers or younger children or in other ways assuming a leadership role in Skillstreaming.

SCHOOLWIDE APPLICATIONS OF SKILLSTREAMING

Although preschool and elementary students are now taught prosocial skills primarily in individual classrooms, Skillstreaming is increasingly a part of the school curriculum on a schoolwide basis. One example of schoolwide use is Edmunds Elementary School in Des Moines, Iowa, where instruction occurs in all preschool through fifth-grade classrooms on a regular basis. Therefore, all teachers and students are aware of the skills and behaviors expected. In addition, because all teachers provide the Skillstreaming instruction, they prompt prosocial skill use throughout the school day.

Polaris K–12 School in Anchorage, Alaska, also uses Skillstreaming in the form of whole-class and group instruction for all students in kindergarten through third grade, as well as providing targeted instruction for students who need to learn positive social behaviors in particular skill areas. This program provides for the prevention of behavior problems by clearly defining behavioral expectations, teaching the skills in a relevant way, and structuring reinforcement of these behaviors by other adults in the school.

The potential for student participation, including generalization and maintenance of learned skills, is greatly enhanced the more the environment is involved in the program. Including entire schools in the skills training process has the potential to increase both student motivation and skill awareness. Large-scale program involvement means that many more teachers and other school staff are involved as instructors, thus providing greater opportunity for students to be rewarded for correct skill use and to receive prompting or coaching following incorrect use. In addition, when entire schools are involved, especially at the lower grade levels, added potential exists for Skillstreaming to operate at a preventive level—before youth get into difficulty in school, at home, or with the law. At the preschool level, implementing such prevention strategies holds special promise to alter the patterns of future aggression.

INTEGRATION IN THE CURRICULUM

As we move into the 21st century, schools are paying more attention to students' emotional health and are more likely to integrate Skillstreaming within the general education curricula. Marx (2006), for example, recommends that schools "expand programs in thinking and reasoning skills as well as civic and character education" (p. 45). As stated by the Partnership for 21st Century Skills (2008), "All Americans must be skilled at interacting competently and respectfully with others" (p. 10). In *Connecting Teachers, Students, and Standards: Strategies for Success in Diverse and Inclusive Classrooms,* and citing the work of Mercer and Pullen (2005), Voltz, Sims, and Nelson (2010) call for including social skills strategy instruction into the curriculum. They state:

[Social skill strategy instruction] . . . is designed to teach students how to interact appropriately with others across a variety of situations and settings. Skills such as resisting pressure, accepting criticism, negotiating, following directions, and asking for help are included. (p. 78)

In addition, it is continuing to become more well-accepted that social skills are essential in achieving needed academic outcomes (Schoenfeld et al., 2008). Indeed, the relationship between problem behavior and low academic skills has been widely investigated (Lassen, Steele, & Sailor, 2006; McIntosh & Mackay, 2008; Rock, Fessler, & Church, 1997; Trzesniewski, Moffit, Caspi, Taylor, & Maughan, 2006). Further, Marzano and Haystead (2008) provide examples for including standards in life skills such as the following:

▶ Expectations for participation (asking questions, staying focused, raising hand, waiting for appropriate time to ask a question)

▶ Work completion (following directions, bringing necessary materials to class)

▶ Behavior (following routines, helping others, treating others with respect such as keeping hands to oneself)

Schoenfeld et al. (2008) describe a way to include social skills instruction into daily academic instruction. Their ENGAGE blueprint includes the following steps:

1. Examine the demands of curriculum and instruction.

2. Note essential social skills (e.g., raising hands, sharing materials). Consider skills for the entire class, small groups, and individual students.

3. Go forward and teach. Implement the teaching plan.

4. Actively monitor (e.g., scan, move about the room, prompt students in skill use, provide positive reinforcement).

5. Gauge progress. Monitor the use of the skills.

6. Exchange reflections. Debrief with students on social skill use and expectations.

It is clear from this brief review that social skills instruction lends itself to being imbedded within the academic curricula as a central goal for all students and that it can be considered as a prevention as well as an intervention strategy.

INCLUSION

Another current initiative in schools today provides for increasing inclusion of youth with special needs in regular education classrooms. The Individuals with Disabilities Education Act (IDEA, 1997, 2004) calls for educating students with disabilities within the least restrictive environment. In other words, as much as possible, students with disabilities should be educated with nondisabled peers within the general education setting. It has been accepted in recent years that if academic or social benefit can be attained in the regular classroom setting, then a student with disabilities should receive his or her instruction there. Yet many experts in the field of special education believe social benefits are unlikely to occur unless planned and systematic instruction in social skills also takes place. Outcomes for preschool students with disabilities required by IDEA include that they have positive social-emotional skills, demonstrate acquisition of use of knowledge and skills, and use appropriate behavior to meet their needs (Bruder, 2010). Students without disabilities may also need instruction in accepting students with differences. Skillstreaming is often used to teach the prosocial behaviors that will enhance successful inclusion. For example, in Placer County, California schools, students with emotional and behavioral disorders receive direct Skillstreaming instruction. In addition, all staff members are involved in the instruction and prompt skill use throughout the school day. In Fayette County Schools, Georgia, Skillstreaming instruction includes students with a variety of disabilities participating in

modeling and role-plays with nondisabled peers. Skillstreaming is also used with students with Asperger's syndrome. This project, Connections Research and Treatment Program, provides services for six hours per day, five days per week, for a period of six weeks. Students receive Skillstreaming for four 20-minute cycles each day. An additional 50 minutes in each cycle is devoted to activities in which children practice the social skills they learned and emotion recognition and expand on their interests.

In the effort to increase prospective teachers' awareness and understanding of students with disabilities, the preservice teaching program at St. Mary's College in Notre Dame, Indiana, implements a field experience called Campus Friends (Turner, 2003). Once per week, students with disabilities come to the campus to interact with college students. Using Skillstreaming, students are taught a variety of prosocial skills. Students also visit areas of the campus community and are prompted to use the prosocial skills they have been taught. In brief, the trend toward inclusion makes it even more important to teach all students (both with and without disabilities) the social skills they need.

MULTI-TIERED SYSTEMS OF SUPPORT

Many schools and districts are developing systems to address both academic and behavioral interventions to meet the learning needs of all students. Tiered systems of support have been evidenced to address student academic concerns through Response to Intervention (RTI) and behavioral concerns through Positive Behavioral Interventions and Supports (PBIS). Recently, social and behavioral concerns have begun to be addressed through RTI in addition to academics. These tiered supports are often composed of three or four levels and offer schools a systematic way to look at the intensity of intervention needed. School teams then develop interventions to address the needs of all and implement academic, behavioral, and social interventions along this continuum. Recognizing that academic needs impact behavior and vice versa, schools and districts are now designing multi-tiered systems of support considering both academic and social-behavioral interventions in such tiered models.

For example, Farmer, Farmer, Estell and Hutchins (2007) offer a three-level system to address both academic and behavioral need. Such systems often include (a) universal strategies to meet the needs of all students, (b) selective or targeted interventions for students who continue to struggle even after high-quality universal instruction is provided, and (c) individual or intense interventions for students not responding to the first two levels. The goal of such systems is to match the intensity of student need with the intensity of interventions.

Positive Behavior Intervention and Supports

PBIS is rapidly gaining acceptance across the country largely because of its strong research base and procedures for training schools in implementation. Funded by a federal grant, The Center on Positive Behavioral Interventions and Supports (www.pbis.org) provides ongoing training assistance to state departments of education and school districts and is a clearinghouse for updated information and new evidence.

The universal (primary) level of prevention includes the development and instruction of school and classroom routines and behavioral expectations through schoolwide social skills training. Skillstreaming is used at this level to instruct all students in skills such as Asking for Help (Skill 2), Listening (Skill 1), and Following Instructions (Skill 5). How these skills look in each area of the school (e.g., cafeteria, hallway, commons, classroom) is demonstrated, and all students in the school have the opportunity to see the skills modeled and to follow through with group role-plays and feedback. New skills are also created depending on the expectations of each school. For example, skills may be developed to teach school routines, such as Passing from Class to Class, Bringing Needed Materials to Class, or Appropriate Talk in the Lunchroom. A new social skill is developed for whatever problem behaviors are experienced by most students. The goal here is to reduce predictable problems so that more time and effort can be directed toward students needing more interventions at the other levels.

Targeted (secondary) prevention provides a system of behavioral supports for those students, fewer in number, who continue to have behavioral difficulties that may result in a school suspension. While still participating in universal interventions, these students experience additionally targeted instruction in Skillstreaming in small groups. At this level, the selection of skills becomes more prescriptive—that is, the specific skills selected for group instruction are those related to the students' problematic behavior. Skills for targeted instruction often include Problem Solving (Skill 41), Using Self-Control (Skill 36), Making a Complaint (Skill 47), and Staying Out of Fights (Skill 40). Other types of targeted interventions may include a staff member's checking in with a group of students to better prepare them for the school day or providing group mentoring activities.

For the few students who remain unresponsive to targeted interventions, individual interventions are designed. Students at this level may experience multiple problems and will therefore need multiple interventions. For example, wraparound supports or a behavior intervention plan (BIP) may be necessary to assist students needing this level of support. At this level, Skillstreaming is a part of the student's overall support program, often implemented to teach the student replacement behaviors (acceptable behaviors that serve the same function and are incompatible with problem behavior), as determined through the functional behavioral assessment (FBA) process. This process is described in more depth in chapter 6, on managing behavioral problems.

Response to Intervention

In part because of dissatisfaction with the discrepancy model for identifying students with learning disabilities, the RTI process is advocated as an alternative method for identifying students who have a learning disability. Used primarily to address academic deficits, it is becoming more common to include behavioral and social deficits within this framework (Sugai, Guardino, & Lathrop, 2007). Most RTI models include these components (Bender, 2009):

- ▶ Universal screening to identify students who are not making adequate progress
- ▶ Increasingly intensive interventions presented in levels or tiers
- ▶ Use of evidence-based strategies at all tiers
- ▶ Progress monitoring of student progress
- ▶ Making data-based decisions when considering moving a student to another tier

What does RTI look like related to social behaviors, and how is Skillstreaming used within this framework? Universal screening for behavior problems and social skills deficits is conducted. This process is often quite easy; most teachers can readily identify the students who are acting out. Reviewing the data from office discipline and counseling referrals is another method of such screening. Once students have been identified, Tier I (or universal social skills instruction) is provided to all students in a manner similar to the PBIS process. The teacher provides whole-class instruction in the skills needed by most students. While continuing to monitor behavioral data, the teacher checks in with a small group of students 10 minutes before school begins and again at the end of the school day (Tier II). This brief check-in time allows the teacher to review the students' behavioral self-monitoring systems and provide encouragement and reinforcement for use of the Tier I skills. Students not making adequate behavioral progress (e.g., continued office referrals) are also assigned to a skills group (Tier II). This group is co-instructed by the teacher and a school counselor or other support staff member and addresses the skills for which those in the group have been sent to the office.

Based on progress monitoring data, students still not making adequate behavioral progress receive more intense Skillstreaming instruction in a Tier III after-school alternative to suspension skills group, along with other strategies as determined on an individual student basis (e.g., counseling support, wraparound supports). A student needing Tier III intervention continues to benefit from interventions at Tiers I and II. As this example shows, Skillstreaming can be a valuable part of a student's program at all three tiers.

NEW INTERVENTION COMBINATIONS

Although Skillstreaming is effective in teaching prosocial skills and interpersonal competencies, quite often the skills learned are not performed by the students where and when needed. Chapter 5 examined the bases for generalization failures, as well as means for their remediation. As discussed earlier, some students fail to display newly learned skill behaviors because earlier learned behaviors, such as aggression, have been well practiced and therefore are more readily available and frequently used.

For this purpose, Goldstein and colleagues (Goldstein & Glick, 1987; Goldstein, Glick, & Gibbs, 1998) developed Aggression Replacement Training (ART). Used primarily for aggressive adolescents, ART incorporates both anger control training (Feindler, 1979, 1995) and moral reasoning (Kohlberg, 1969, 1973). Students learn what to do from Skillstreaming and what not to do from anger control training. The final component, moral reasoning, is designed to engage students in discussion of values to increase motivation to choose prosocial skill alternatives. A third edition of this widely used program is available (Glick & Gibbs, 2010). The Prepare Curriculum (Goldstein, 1999b) expands the three components of ART to include such areas as empathy training, situational perception training, and problem solving.

Based on ART, The Peace4Kids and Families Program (centerforsafeschools.org) was developed for use in schools in grades prekindergarten through 12. The program includes the four components of social skills training, empathy, anger control, and character education. Peace4Kids provides strategies for all students (universal interventions); targeted strategies for students who are at risk; and intensive, individualized interventions for students who do not show improved behavior through the first two levels of intervention. The goal of the program is to implement an effective prevention program, creating a culture of learning and behaving and is used in schools, community-based programs, day treatment, and residential services. An effective parent empowerment component is also included.

Skill Outlines
and Homework Reports

Group 1

Classroom Survival Skills

Skills 1–13

Skill 1: Listening

SKILL STEPS

1. **Look at the person who is talking.**

   Point out to students that sometimes others may think someone isn't listening, even though he/she has heard what was said.

2. **Sit quietly.**

   These steps are to show someone that you really are listening.

3. **Think about what is being said.**

   Tell students to sit (or stand) facing the person and remember not to laugh, fidget, play with something, and so on.

4. **Say yes or nod your head.**

   Discuss with students that both verbal and nonverbal messages are important to show that a person is listening.

5. **Ask a question about the topic to find out more.**

   Discuss relevant questions (i.e., ones that do not change the topic).

SUGGESTED MODELING SITUATIONS

- ▶ *School:* Your teacher explains an assignment.
- ▶ *Home:* Your parents are talking with you about how to do a chore.
- ▶ *Peer group:* Another student tells about a story he/she read or what he/she did over the weekend.
- ▶ *Community:* A store manager is telling you the rules about kids being in the store.

COMMENTS

This is an excellent skill with which to begin your Skillstreaming group. Once students learn the skill of Listening, it can be incorporated into group or classroom rules. You can emphasize the behaviors that show someone is listening by modeling listening behaviors yourself.

From *Skillstreaming the Elementary School Child: Teaching Prosocial Skills* (3rd ed.), © 2012 by E. McGinnis, Champaign, IL: Research Press (www.researchpress.com, 800-519-2707).

Skill 1: Listening

Name _____ Date _____

SKILL STEPS

1. Look at the person who is talking.

2. Sit quietly.

3. Think about what is being said.

4. Say yes or nod your head.

5. Ask a question about the topic to find out more.

FILL IN NOW

With whom will I try this? _____

When? _____

FILL IN AFTER YOU PRACTICE THE SKILL

What happened? _____

_____

_____

How did I do?   ☺   😐   ☹

Why did I circle this? _____

_____

Skillstreaming

From *Skillstreaming the Elementary School Child: Teaching Prosocial Skills* (3rd ed.), © 2012 by E. McGinnis, Champaign, IL: Research Press (www.researchpress.com, 800-519-2707).

Skill 1: Listening

Name _____ Date _____

SKILL STEPS

1. Look at the person who is talking.

2. Sit quietly.

3. Think about what is being said.

4. Say yes or nod your head.

5. Ask a question about the topic to find out more.

When did I practice?   How did I do?

_____

_____

_____

_____

Skillstreaming From *Skillstreaming the Elementary School Child: Teaching Prosocial Skills* (3rd ed.), © 2012 by E. McGinnis, Champaign, IL: Research Press (www.researchpress.com, 800-519-2707).

Skill 2: Asking for Help

SKILL STEPS

1. **Ask yourself, "Can I do this alone?"**

   Students should be sure to read directions and try the task on their own (at least one problem or question) before going on to the next skill step.

2. **If not, raise your hand.**

   Discuss that this is appropriate in class, not at home or with friends.

3. **Wait. Say to yourself, "I know I can wait without talking."**

   Instruct the students to say this to themselves until the desired help is given.

4. **Ask for help in a friendly way.**

   Discuss what constitutes a friendly manner (tone of voice, facial expression, content).

SUGGESTED MODELING SITUATIONS

- ► *School:* You want help with an assignment, or you don't understand what you are supposed to do.

- ► *Home:* You can't find your favorite video game and ask your brother to help look for it.

- ► *Peer group:* You want your friend to teach you a new dance that everyone is doing.

- ► *Community:* You need some help finding something in the store.

COMMENTS

It is very important to discuss body language throughout Skillstreaming. When first introducing terminology such as "in a friendly way," discussing and modeling friendly behaviors and nonverbal communicators are essential. Nonverbal behaviors include voice tone and volume, body posture, gestures, and facial expression.

Skillstreaming From *Skillstreaming the Elementary School Child: Teaching Prosocial Skills* (3rd ed.), © 2012 by E. McGinnis, Champaign, IL: Research Press (www.researchpress.com, 800-519-2707).

Skill 2: Asking for Help

Name _____ Date _____

SKILL STEPS

1. Ask yourself, "Can I do this alone?"

2. If not, raise your hand.

3. Wait. Say to yourself, "I know I can wait without talking."

4. Ask for help in a friendly way.

FILL IN NOW

With whom will I try this? _____

When? _____

FILL IN AFTER YOU PRACTICE THE SKILL

What happened? _____

_____

_____

How did I do?   ☺ 😐 ☹

Why did I circle this? _____

_____

Skill 2: Asking for Help

Name _____ Date _____

SKILL STEPS

1. Ask yourself, "Can I do this alone?"

2. If not, raise your hand.

3. Wait. Say to yourself, "I know I can wait without talking."

4. Ask for help in a friendly way.

When did I practice?   How did I do?

<table>
<tr><td></td><td>☺</td><td>😐</td><td>☹</td></tr>
<tr><td></td><td>☺</td><td>😐</td><td>☹</td></tr>
<tr><td></td><td>☺</td><td>😐</td><td>☹</td></tr>
<tr><td></td><td>☺</td><td>😐</td><td>☹</td></tr>
</table>

Skillstreaming

From *Skillstreaming the Elementary School Child: Teaching Prosocial Skills* (3rd ed.), © 2012 by E. McGinnis, Champaign, IL: Research Press (www.researchpress.com, 800-519-2707).

Skill 3: Saying Thank You

SKILL STEPS

1. **Decide if you want to thank someone.**

   Discuss the purpose of saying thank you (i.e., it is a way of telling someone that you appreciate what he/she did). Emphasize sincerity. You thank someone when you want to or feel it is deserved—for example, for a favor, help given, or a compliment.

2. **Choose a good time and place.**

   Discuss how to choose a good time (when the person is not busy with something or someone else).

3. **Thank the person in a friendly way.**

   Let students know that it is OK to tell why you are thanking the person (that they really needed the help or that something the person did made them feel good).

SUGGESTED MODELING SITUATIONS

► *School:* Someone helps you with your schoolwork or a computer activity.

► *Home:* Your parents help you with your chores or homework, or they let you do something you have asked to do.

► *Peer group:* Someone lends you a music DVD or compliments you.

► *Community:* A person in the store helps by giving you directions.

COMMENTS

Students may begin to use this skill frequently, and somewhat mechanically, following initial instruction. This is natural and should not be interpreted as insincere use of the skill. It may be useful to discuss and practice different ways of saying thank you (e.g., "It made me feel good when you . . ." or doing something nice for the person).

Skill 3: Saying Thank You

Name _____ Date _____

SKILL STEPS

1. Decide if you want to thank someone.

2. Choose a good time and place.

3. Thank the person in a friendly way.

FILL IN NOW

With whom will I try this? _____

When? _____

FILL IN AFTER YOU PRACTICE THE SKILL

What happened? _____

_____

_____

How did I do?   ☺   😐   ☹

Why did I circle this? _____

_____

Skillstreaming

From *Skillstreaming the Elementary School Child: Teaching Prosocial Skills* (3rd ed.), © 2012 by E. McGinnis, Champaign, IL: Research Press (www.researchpress.com, 800-519-2707).

Skill 3: Saying Thank You

Name _____ Date _____

SKILL STEPS

1. Decide if you want to thank someone.

2. Choose a good time and place.

3. Thank the person in a friendly way.

When did I practice?   How did I do?

_____

_____

_____

_____

From *Skillstreaming the Elementary School Child: Teaching Prosocial Skills* (3rd ed.), © 2012
by E. McGinnis, Champaign, IL: Research Press (www.researchpress.com, 800-519-2707).

Skill 4: Bringing Materials to Class

SKILL STEPS

1. **Ask yourself, "What materials do I need for this class?"**

   Students may have to make a list of needed items, such as pencil, crayons, paper, or notebook.

2. **Gather the materials together.**

   Students should remember not to take things that aren't needed—for example, toys.

3. **Ask yourself, "Do I have everything I need?"**

4. **Recheck your materials and pack them up.**

SUGGESTED MODELING SITUATIONS

▶ *School:* You are going to a special area class (art, music, physical education) or attending a class in another classroom.

▶ *Home:* You are going to attend an outside club event or activity, or you are getting your backpack ready for school in the morning.

▶ *Peer group:* You will be staying overnight at a friend's house.

▶ *Community:* You are going on a school field trip to a museum.

COMMENTS

This skill helps students become more organized. For some students, at first you may need to provide a written list of what is needed. Also, providing a notebook or folder where the materials can be kept may help students perform this skill.

Placing a poster of the skill steps near the classroom door may help students remember to check for the materials they will need before they leave the classroom.

Skillstreaming

From *Skillstreaming the Elementary School Child: Teaching Prosocial Skills* (3rd ed.), © 2012 by E. McGinnis, Champaign, IL: Research Press (www.researchpress.com, 800-519-2707).

Skill 4: Bringing Materials to Class

Name _____ Date _____

SKILL STEPS

1. Ask yourself, "What materials do I need for this class?"

2. Gather the materials together.

3. Ask yourself, "Do I have everything I need?"

4. Recheck your materials and pack them up.

FILL IN NOW

With whom will I try this? _____

When? _____

FILL IN AFTER YOU PRACTICE THE SKILL

What happened? _____

_____

_____

How did I do?   ☺ 😐 ☹

Why did I circle this? _____

_____

 From *Skillstreaming the Elementary School Child: Teaching Prosocial Skills* (3rd ed.), © 2012 by E. McGinnis, Champaign, IL: Research Press (www.researchpress.com, 800-519-2707).

Skill 4: Bringing Materials to Class

Name_____ Date_____

SKILL STEPS

1. Ask yourself, "What materials do I need for this class?"

2. Gather the materials together.

3. Ask yourself, "Do I have everything I need?"

4. Recheck your materials and pack them up.

When did I practice?   How did I do?

Skillstreaming

From *Skillstreaming the Elementary School Child: Teaching Prosocial Skills* (3rd ed.), © 2012 by E. McGinnis, Champaign, IL: Research Press (www.researchpress.com, 800-519-2707).

Skill 5: Following Instructions

SKILL STEPS

1. **Listen carefully to the instructions.**

   Remind students that they should think about what is being said.

2. **Ask questions about anything you don't understand.**

   Teach students Asking for Help (Skill 2) or Asking a Question (Skill 9).

3. **Repeat the instructions to the person (or to yourself).**

   This step is necessary to be sure students clearly understand the directions.

4. **Follow the instructions.**

SUGGESTED MODELING SITUATIONS

- ► *School:* A teacher explains an assignment.
- ► *Home:* Your mom or dad gives you instructions on how to cook or how to do a chore.
- ► *Peer group:* A friend gives you directions for getting to his/her house.
- ► *Community:* A security guard at the mall explains rules for behavior.

COMMENTS

For students to perform this skill successfully, they must be able to complete the task required of them independently. The skill will only frustrate them if they follow the steps and then find that the task is too difficult.

Skill 5: Following Instructions

Name _____ Date _____

SKILL STEPS

1. Listen carefully to the instructions.

2. Ask questions about anything you don't understand.

3. Repeat the instructions to the person (or to yourself).

4. Follow the instructions.

FILL IN NOW

With whom will I try this? _____

When? _____

FILL IN AFTER YOU PRACTICE THE SKILL

What happened? _____

_____

_____

How did I do?   ☺   😐   ☹

Why did I circle this? _____

_____

Skillstreaming From *Skillstreaming the Elementary School Child: Teaching Prosocial Skills* (3rd ed.), © 2012 by E. McGinnis, Champaign, IL: Research Press (www.researchpress.com, 800-519-2707).

Skill 5: Following Instructions

Name _____ Date _____

SKILL STEPS

1. Listen carefully to the instructions.

2. Ask questions about anything you don't understand.

3. Repeat the instructions to the person (or to yourself).

4. Follow the instructions.

When did I practice?   How did I do?

Skill 6: Completing Assignments

SKILL STEPS

1. **Ask yourself, "Is my work finished?"**

   Have students practice reviewing each item to be certain that all questions are answered.

2. **Look over each question to be sure.**

   Remind students to fill in the missing answers if items aren't complete.

3. **When you are sure your work is finished, hand it in.**

   Specific classroom rules for handing in completed work can be included in this step.

4. **Say to yourself, "Good for me! I finished it!"**

   Discuss ways of rewarding yourself.

SUGGESTED MODELING SITUATIONS

▶ *School:* Complete academic assignments given by the teacher.

▶ *Home:* Finish a project or activity you started at home (making a model car from a kit or cleaning your room).

▶ *Peer group:* Complete a project or a chore you promised to do for a friend.

▶ *Community:* Complete an activity at a learning or community center.

COMMENTS

This skill facilitates organizational ability and is particularly useful for the student with a learning disability or others who have specific difficulties in task completion. Ideally, this skill should be practiced in the setting where the skill is needed. For example, if practice in seatwork completion is needed, the student should practice this skill at his or her desk.

Again, it is important for students to be able to complete the task independently. Rewarding Yourself (Skill 35) is a part of this skill (Step 4). Self-reinforcement may be necessary until the skill can be reinforced by teachers or parents.

From *Skillstreaming the Elementary School Child: Teaching Prosocial Skills* (3rd ed.), © 2012 by E. McGinnis, Champaign, IL: Research Press (www.researchpress.com, 800-519-2707).

Skill 6: Completing Assignments

Name _____ Date _____

SKILL STEPS

1. Ask yourself, "Is my work finished?"

2. Look over each question to be sure.

3. When you are sure your work is finished, hand it in.

4. Say to yourself, "Good for me! I finished it!"

FILL IN NOW

With whom will I try this? _____

When? _____

FILL IN AFTER YOU PRACTICE THE SKILL

What happened? _____

_____

_____

How did I do?   ☺   😐   ☹

Why did I circle this? _____

_____

From *Skillstreaming the Elementary School Child: Teaching Prosocial Skills* (3rd ed.), © 2012 by E. McGinnis, Champaign, IL: Research Press (www.researchpress.com, 800-519-2707).

Skill 6: Completing Assignments

Name _____ Date _____

SKILL STEPS

1. Ask yourself, "Is my work finished?"

2. Look over each question to be sure.

3. When you are sure your work is finished, hand it in.

4. Say to yourself, "Good for me! I finished it!"

When did I practice?   How did I do?

Skillstreaming   From *Skillstreaming the Elementary School Child: Teaching Prosocial Skills* (3rd ed.), © 2012 by E. McGinnis, Champaign, IL: Research Press (www.researchpress.com, 800-519-2707).

Skill 7: Contributing to Discussions

SKILL STEPS

1. **Decide if you have something you want to say.**

   Discuss that the comments must be relevant to the discussion. Give examples of relevant comments.

2. **Ask yourself, "Is this related to the discussion?"**

   Students may need the additional step of deciding how to say it.

3. **Decide exactly what you want to say.**

4. **Raise your hand.**

5. **When you are called on, say what you want to say.**

   Steps 4 and 5 should be in accordance with your classroom rules. Explain that students should eliminate these steps at home or with friends.

SUGGESTED MODELING SITUATIONS

- ► *School:* Say something in a class discussion when you have something you want to say.
- ► *Home:* Say something in a family meeting or during dinner.
- ► *Peer group:* Say something in a discussion with friends after school.
- ► *Community:* Say something in an activity at church or community event.

COMMENTS

Discussion should include times this skill is appropriate to use. Students must learn which teacher cues indicate when contributions are and are not welcome. Students will also need to discriminate among the persons with whom the skill is used. For example, contributing to a discussion among friends would be very different from contributing to a discussion in class.

When providing the opportunities for students to practice this skill, choose familiar and interesting topics for discussion.

Skill 7: Contributing to Discussions

Name _____ Date _____

SKILL STEPS

1. Decide if you have something you want to say.

2. Ask yourself, "Is this related to the discussion?"

3. Decide exactly what you want to say.

4. Raise your hand.

5. When you are called on, say what you want to say.

FILL IN NOW

With whom will I try this? _____

When? _____

FILL IN AFTER YOU PRACTICE THE SKILL

What happened? _____

_____

_____

How did I do?   ☺   😐   ☹

Why did I circle this? _____

_____

Skillstreaming   From *Skillstreaming the Elementary School Child: Teaching Prosocial Skills* (3rd ed.), © 2012 by E. McGinnis, Champaign, IL: Research Press (www.researchpress.com, 800-519-2707).

Skill 7: Contributing to Discussions

Name _____ Date _____

SKILL STEPS

1. Decide if you have something you want to say.

2. Ask yourself, "Is this related to the discussion?"

3. Decide exactly what you want to say.

4. Raise your hand.

5. When you are called on, say what you want to say.

When did I practice?   How did I do?

  From *Skillstreaming the Elementary School Child: Teaching Prosocial Skills* (3rd ed.), © 2012 by E. McGinnis, Champaign, IL: Research Press (www.researchpress.com, 800-519-2707).

Skill 8: Offering Help to an Adult

SKILL STEPS

1. **Decide if the adult needs your help.**

   Discuss how the adult might act if he or she needed help. Discuss different ways of asking—for example, "May I help you do that?"

2. **Decide how to ask if you can help.**

3. **Ask yourself, "Is this a good time to offer help?"**

   Remind students to be sure that their work is completed and there isn't something else they are supposed to do. If this is not a good time, they should wait until it is a good time.

4. **Ask the adult if you may help.**

   Discuss the importance of following through with help.

SUGGESTED MODELING SITUATIONS

- ▶ *School:* The teacher is making a bulletin board or rearranging the classroom.
- ▶ *Home:* Your mom or dad is fixing dinner.
- ▶ *Community:* Your neighbor is raking leaves or shoveling snow.

COMMENTS

With some students, it is especially important to emphasize Step 1, deciding if the teacher or parent needs the help. A student who frequently requests to help may be attempting to gain attention or avoid academic tasks. In such cases this skill can be useful to teach the student when offering assistance is appropriate.

Skillstreaming From *Skillstreaming the Elementary School Child: Teaching Prosocial Skills* (3rd ed.), © 2012 by E. McGinnis, Champaign, IL: Research Press (www.researchpress.com, 800-519-2707).

Skill 8: Offering Help to an Adult

Name _____ Date _____

SKILL STEPS

1. Decide if the adult needs your help.

2. Decide how to ask if you can help.

3. Ask yourself, "Is this a good time to offer help?"

4. Ask the adult if you may help.

FILL IN NOW

With whom will I try this? _____

When? _____

FILL IN AFTER YOU PRACTICE THE SKILL

What happened? _____

_____

_____

How did I do?   ☺   😐   ☹

Why did I circle this? _____

_____

 From *Skillstreaming the Elementary School Child: Teaching Prosocial Skills* (3rd ed.), © 2012 by E. McGinnis, Champaign, IL: Research Press (www.researchpress.com, 800-519-2707).

139

Skill 8: Offering Help to an Adult

Name _____ Date _____

SKILL STEPS

1. Decide if the adult needs your help.

2. Decide how to ask if you can help.

3. Ask yourself, "Is this a good time to offer help?"

4. Ask the adult if you may help.

When did I practice?   How did I do?

Skillstreaming

From *Skillstreaming the Elementary School Child: Teaching Prosocial Skills* (3rd ed.), © 2012 by E. McGinnis, Champaign, IL: Research Press (www.researchpress.com, 800-519-2707).

Skill 9: Asking a Question

SKILL STEPS

1. **Decide what you need to ask.**

   Discuss how students can decide whether they really need to ask this question.

2. **Decide whom you will ask.**

   Discuss how to decide whether to ask the teacher, an aide, a classmate, or someone else.

3. **Decide what to say.**

   Stress asking in a friendly way—it is not only what you say but how you say it.

4. **Choose a good time.**

   Discuss how to choose a good time (when the other person isn't busy or talking with someone else).

5. **Ask your question.**

   Teach students Saying Thank You (Skill 3) and encourage them to use it when they receive the answer to their question.

SUGGESTED MODELING SITUATIONS

- ▶ *School:* Ask the teacher about something you don't understand.
- ▶ *Home:* Ask your mom and dad about their work or hobbies.
- ▶ *Peer group:* Ask another student how to play a game.
- ▶ *Community:* You ask the librarian about a book or a movie you want to check out.

COMMENTS

Discuss the times when it is necessary to ask a question. Encourage students to use this skill only when they have a legitimate question. Discussion should include other ways of finding needed information—for example, consulting a dictionary, encyclopedia, or the Internet.

Skill 9: Asking a Question

Name _____ Date _____

SKILL STEPS

1. Decide what you need to ask.

2. Decide whom you will ask.

3. Decide what to say.

4. Choose a good time.

5. Ask your question.

FILL IN NOW

With whom will I try this? _____

When? _____

FILL IN AFTER YOU PRACTICE THE SKILL

What happened? _____

_____

_____

How did I do?   ☺   😐   ☹

Why did I circle this? _____

_____

From *Skillstreaming the Elementary School Child: Teaching Prosocial Skills* (3rd ed.), © 2012 by E. McGinnis, Champaign, IL: Research Press (www.researchpress.com, 800-519-2707).

Skill 9: Asking a Question

Name _____ Date _____

SKILL STEPS

1. Decide what you need to ask.

2. Decide whom you will ask.

3. Decide what to say.

4. Choose a good time.

5. Ask your question.

When did I practice?   How did I do?

_____	☺	😐	☹
_____	☺	😐	☹
_____	☺	😐	☹
_____	☺	😐	☹

Skillstreaming From *Skillstreaming the Elementary School Child: Teaching Prosocial Skills* (3rd ed.), © 2012 by E. McGinnis, Champaign, IL: Research Press (www.researchpress.com, 800-519-2707).

Skill 10: Ignoring Distractions

SKILL STEPS

1. **Count to five.**

   Discuss that counting to five will give the student the time to calm down if frustrated and to recall the rest of the skill steps.

2. **Say to yourself, "I won't look. I'll keep on working."**

   Statements should be spoken aloud during modeling and role-playing.

3. **Continue to work.**

4. **Say to yourself, "Good for me. I did it!"**

   Discuss ways of rewarding yourself.

SUGGESTED MODELING SITUATIONS

- ► *School:* Another teacher comes into the room to talk with your teacher.
- ► *Home:* Your brother or sister tries to distract you from your chores or homework.
- ► *Peer group:* A classmate tries to get your attention in class or to distract you from a game at recess.
- ► *Community:* Kids are making noise in the movie, in the library, or in another community place.

COMMENTS

Each time students ignore a distraction, they may make a check mark on an index card or color a space on one of the self-recording forms (Appendix A). Self-recording efforts can then be reinforced if needed.

Rewarding Yourself (Skill 35) is a part of this skill (Step 4). Self-reinforcement may be necessary until the skill can be reinforced by teachers or parents.

Skillstreaming From *Skillstreaming the Elementary School Child: Teaching Prosocial Skills* (3rd ed.), © 2012 by E. McGinnis, Champaign, IL: Research Press (www.researchpress.com, 800-519-2707).

Skill 10: Ignoring Distractions

Name_____ Date_____

SKILL STEPS

1. Count to five.

2. Say to yourself, "I won't look. I'll keep on working."

3. Continue to work.

4. Say to yourself, "Good for me. I did it!"

FILL IN NOW

With whom will I try this? _____

When?_____

FILL IN AFTER YOU PRACTICE THE SKILL

What happened?_____

_____

_____

How did I do?   ☺   😐   ☹

Why did I circle this?_____

_____

From *Skillstreaming the Elementary School Child: Teaching Prosocial Skills* (3rd ed.), © 2012 by E. McGinnis, Champaign, IL: Research Press (www.researchpress.com, 800-519-2707).

Skill 10: Ignoring Distractions

Name _____ Date _____

SKILL STEPS

1. Count to five.

2. Say to yourself, "I won't look. I'll keep on working."

3. Continue to work.

4. Say to yourself, "Good for me. I did it!"

When did I practice?	How did I do?		
	☺	😐	☹
	☺	😐	☹
	☺	😐	☹
	☺	😐	☹

Skillstreaming

From *Skillstreaming the Elementary School Child: Teaching Prosocial Skills* (3rd ed.), © 2012 by E. McGinnis, Champaign, IL: Research Press (www.researchpress.com, 800-519-2707).

Skill 11: Making Corrections

SKILL STEPS

1. **Look at the first correction.**

   Discuss dealing with one correction at a time rather than looking at them all. This will help lessen frustration and make the task seem less overwhelming.

2. **Try to answer the question (or do the task) again.**

3. **If you don't understand the question, ask someone.**

   Teach students Asking for Help (Skill 2).

4. **Write in your new answer.**

5. **Say to yourself, "Good. That one is done."**

6. **Go on to the next correction.**

SUGGESTED MODELING SITUATIONS

- *School:* Your teacher gives your math assignment back for you to correct.
- *Home:* You must do a chore over again.
- *Peer group:* You made something for a friend, but it didn't turn out right.
- *Community:* You made a project for a community event, but it doesn't look like you wanted.

COMMENTS

Redoing tasks or academic assignments can be extremely frustrating for children. Discuss the normal feeling of frustration when tasks must be done again.

If many errors are made on any assignment, it is important to analyze these errors and reteach the necessary skills. This skill is most useful following such a reteaching effort or for assignments that are completed carelessly, not for assignments beyond the student's abilities.

From *Skillstreaming the Elementary School Child: Teaching Prosocial Skills* (3rd ed.), © 2012 by E. McGinnis, Champaign, IL: Research Press (www.researchpress.com, 800-519-2707).

Skill 11: Making Corrections

Name _____ Date _____

SKILL STEPS

1. Look at the first correction.

2. Try to answer the question (or do the task) again.

3. If you don't understand the question, ask someone.

4. Write in your new answer.

5. Say to yourself, "Good. That one is done."

6. Go on to the next correction.

FILL IN NOW

With whom will I try this? _____

When?_____

FILL IN AFTER YOU PRACTICE THE SKILL

What happened?_____

_____

_____

How did I do?   ☺   😐   ☹

Why did I circle this?_____

_____

Skillstreaming From *Skillstreaming the Elementary School Child: Teaching Prosocial Skills* (3rd ed.), © 2012 by E. McGinnis, Champaign, IL: Research Press (www.researchpress.com, 800-519-2707).

Skill 11: Making Corrections

Name _____ Date _____

SKILL STEPS

1. Look at the first correction.

2. Try to answer the question (or do the task) again.

3. If you don't understand the question, ask someone.

4. Write in your new answer.

5. Say to yourself, "Good. That one is done."

6. Go on to the next correction.

When did I practice?	How did I do?		
	☺	😐	☹
	☺	😐	☹
	☺	😐	☹
	☺	😐	☹

Skillstreaming From *Skillstreaming the Elementary School Child: Teaching Prosocial Skills* (3rd ed.), © 2012 by E. McGinnis, Champaign, IL: Research Press (www.researchpress.com, 800-519-2707).

Skill 12: Deciding on Something to Do

SKILL STEPS

1. **Check to be sure you have finished all of your work.**

   An assignment sheet to check off work as it is completed will help many students with this first step.

2. **Think of the activities you would like to do.**

   Guide students to generate a list of acceptable activities.

3. **Choose one.**

4. **Start the activity.**

   Students should be sure the activity chosen will not disrupt classmates who have not yet completed their schoolwork (or brothers or sisters if the students are at home).

SUGGESTED MODELING SITUATIONS

▶ *School:* Decide on an activity during free time in the classroom or when you have a few minutes after finishing your work.

▶ *Home:* Choose something to do after you have finished your homework and chores.

▶ *Community:* You are attending a community event with your parents (select an event the students typically attend).

COMMENTS

Encourage students to list both quiet activities (those in which they could engage when other students are still working on their academic assignments) and less quiet activities (those in which they can participate during a free activity period for the entire class). This list, along with the behavioral steps for this skill, can then be displayed in the classroom for easy student reference. Dealing with Boredom (Skill 45) is a similar skill geared for use outside of the academic setting.

Skillstreaming

From *Skillstreaming the Elementary School Child: Teaching Prosocial Skills* (3rd ed.), © 2012 by E. McGinnis, Champaign, IL: Research Press (www.researchpress.com, 800-519-2707).

Skill 12: Deciding on Something to Do

Name _____ Date _____

SKILL STEPS

1. Check to be sure you have finished all of your work.

2. Think of the activities you would like to do.

3. Choose one.

4. Start the activity.

FILL IN NOW

With whom will I try this? _____

When? _____

FILL IN AFTER YOU PRACTICE THE SKILL

What happened? _____

_____

_____

How did I do?   ☺   😐   ☹

Why did I circle this? _____

_____

Skill 12: Deciding on Something to Do

Name _____ Date _____

SKILL STEPS

1. Check to be sure you have finished all of your work.

2. Think of the activities you would like to do.

3. Choose one.

4. Start the activity.

When did I practice?   How did I do?

Skillstreaming From *Skillstreaming the Elementary School Child: Teaching Prosocial Skills* (3rd ed.), © 2012 by E. McGinnis, Champaign, IL: Research Press (www.researchpress.com, 800-519-2707).

Skill 13: Setting a Goal

SKILL STEPS

1. **Decide on a goal you want to reach.**

   Discuss choosing a realistic goal (considering content, time frame).

2. **Decide on the steps you will need to take to get there.**

   It may be helpful to list these steps on a bulletin board, include them in a student folder, or write them on a card taped to students' desks.

3. **Take the first step.**

4. **Take all other steps, one at a time.**

   Encourage students to mark off each step as it is achieved. (This also gives students practice in organization.)

5. **Reward yourself when your goal is reached.**

   Discuss ways of rewarding yourself.

SUGGESTED MODELING SITUATIONS

- ► *School:* Set and reach an academic, behavioral, or social skills goal.
- ► *Home:* Clean your room or the garage.
- ► *Peer group:* Make a new friend.
- ► *Community:* You decide you want to help someone in the community.

COMMENTS

Many elementary-age students enjoy setting academic goals (e.g., learning addition facts, reading a given number of books). Setting small goals that can be easily achieved in a relatively short period of time (e.g., reading one book) is more beneficial than setting less attainable goals. Goal setting is also useful for nonacademic areas, such as prosocial skills development. Examples include practicing a given skill a certain number of times or using it at home or with peers.

Rewarding Yourself (Skill 35) is a part of this skill (Step 5). Self-reinforcement may be necessary until the skill can be reinforced by teachers or parents.

Skill 13: Setting a Goal

Name _____ Date _____

SKILL STEPS

1. Decide on a goal you want to reach.

2. Decide on the steps you will need to take to get there.

3. Take the first step.

4. Take all other steps, one at a time.

5. Reward yourself when your goal is reached.

FILL IN NOW

With whom will I try this? _____

When? _____

FILL IN AFTER YOU PRACTICE THE SKILL

What happened? _____

_____

_____

How did I do? ☺ 😐 ☹

Why did I circle this? _____

_____

Skillstreaming

From *Skillstreaming the Elementary School Child: Teaching Prosocial Skills* (3rd ed.), © 2012 by E. McGinnis, Champaign, IL: Research Press (www.researchpress.com, 800-519-2707).

Skill 13: Setting a Goal

Name _____ Date _____

SKILL STEPS

1. Decide on a goal you want to reach.

2. Decide on the steps you will need to take to get there.

3. Take the first step.

4. Take all other steps, one at a time.

5. Reward yourself when your goal is reached.

When did I practice?   How did I do?

Group II

Friendship-Making Skills

Skills 14–25

Skill 14: Introducing Yourself

SKILL STEPS

1. **Decide if you want to meet the person.**

   Discuss why students might want to meet a person: The person looks friendly, is new to the school, and so forth.

2. **Decide if it is a good time.**

   Discuss how to choose a good time: The person is not busy with something or someone else.

3. **Walk up to the person.**

   Watch for appropriate distance.

4. **Introduce yourself.**

   Discuss ways to introduce yourself (say, "Hi, my name is _____").

5. **Wait for the person to tell you his/her name. (If he/she doesn't tell you, ask.)**

   Discuss appropriate ways to ask a person's name.

SUGGESTED MODELING SITUATIONS

- ▶ *School:* There is a new student in your classroom.
- ▶ *Home:* A friend of your parents is visiting your home.
- ▶ *Peer group:* A new boy or girl moves into your neighborhood.
- ▶ *Community:* You're with your parent and they stop to talk with someone you don't know.

COMMENTS

Practicing this skill also helps students know what to do when someone else introduces himself or herself. A logical next skill to teach is Beginning a Conversation (Skill 15). Students may then practice putting the two skills together in one role-play.

Skill 14: Introducing Yourself

Name _____ Date _____

SKILL STEPS

1. Decide if you want to meet the person.

2. Decide if it is a good time.

3. Walk up to the person.

4. Introduce yourself.

5. Wait for the person to tell you his/her name. (If he/she doesn't tell you, ask.)

FILL IN NOW

With whom will I try this? _____

When? _____

FILL IN AFTER YOU PRACTICE THE SKILL

What happened? _____

_____

_____

How did I do?   ☺   😐   ☹

Why did I circle this? _____

_____

Skillstreaming

From *Skillstreaming the Elementary School Child: Teaching Prosocial Skills* (3rd ed.), © 2012 by E. McGinnis, Champaign, IL: Research Press (www.researchpress.com, 800-519-2707).

Skill 14: Introducing Yourself

Name _____ Date _____

SKILL STEPS

1. Decide if you want to meet the person.

2. Decide if it is a good time.

3. Walk up to the person.

4. Introduce yourself.

5. Wait for the person to tell you his/her name. (If he/she doesn't tell you, ask.)

When did I practice?   How did I do?

_____

_____

_____

_____

Skill 15: Beginning a Conversation

SKILL STEPS

1. **Choose the person with whom you want to talk.**

   Remind students to consider whether their talking is going to bother someone else—for example, someone who is trying to work.

2. **Decide what you want to say.**

   Suggest topics like something students did during the weekend, a hobby, or a favorite sport.

3. **Choose a good time and place.**

   Discuss how to choose a good time: when the other person isn't busy or when the student isn't supposed to be doing something else.

4. **Start talking in a friendly way.**

   Discuss the body language and nonverbal communicators that show a friendly attitude and suggest watching the person to see if he or she seems interested. Stress not talking too long without giving the other person a chance to talk.

SUGGESTED MODELING SITUATIONS

► *School:* Tell a classmate about an art project you did.

► *Home:* Tell your parents what happened at school.

► *Peer group:* Tell a friend what you did during the weekend.

► *Community:* You see a classmate at the library or the arcade.

COMMENTS

Students should role-play this skill with both adults and peers to determine language and nonverbal signals appropriate for persons in different roles—for example, teachers, parents, friends. This skill can be taught directly following Skill 14 (Introducing Yourself). Skill 16 (Ending a Conversation) may follow this skill as needed.

From *Skillstreaming the Elementary School Child: Teaching Prosocial Skills* (3rd ed.), © 2012 by E. McGinnis, Champaign, IL: Research Press (www.researchpress.com, 800-519-2707).

Skill 15: Beginning a Conversation

Name _____ Date _____

SKILL STEPS

1. Choose the person with whom you want to talk.

2. Decide what you want to say.

3. Choose a good time and place.

4. Start talking in a friendly way.

FILL IN NOW

With whom will I try this? _____

When? _____

FILL IN AFTER YOU PRACTICE THE SKILL

What happened? _____

_____

_____

How did I do?   ☺   😐   ☹

Why did I circle this? _____

_____

From *Skillstreaming the Elementary School Child: Teaching Prosocial Skills* (3rd ed.), © 2012 by E. McGinnis, Champaign, IL: Research Press (www.researchpress.com, 800-519-2707).

Skill 15: Beginning a Conversation

Name _____ Date _____

SKILL STEPS

1. Choose the person with whom you want to talk.

2. Decide what you want to say.

3. Choose a good time and place.

4. Start talking in a friendly way.

When did I practice?	How did I do?		
	☺	😐	☹
	☺	😐	☹
	☺	😐	☹
	☺	😐	☹

Skillstreaming

From *Skillstreaming the Elementary School Child: Teaching Prosocial Skills* (3rd ed.), © 2012 by E. McGinnis, Champaign, IL: Research Press (www.researchpress.com, 800-519-2707).

Skill 16: Ending a Conversation

SKILL STEPS

1. **Decide if you need to end the conversation.**

   Students should decide why they need to end the conversation.

2. **Decide what to say.**

   Tell students to ask themselves, What is the reason? Give examples: "I have to go now, but I'll talk with you later"; "I have to do my work."

3. **Wait until the other person stops talking.**

   Discuss the importance of not interrupting and of thinking whether or not this is a good time to end the conversation.

4. **Say it in a friendly way.**

   Remind students of the body language and nonverbal communicators that show a friendly attitude.

SUGGESTED MODELING SITUATIONS

- ► *School:* Recess or free time in the classroom is over.
- ► *Home:* You are talking with your parents, and a friend is waiting for you.
- ► *Peer group:* Your mother tells you to come inside or to stop talking on the telephone.
- ► *Community:* You are talking with a friend at the library, but it's time for you to leave.

COMMENTS

Learning how to end a conversation may help students stay out of trouble—for example, be on time to class, be home on time, not disrupt the class. Discussing such situations helps students understand the purpose of this skill. After practicing Skills 14, 15, and 16 separately, give students practice in using these skills successively.

Skill 16: Ending a Conversation

Name _____ Date _____

SKILL STEPS

1. Decide if you need to end the conversation.

2. Decide what to say.

3. Wait until the other person stops talking.

4. Say it in a friendly way.

FILL IN NOW

With whom will I try this? _____

When? _____

FILL IN AFTER YOU PRACTICE THE SKILL

What happened? _____

_____

_____

How did I do?   ☺   😐   ☹

Why did I circle this? _____

_____

Skillstreaming

From *Skillstreaming the Elementary School Child: Teaching Prosocial Skills* (3rd ed.), © 2012 by E. McGinnis, Champaign, IL: Research Press (www.researchpress.com, 800-519-2707).

Skill 16: Ending a Conversation

Name _____ Date _____

SKILL STEPS

1. Decide if you need to end the conversation.

2. Decide what to say.

3. Wait until the other person stops talking.

4. Say it in a friendly way.

When did I practice?   How did I do?

☺	😐	☹
☺	😐	☹
☺	😐	☹
☺	😐	☹

From *Skillstreaming the Elementary School Child: Teaching Prosocial Skills* (3rd ed.), © 2012 by E. McGinnis, Champaign, IL: Research Press (www.researchpress.com, 800-519-2707).

Skill 17: Joining In

SKILL STEPS

1. **Decide if you want to join in.**

   Students should decide whether they really want to participate.

2. **Decide what to say.**

   Suggest possible things to say: "Can one more person play?"; "Can I play, too?"

3. **Choose a good time.**

   Discuss how to choose a good time: during a break in the activity or before the activity has begun.

4. **Say it in a friendly way.**

   Discuss the body language and nonverbal communicators that show a friendly attitude.

SUGGESTED MODELING SITUATIONS

- ► *School:* Ask to join in a group game at recess.
- ► *Home:* Ask to join a game with parents or brothers and sisters.
- ► *Peer group:* Ask to join an activity in the neighborhood.
- ► *Community:* Ask to join in a community project.

COMMENTS

This skill is very useful for students who have difficulty deciding what to do in social play situations. The skill gives them the opportunity to join peers in an ongoing activity. Encourage students to try out this skill first with peers or adults they feel will accept their overtures.

Skillstreaming From *Skillstreaming the Elementary School Child: Teaching Prosocial Skills* (3rd ed.), © 2012 by E. McGinnis, Champaign, IL: Research Press (www.researchpress.com, 800-519-2707).

Skill 17: Joining In

Name _____ Date _____

SKILL STEPS

1. Decide if you want to join in.

2. Decide what to say.

3. Choose a good time.

4. Say it in a friendly way.

FILL IN NOW

With whom will I try this? _____

When? _____

FILL IN AFTER YOU PRACTICE THE SKILL

What happened? _____

_____

_____

How did I do?   ☺   😐   ☹

Why did I circle this? _____

_____

Skill 17: Joining In

Name _____ Date _____

SKILL STEPS

1. Decide if you want to join in.

2. Decide what to say.

3. Choose a good time.

4. Say it in a friendly way.

When did I practice?   How did I do?

When did I practice?	☺	😐	☹
_____	☺	😐	☹
_____	☺	😐	☹
_____	☺	😐	☹
_____	☺	😐	☹

Skillstreaming

From *Skillstreaming the Elementary School Child: Teaching Prosocial Skills* (3rd ed.), © 2012 by E. McGinnis, Champaign, IL: Research Press (www.researchpress.com, 800-519-2707).

Skill 18: Playing a Game

SKILL STEPS

1. **Be sure you know the rules.**

   Discuss what to do if students don't know the rules (ask someone to explain them).

2. **Decide who starts the game.**

   Discuss methods of deciding who begins the game—for example, roll the dice or offer to let the other person go first.

3. **Remember to wait your turn.**

   Suggest that students repeat silently to themselves, "I can wait until it's my turn."

4. **When the game is over, say something nice to the other person.**

   Discuss and practice appropriate ways of handling winning (tell the person he/she played a good game) and losing (congratulate the other person).

SUGGESTED MODELING SITUATIONS

► *School:* Play a board or computer game with a classmate or a group game at recess.

► *Home:* Play a board or video game with your parents, brother, or sister.

► *Peer group:* Play a group game with friends in the neighborhood.

► *Community:* Play a game at a community event.

COMMENTS

It may be helpful to coach students in how to play a variety of board games and group games played at recess or in the neighborhood so they will feel confident playing. Posting lists of familiar classroom and recess games may also encourage them to play acceptable games. Good skills to teach following this one are Dealing with Losing (Skill 49) and Being a Good Sport (Skill 50).

From *Skillstreaming the Elementary School Child: Teaching Prosocial Skills* (3rd ed.), © 2012 by E. McGinnis, Champaign, IL: Research Press (www.researchpress.com, 800-519-2707).
171

Skill 18: Playing a Game

Name _____ Date _____

SKILL STEPS

1. Be sure you know the rules.

2. Decide who starts the game.

3. Remember to wait your turn.

4. When the game is over, say something nice to the other person.

FILL IN NOW

With whom will I try this? _____

When? _____

FILL IN AFTER YOU PRACTICE THE SKILL

What happened? _____

_____

_____

How did I do? ☺ 😐 ☹

Why did I circle this? _____

_____

Skillstreaming From *Skillstreaming the Elementary School Child: Teaching Prosocial Skills* (3rd ed.), © 2012 by E. McGinnis, Champaign, IL: Research Press (www.researchpress.com, 800-519-2707).

Skill 18: Playing a Game

Name_____ Date_____

SKILL STEPS

1. Be sure you know the rules.

2. Decide who starts the game.

3. Remember to wait your turn.

4. When the game is over, say something nice to the other person.

When did I practice?   How did I do?

 From *Skillstreaming the Elementary School Child: Teaching Prosocial Skills* (3rd ed.), © 2012 by E. McGinnis, Champaign, IL: Research Press (www.researchpress.com, 800-519-2707).

Skill 19: Asking a Favor

SKILL STEPS

1. **Decide if you want or need to ask a favor.**

   Discuss what to do if students don't know the rules (ask someone to explain them).

2. **Plan what you want to say.**

   Discuss methods of deciding who begins the game—for example, roll the dice or offer to let the other person go first.

3. **Ask the favor in a friendly way.**

   Suggest that students repeat silently to themselves, "I can wait until it's my turn."

4. **Remember to thank the person.**

   Teach the skill Saying Thank You (Skill 3).

SUGGESTED MODELING SITUATIONS

▶ *School:* You would like to join a group and someone must move over to make room for you, or someone is making a noise that interferes with your work.

▶ *Home:* The television is too loud for you to do your homework.

▶ *Peer group:* A friend is going to a movie and you'd like to go along, or you would like to borrow something from a friend.

▶ *Community:* You need help with using the computer at the library.

COMMENTS

The definition of a "favor," as used in this skill, is anything a student needs help with, varying from problems with other people to school and other informational problems. Students may need guidance in deciding on the individual they should ask in different situations. Teach students to use Accepting No (Skill 54) if the person they ask can't help.

Skillstreaming From *Skillstreaming the Elementary School Child: Teaching Prosocial Skills* (3rd ed.), © 2012 by E. McGinnis, Champaign, IL: Research Press (www.researchpress.com, 800-519-2707).

Skill 19: Asking a Favor

Name_____ Date_____

SKILL STEPS

1. Decide if you want or need to ask a favor.

2. Plan what you want to say.

3. Ask the favor in a friendly way.

4. Remember to thank the person.

FILL IN NOW

With whom will I try this?_____

When?_____

FILL IN AFTER YOU PRACTICE THE SKILL

What happened?_____

_____

_____

How did I do?   ☺   😐   ☹

Why did I circle this?_____

_____

From *Skillstreaming the Elementary School Child: Teaching Prosocial Skills* (3rd ed.), © 2012 by E. McGinnis, Champaign, IL: Research Press (www.researchpress.com, 800-519-2707).

Skill 19: Asking a Favor

Name _____ Date _____

SKILL STEPS

1. Decide if you want or need to ask a favor.

2. Plan what you want to say.

3. Ask the favor in a friendly way.

4. Remember to thank the person.

When did I practice?   How did I do?

Skillstreaming   From *Skillstreaming the Elementary School Child: Teaching Prosocial Skills* (3rd ed.), © 2012 by E. McGinnis, Champaign, IL: Research Press (www.researchpress.com, 800-519-2707).

Skill 20: Offering Help to a Classmate

SKILL STEPS

1. **Decide if the person needs or wants help.**

   Discuss how to determine if another student needs help: How does he look? What is she doing or saying?

2. **Think of how you can help.**

   Observing the person can help the student decide whether to offer physical help or verbal guidance.

3. **Decide what to say.**

   Discuss a variety of ways to offer help.

4. **Choose a good time.**

   Remind students to be sure that they are not supposed to be doing something else.

5. **Ask in a friendly way.**

   Discuss the body language and nonverbal communicators that show a friendly attitude.

SUGGESTED MODELING SITUATIONS

▶ *School:* A classmate drops his/her books or is having difficulty with an assignment or a project.

▶ *Peer group:* A friend is having difficulty completing a chore or project.

COMMENTS

Discuss how people feel when helping someone or being helped. Emphasize not feeling hurt or offended if the person says no or asks someone else for help. If the person wants help, the student should follow through.

Skill 20: Offering Help to a Classmate

Name _____ Date _____

SKILL STEPS

1. Decide if the person needs or wants help.

2. Think of how you can help.

3. Decide what to say.

4. Choose a good time.

5. Ask in a friendly way.

FILL IN NOW

With whom will I try this? _____

When? _____

FILL IN AFTER YOU PRACTICE THE SKILL

What happened? _____

_____

_____

How did I do? ☺ 😐 ☹

Why did I circle this? _____

_____

Skillstreaming

From *Skillstreaming the Elementary School Child: Teaching Prosocial Skills* (3rd ed.), © 2012 by E. McGinnis, Champaign, IL: Research Press (www.researchpress.com, 800-519-2707).

Skill 20: Offering Help to a Classmate

Name _____ Date _____

SKILL STEPS

1. Decide if the person needs or wants help.

2. Think of how you can help.

3. Decide what to say.

4. Choose a good time.

5. Ask in a friendly way.

When did I practice?   How did I do?

_____

_____

_____

_____

Skillstreaming From *Skillstreaming the Elementary School Child: Teaching Prosocial Skills* (3rd ed.), © 2012 by E. McGinnis, Champaign, IL: Research Press (www.researchpress.com, 800-519-2707).

Skill 21: Giving a Compliment

SKILL STEPS

1. **Decide what you want to tell the other person.**

   Discuss the types of things students may want to compliment someone on: appearance, behavior, an achievement.

2. **Decide what to say.**

   Give examples of compliments.

3. **Choose a good time and place.**

   Discuss how to choose: when the student and the other person aren't busy and perhaps when a lot of other people aren't around.

4. **Give the compliment in a friendly way.**

   Emphasize giving the compliment in a sincere manner. Discuss the body language and facial expressions associated with sincerity.

SUGGESTED MODELING SITUATIONS

- ▶ *School:* A classmate has done really well on an assignment or has worked very hard on a project.
- ▶ *Home:* Your mom or dad makes a good dinner.
- ▶ *Peer group:* You like what someone is wearing.
- ▶ *Community:* An adult organized to help a community member.

COMMENTS

When students first begin using this skill, it may appear mechanical and insincere. Once they have had sufficient practice, their skill use will be more natural. Discuss the way both the giver and recipient of the compliment might feel (e.g., embarrassed, pleased).

Skillstreaming From *Skillstreaming the Elementary School Child: Teaching Prosocial Skills* (3rd ed.), © 2012 by E. McGinnis, Champaign, IL: Research Press (www.researchpress.com, 800-519-2707).

Skill 21: Giving a Compliment

Name _____ Date _____

SKILL STEPS

1. Decide what you want to tell the other person.

2. Decide what to say.

3. Choose a good time and place.

4. Give the compliment in a friendly way.

FILL IN NOW

With whom will I try this? _____

When?_____

FILL IN AFTER YOU PRACTICE THE SKILL

What happened?_____

_____

_____

How did I do?   ☺ 😐 ☹

Why did I circle this?_____

_____

 From *Skillstreaming the Elementary School Child: Teaching Prosocial Skills* (3rd ed.), © 2012 by E. McGinnis, Champaign, IL: Research Press (www.researchpress.com, 800-519-2707).

Skill 21: Giving a Compliment

Name _____ Date _____

SKILL STEPS

1. Decide what you want to tell the other person.

2. Decide what to say.

3. Choose a good time and place.

4. Give the compliment in a friendly way.

When did I practice?   How did I do?

Skillstreaming From *Skillstreaming the Elementary School Child: Teaching Prosocial Skills* (3rd ed.), © 2012 by E. McGinnis, Champaign, IL: Research Press (www.researchpress.com, 800-519-2707).

Skill 22: Accepting a Compliment

SKILL STEPS

1. **Decide if someone has given you a compliment.**

   Discuss ways students can tell whether someone has given them a compliment—for instance, how the person looked and sounded when making the comment.

2. **Say thank you.**

   If necessary, teach students Saying Thank You (Skill 3).

3. **Say something else if you want to.**

   Give an example: "Yes, I tried hard." Encourage students to give credit to someone else who may have helped also: "Joey helped, too."

SUGGESTED MODELING SITUATIONS

- ► *School:* The teacher compliments you on work well done.
- ► *Home:* Your parents compliment you on how well you did your chores.
- ► *Peer group:* A friend compliments you on the way you look.
- ► *Community:* A friend of your parent compliments you on your behavior in the community.

COMMENTS

This skill is important because children are frequently embarrassed when given a compliment. Children with low self-esteem may also interpret compliments as negative and become defensive, as if they don't believe what the person is saying. When receiving a compliment is presented as a skill to be learned, such children are frequently more accepting.

From *Skillstreaming the Elementary School Child: Teaching Prosocial Skills* (3rd ed.), © 2012 by E. McGinnis, Champaign, IL: Research Press (www.researchpress.com, 800-519-2707).

Skill 22: Accepting a Compliment

Name _____ Date _____

SKILL STEPS

1. Decide if someone has given you a compliment.

2. Say thank you.

3. Say something else if you want to.

FILL IN NOW

With whom will I try this? _____

When?_____

FILL IN AFTER YOU PRACTICE THE SKILL

What happened?_____

_____

_____

How did I do?

Why did I circle this?_____

_____

From *Skillstreaming the Elementary School Child: Teaching Prosocial Skills* (3rd ed.), © 2012 by E. McGinnis, Champaign, IL: Research Press (www.researchpress.com, 800-519-2707).

Skill 22: Accepting a Compliment

Name _____ Date _____

SKILL STEPS

1. Decide if someone has given you a compliment.

2. Say thank you.

3. Say something else if you want to.

When did I practice?   How did I do?

_____   ☺   😐   ☹

_____   ☺   😐   ☹

_____   ☺   😐   ☹

_____   ☺   😐   ☹

 From *Skillstreaming the Elementary School Child: Teaching Prosocial Skills* (3rd ed.), © 2012 by E. McGinnis, Champaign, IL: Research Press (www.researchpress.com, 800-519-2707).

Skill 23: Suggesting an Activity

SKILL STEPS

1. **Decide on an activity you want to suggest.**

   Discuss a variety of appropriate activities in various settings (playground, during free time in the classroom, etc.).

2. **Decide what to say.**

   Give an example: "Would you like to _____?"

3. **Choose a good time.**

   Discuss how to choose a good time: when others aren't involved with another activity.

4. **Say it in a friendly way.**

   Discuss the body language and nonverbal communicators that show a friendly attitude.

SUGGESTED MODELING SITUATIONS

- ► *School:* Suggest a group game to be played at recess.
- ► *Home:* Suggest an evening out with your parents—for example, going to a movie.
- ► *Peer group:* Suggest a game or an activity to a friend.
- ► *Community:* Suggest an activity to peers at an adult community event.

COMMENTS

It may be helpful to coach students in how to play a variety of games. The activity must be appropriate to the setting (e.g., the classroom versus the playground or neighborhood) and to the number of students involved (group versus individual) so certain individuals are not left out. Discuss what to say if someone says no to a suggested activity: Students could ask, "What would you like to do?" or invite someone else.

From *Skillstreaming the Elementary School Child: Teaching Prosocial Skills* (3rd ed.), © 2012 by E. McGinnis, Champaign, IL: Research Press (www.researchpress.com, 800-519-2707).

Skill 23: Suggesting an Activity

Name _____ Date _____

SKILL STEPS

1. Decide on an activity you want to suggest.

2. Decide what to say.

3. Choose a good time.

4. Say it in a friendly way.

FILL IN NOW

With whom will I try this? _____

When? _____

FILL IN AFTER YOU PRACTICE THE SKILL

What happened? _____

_____

_____

How did I do?   ☺   😐   ☹

Why did I circle this? _____

_____

Skill 23: Suggesting an Activity

Name _____ Date _____

SKILL STEPS

1. Decide on an activity you want to suggest.

2. Decide what to say.

3. Choose a good time.

4. Say it in a friendly way.

When did I practice?   How did I do?

_____   ☺   😐   ☹

_____   ☺   😐   ☹

_____   ☺   😐   ☹

_____   ☺   😐   ☹

Skillstreaming

From *Skillstreaming the Elementary School Child: Teaching Prosocial Skills* (3rd ed.), © 2012 by E. McGinnis, Champaign, IL: Research Press (www.researchpress.com, 800-519-2707).

Skill 24: Sharing

SKILL STEPS

1. **Decide if you want to share something.**

   Talk about how the other person might feel if the student does or doesn't share.

2. **Decide on the person with whom you want to share.**

   If the student can share with only one person, point out that others around may feel left out.

3. **Choose a good time and place.**

   Discuss how to choose a good time: when another person needs or would enjoy using something of the student.

4. **Offer to share in a friendly and sincere way.**

   Discuss appropriate body language, voice tone, and facial expression.

SUGGESTED MODELING SITUATIONS

▶ *School:* Offer to share your materials (crayons, pencils, paper) with a classmate.

▶ *Home:* Offer to share a treat with a friend, brother, or sister.

▶ *Peer group:* Offer to share a game or toys with a friend.

▶ *Community:* Offer to share a treat with a friend at a ballgame or other event.

COMMENTS

Teachers should create opportunities in the classroom for students to share work materials, information, and other items. Doing so will not only increase the chances that students will master this skill but also enhance a sense of community within the instructional setting.

Skill 24: Sharing

Name _____ Date _____

SKILL STEPS

1. Decide if you want to share something.

2. Decide on the person with whom you want to share.

3. Choose a good time and place.

4. Offer to share in a friendly and sincere way.

FILL IN NOW

With whom will I try this? _____

When? _____

FILL IN AFTER YOU PRACTICE THE SKILL

What happened? _____

_____

_____

How did I do?   ☺ ☺ ☹

Why did I circle this? _____

_____

Skillstreaming

From *Skillstreaming the Elementary School Child: Teaching Prosocial Skills* (3rd ed.), © 2012 by E. McGinnis, Champaign, IL: Research Press (www.researchpress.com, 800-519-2707).

Skill 24: Sharing

Name _____ Date _____

SKILL STEPS

1. Decide if you want to share something.

2. Decide on the person with whom you want to share.

3. Choose a good time and place.

4. Offer to share in a friendly and sincere way.

When did I practice?   How did I do?

From *Skillstreaming the Elementary School Child: Teaching Prosocial Skills* (3rd ed.), © 2012 by E. McGinnis, Champaign, IL: Research Press (www.researchpress.com, 800-519-2707).

Skill 25: Apologizing

SKILL STEPS

1. **Decide if you need to apologize.**

   Discuss how we sometimes do things for which we are later sorry. Apologizing is something we can do to let other people know we are sorry. It also often makes us feel better.

2. **Think about your choices:**

   a. **Say it out loud to the person.**

      Discuss when it is best to use verbal or written ways to apologize.

   b. **Write the person a note.**

3. **Choose a good time and place.**

   Discuss how to choose a good time (i.e., soon after the problem). The student may want to be alone with the person for a verbal apology.

4. **Carry out your best choice in a sincere way.**

   Discuss the body language, voice tone, and facial expressions associated with sincerity.

SUGGESTED MODELING SITUATIONS

► *School:* You are late for a class.

► *Home:* You accidentally break something.

► *Peer group:* You said something cruel because you were angry, or you had planned to do something with a friend but you had to go somewhere with your parents instead.

► *Community:* You bump into someone on the street.

COMMENTS

It may be beneficial to discuss how difficult it might be to apologize. Discussion of how a person might feel before apologizing (e.g., anxious, afraid), as well as how a person might feel receiving the apology (e.g., relieved, less upset, less angry), may make students more willing to use this skill.

Skillstreaming

From *Skillstreaming the Elementary School Child: Teaching Prosocial Skills* (3rd ed.), © 2012 by E. McGinnis, Champaign, IL: Research Press (www.researchpress.com, 800-519-2707).

Skill 25: Apologizing

Name_____ Date_____

SKILL STEPS

1. Decide if you need to apologize.

2. Think about your choices:

   a. Say it out loud to the person.

   b. Write the person a note.

3. Choose a good time and place.

4. Carry out your best choice in a sincere way.

FILL IN NOW

With whom will I try this? _____

When?_____

FILL IN AFTER YOU PRACTICE THE SKILL

What happened?_____

_____

_____

How did I do?   ☺   😐   ☹

Why did I circle this?_____

_____

Skill 25: Apologizing

Name _____ Date _____

SKILL STEPS

1. Decide if you need to apologize.

2. Think about your choices:

   a. Say it out loud to the person.

   b. Write the person a note.

3. Choose a good time and place.

4. Carry out your best choice in a sincere way.

When did I practice?   How did I do?

_____   ☺   😐   ☹

_____   ☺   😐   ☹

_____   ☺   😐   ☹

_____   ☺   😐   ☹

Skillstreaming

From *Skillstreaming the Elementary School Child: Teaching Prosocial Skills* (3rd ed.), © 2012 by E. McGinnis, Champaign, IL: Research Press (www.researchpress.com, 800-519-2707).

Group III

Skills for Dealing with Feelings

Skills 26–35

Skill 26: Knowing Your Feelings

SKILL STEPS

1. **Think of how your body feels.**

   Discuss the cues students' bodies may give—for example, blushing, tight muscles, or queasy stomach.

2. **Decide what you could call the feeling.**

   Discuss feelings such as frustration, fear, and embarrassment and their associated physical reactions.

3. **Say to yourself, "I feel _____."**

SUGGESTED MODELING SITUATIONS

▶ *School:* You are frustrated with a difficult assignment, or you are embarrassed about a grade.

▶ *Home:* You are disappointed because your parents forgot to do something they had promised.

▶ *Peer group:* You are disappointed because a friend promised to go to a movie with you but now can't go.

▶ *Community:* An older kid says mean things to you at a game or other event.

COMMENTS

Additional activities specific to identifying and labeling feelings will likely be needed. Such activities might include generating a list of feeling words to be displayed in the classroom, finding pictures in magazines of persons expressing those feelings, and discussing different situations and how people might feel in them.

Skill 26: Knowing Your Feelings

Name _____ Date _____

SKILL STEPS

1. Think of how your body feels.

2. Decide what you could call the feeling.

3. Say to yourself, "I feel _____."

FILL IN NOW

With whom will I try this? _____

When? _____

FILL IN AFTER YOU PRACTICE THE SKILL

What happened? _____

_____

_____

How did I do?   ☺   😐   ☹

Why did I circle this? _____

_____

Skillstreaming

From *Skillstreaming the Elementary School Child: Teaching Prosocial Skills* (3rd ed.), © 2012 by E. McGinnis, Champaign, IL: Research Press (www.researchpress.com, 800-519-2707).

Skill 26: Knowing Your Feelings

Name _____ Date _____

SKILL STEPS

1. Think of how your body feels.

2. Decide what you could call the feeling.

3. Say to yourself, "I feel _____."

When did I practice?   How did I do?

From *Skillstreaming the Elementary School Child: Teaching Prosocial Skills* (3rd ed.), © 2012 by E. McGinnis, Champaign, IL: Research Press (www.researchpress.com, 800-519-2707).

Skill 27: Expressing Your Feelings

SKILL STEPS

1. **Stop and think of how your body feels.**

   Discuss how students can identify feelings by paying attention to body cues.

2. **Decide what to call the feeling.**

   Display a list of feeling words. Discuss what events may have contributed to the feeling.

3. **Think about your choices:**

   a. **Say to the person, "I feel _____."**

   Consider when and where the student may be able to talk about the feeling.

   b. **Walk away for now.**

   Suggest this alternative as a way to calm down.

   c. **Get involved in an activity.**

   Discuss alternative activities.

4. **Act out your best choice.**

   If the student is still having an intense feeling—such as anger—after following these steps, he or she should wait until the feeling isn't so intense before acting on the best choice. If one choice doesn't work, the student should try another one.

SUGGESTED MODELING SITUATIONS

▶ *School:* You want to answer in class, but you are afraid your answer will be wrong.

▶ *Home:* Your parents won't allow you to watch a movie on TV that many of your friends are going to watch.

▶ *Peer group:* Someone calls you a name or ignores you.

▶ *Community:* The store clerk follows you around in the store.

COMMENTS

You can model this skill throughout the year by expressing your own feelings to the class in an appropriate manner.

Skillstreaming From *Skillstreaming the Elementary School Child: Teaching Prosocial Skills* (3rd ed.), © 2012 by E. McGinnis, Champaign, IL: Research Press (www.researchpress.com, 800-519-2707).

Skill 27: Expressing Your Feelings

Name _____ Date _____

SKILL STEPS

1. Stop and think of how your body feels.

2. Decide what to call the feeling.

3. Think about your choices:

   a. Say to the person, "I feel _____."

   b. Walk away for now.

   c. Get involved in an activity.

4. Act out your best choice.

FILL IN NOW

With whom will I try this? _____

When? _____

FILL IN AFTER YOU PRACTICE THE SKILL

What happened? _____

_____

_____

How did I do?   ☺   😐   ☹

Why did I circle this? _____

_____

 From *Skillstreaming the Elementary School Child: Teaching Prosocial Skills* (3rd ed.), © 2012 by E. McGinnis, Champaign, IL: Research Press (www.researchpress.com, 800-519-2707).   **201**

Skill 27: Expressing Your Feelings

Name _____ Date _____

SKILL STEPS

1. Stop and think of how your body feels.

2. Decide what to call the feeling.

3. Think about your choices:

   a. Say to the person, "I feel _____."

   b. Walk away for now.

   c. Get involved in an activity.

4. Act out your best choice.

When did I practice?   How did I do?

Skillstreaming

From *Skillstreaming the Elementary School Child: Teaching Prosocial Skills* (3rd ed.), © 2012 by E. McGinnis, Champaign, IL: Research Press (www.researchpress.com, 800-519-2707).

Skill 28: Recognizing Another's Feelings

SKILL STEPS

1. **Watch the person.**

   Discuss paying attention to the way the person looks (posture, facial expression), what the person does and says, and how the person says it.

2. **Name what you think the person is feeling.**

   Display a list of feeling words for reference.

3. **Decide whether or not to ask the person if he/she is feeling that way.**

   If the person seems very angry or upset, it may be best to wait until the person has calmed down.

4. **Ask in a concerned way.**

   Discuss desirable ways to ask: facial expression, voice tone, and so on that show concern.

SUGGESTED MODELING SITUATIONS

▶ *School:* After assignments are handed back, a student puts his head on the desk.

▶ *Home:* Your dad or mom is slamming doors and muttering to himself/herself.

▶ *Peer group:* A friend wasn't chosen for a game, or a classmate is watching a game instead of asking to join in.

▶ *Community:* A kid from your school strikes out at the baseball game.

COMMENTS

Include role-plays targeted toward both adults and peers. This skill should precede Showing Understanding of Another's Feelings (Skill 29).

Skill 28: Recognizing Another's Feelings

Name _____ Date _____

SKILL STEPS

1. Watch the person.

2. Name what you think the person is feeling.

3. Decide whether or not to ask the person if he/she is feeling that way.

4. Ask in a concerned way.

FILL IN NOW

With whom will I try this? _____

When?_____

FILL IN AFTER YOU PRACTICE THE SKILL

What happened?_____

_____

_____

How did I do?

Why did I circle this?_____

_____

Skillstreaming
From *Skillstreaming the Elementary School Child: Teaching Prosocial Skills* (3rd ed.), © 2012 by E. McGinnis, Champaign, IL: Research Press (www.researchpress.com, 800-519-2707).

Skill 28: Recognizing Another's Feelings

Name _____ Date _____

SKILL STEPS

1. Watch the person.

2. Name what you think the person is feeling.

3. Decide whether or not to ask the person if he/she is feeling that way.

4. Ask in a concerned way.

When did I practice?   How did I do?

	☺	😐	☹
_____	☺	😐	☹
_____	☺	😐	☹
_____	☺	😐	☹

Skillstreaming From *Skillstreaming the Elementary School Child: Teaching Prosocial Skills* (3rd ed.), © 2012 by E. McGinnis, Champaign, IL: Research Press (www.researchpress.com, 800-519-2707).

Skill 29: Showing Understanding of Another's Feelings

SKILL STEPS

1. **Name what you think the person is feeling.**

    Discuss how the student might feel if he or she were in that situation.

2. **Think about your choices:**

    Discuss how the student should base the choice on how well he or she knows the other person and on the cues the person is giving.

    a. **Ask the person if he/she feels this way.**

    b. **Ask the person if you can help.**

    c. **Leave the person alone.**

        If the person seems very upset or angry, it may be best to leave the person alone and then make another choice when the person is less upset.

3. **Act out your best choice.**

    If one choice doesn't work, the student should try another one.

SUGGESTED MODELING SITUATIONS

▶ *School:* A classmate is crying because someone teased her.

▶ *Home:* Your brother or sister won't talk to anyone after having a talk with a parent.

▶ *Peer group:* A friend throws a board game after losing.

▶ *Community:* A friend lost his money on the street.

COMMENTS

Teach Recognizing Another's Feelings (Skill 28) prior to this skill. It will then be beneficial to have students practice using the two skills together.

Skillstreaming

From *Skillstreaming the Elementary School Child: Teaching Prosocial Skills* (3rd ed.), © 2012 by E. McGinnis, Champaign, IL: Research Press (www.researchpress.com, 800-519-2707).

Skill 29: Showing Understanding of Another's Feelings

Name_____ Date_____

SKILL STEPS

1. Name what you think the person is feeling.

2. Think about your choices:

   a. Ask the person if he/she feels this way.

   b. Ask the person if you can help.

   c. Leave the person alone.

3. Act out your best choice.

FILL IN NOW

With whom will I try this? _____

When?_____

FILL IN AFTER YOU PRACTICE THE SKILL

What happened?_____

_____

_____

How did I do?   ☺   😐   ☹

Why did I circle this?_____

_____

 From *Skillstreaming the Elementary School Child: Teaching Prosocial Skills* (3rd ed.), © 2012 by E. McGinnis, Champaign, IL: Research Press (www.researchpress.com, 800-519-2707).

Skill 29: Showing Understanding of Another's Feelings

Name_____ Date_____

SKILL STEPS

1. Name what you think the person is feeling.

2. Think about your choices:

   a. Ask the person if he/she feels this way.

   b. Ask the person if you can help.

   c. Leave the person alone.

3. Act out your best choice.

When did I practice?   How did I do?

_____   ☺ 😐 ☹

_____   ☺ 😐 ☹

_____   ☺ 😐 ☹

_____   ☺ 😐 ☹

Skillstreaming From *Skillstreaming the Elementary School Child: Teaching Prosocial Skills* (3rd ed.), © 2012 by E. McGinnis, Champaign, IL: Research Press (www.researchpress.com, 800-519-2707).

Skill 30: Expressing Concern for Another

SKILL STEPS

1. **Decide if someone is having a problem.**

   Discuss ways to determine if someone is having a problem: What is the person doing? How does he or she look? Discuss the meaning of empathy and its importance in using this skill.

2. **Think about your choices:**

   a. **Say, "Can I help you?"**

      Emphasize sincerity.

   b. **Do something nice for the person.**

      Suggest sharing something with the person or asking the person to join an activity.

3. **Act out your best choice.**

   If one choice doesn't work, the student should try another one.

SUGGESTED MODELING SITUATIONS

▶ *School:* A classmate is struggling with a difficult assignment.

▶ *Home:* A parent is having difficulty with a chore.

▶ *Peer group:* A friend has hurt himself/herself.

▶ *Community:* A friend left his homework at the library.

COMMENTS

Students may need instruction in the skill of Recognizing Another's Feelings (Skill 28) before using this one.

Skill 30: Expressing Concern for Another

Name _____ Date _____

SKILL STEPS

1. Decide if someone is having a problem.

2. Think about your choices:

    a. Say, "Can I help you?"

    b. Do something nice for the person.

3. Act out your best choice.

FILL IN NOW

With whom will I try this? _____

When?_____

FILL IN AFTER YOU PRACTICE THE SKILL

What happened?_____

_____

_____

How did I do?   ☺   😐   ☹

Why did I circle this?_____

_____

Skillstreaming From *Skillstreaming the Elementary School Child: Teaching Prosocial Skills* (3rd ed.), © 2012 by E. McGinnis, Champaign, IL: Research Press (www.researchpress.com, 800-519-2707).

Skill 30: Expressing Concern for Another

Name _____ Date _____

SKILL STEPS

1. Decide if someone is having a problem.

2. Think about your choices:

    a. Say, "Can I help you?"

    b. Do something nice for the person.

3. Act out your best choice.

When did I practice?   How did I do?

_____   😊   😐   ☹️

_____   😊   😐   ☹️

_____   😊   😐   ☹️

                                             😊   😐   ☹️

From *Skillstreaming the Elementary School Child: Teaching Prosocial Skills* (3rd ed.), © 2012 by E. McGinnis, Champaign, IL: Research Press (www.researchpress.com, 800-519-2707).

Skill 31: Dealing with Your Anger

SKILL STEPS

1. **Stop and count to 10.**

   Discuss the importance of allowing yourself time to cool off and think.

2. **Think about your choices:**

   a. **Tell the person in words why you are angry.**

      Discuss how to tell the person in a way that won't get that person angry, too.

   b. **Walk away for now.**

      Students may need to ask the teacher if they can leave the classroom and run an errand or take a break.

   c. **Do a relaxation exercise.**

      Teach students Relaxing (Skill 56).

3. **Act out your best choice.**

   If one choice doesn't work, the student should try another one.

SUGGESTED MODELING SITUATIONS

▶ *School:* You don't think the teacher has been fair to you, you are angry at yourself for forgetting your homework, or you are having a day where everything seems to go wrong.

▶ *Home:* Your parents won't let you have a friend over or won't let you leave the house.

▶ *Peer group:* A friend talks about you behind your back.

▶ *Community:* An older kid is picking on you and your friend at the mall.

COMMENTS

For a child who directs anger inward, additional choices may be necessary. Such choices might include "Write about how you feel" or "Decide what you can change to keep this from happening again." Skills such as Problem Solving (Skill 41) may also help children who direct anger toward themselves.

.Skillstreaming From *Skillstreaming the Elementary School Child: Teaching Prosocial Skills* (3rd ed.), © 2012 by E. McGinnis, Champaign, IL: Research Press (www.researchpress.com, 800-519-2707).

Skill 31: Dealing with Your Anger

Name _____ Date _____

SKILL STEPS

1. Stop and count to 10.

2. Think about your choices:

   a. Tell the person in words why you are angry.

   b. Walk away for now.

   c. Do a relaxation exercise.

3. Act out your best choice.

FILL IN NOW

With whom will I try this? _____

When? _____

FILL IN AFTER YOU PRACTICE THE SKILL

What happened? _____

_____

_____

How did I do?   ☺   😐   ☹

Why did I circle this? _____

_____

From *Skillstreaming the Elementary School Child: Teaching Prosocial Skills* (3rd ed.), © 2012 by E. McGinnis, Champaign, IL: Research Press (www.researchpress.com, 800-519-2707).

Skill 31: Dealing with Your Anger

Name _____ Date _____

SKILL STEPS

1. Stop and count to 10.

2. Think about your choices:

   a. Tell the person in words why you are angry.

   b. Walk away for now.

   c. Do a relaxation exercise.

3. Act out your best choice.

When did I practice?   How did I do?

Skillstreaming

From *Skillstreaming the Elementary School Child: Teaching Prosocial Skills* (3rd ed.), © 2012 by E. McGinnis, Champaign, IL: Research Press (www.researchpress.com, 800-519-2707).

Skill 32: Dealing with Another's Anger

SKILL STEPS

1. **Listen to what the person has to say.**

   Discuss the importance of not interrupting or becoming defensive. If needed, students may say to themselves, "I can stay calm."

2. **Think about your choices:**

   Discuss the possible consequences of each choice.

   a. **Keep listening.**

   b. **Ask why the person is angry.**

   c. **Give the person an idea to fix the problem.**

   d. **Walk away for now.**

      If the student begins to feel angry, too, he/she should walk away until feeling calmer. This action will not fix the problem but will keep the student out of trouble. Later, the student can make a different choice.

3. **Act out your best choice.**

SUGGESTED MODELING SITUATIONS

- *School:* The teacher is angry at you for not doing well on a test.
- *Home:* Your parents are angry because you didn't clean your room.
- *Peer group:* Another student is angry at you because you didn't choose him to play a game.
- *Community:* An adult seems angry with you for making noise and being silly at a community event.

COMMENTS

Students need to know that it may be OK to delay discussing the situation when a peer is angry. If an adult is angry, delaying may only create more problems for the student. Stress the importance of adjusting one's behavior according to the role of the person with whom the problem exists.

Skill 32: Dealing with Another's Anger

Name _____ Date _____

SKILL STEPS

1. Listen to what the person has to say.

2. Think about your choices:

   a. Keep listening.

   b. Ask why the person is angry.

   c. Give the person an idea to fix the problem.

   d. Walk away for now.

3. Act out your best choice.

FILL IN NOW

With whom will I try this? _____

When? _____

FILL IN AFTER YOU PRACTICE THE SKILL

What happened? _____

_____

_____

How did I do?

Why did I circle this? _____

_____

Skillstreaming From *Skillstreaming the Elementary School Child: Teaching Prosocial Skills* (3rd ed.), © 2012 by E. McGinnis, Champaign, IL: Research Press (www.researchpress.com, 800-519-2707).

Skill 32: Dealing with Another's Anger

Name _____ Date _____

SKILL STEPS

1. Listen to what the person has to say.

2. Think about your choices:

   a. Keep listening.

   b. Ask why the person is angry.

   c. Give the person an idea to fix the problem.

   d. Walk away for now.

3. Act out your best choice.

When did I practice?   How did I do?

Skill 33: Expressing Affection

SKILL STEPS

1. **Decide if you have good feelings about the other person.**

   Discuss these feelings.

2. **Decide if you think the other person would like to know you feel this way.**

   Discuss possible consequences of telling the person—for example, the person may become embarrassed or feel good.

3. **Decide what to say.**

4. **Choose a good time and place.**

   Discuss how to choose a good time: Being alone may make it easier to express affection.

5. **Tell the person in a friendly way.**

   Discuss the body language and nonverbal communicators that show a friendly attitude.

SUGGESTED MODELING SITUATIONS

▶ *School:* Thank a teacher for something he/she has done.

▶ *Home:* Tell your parents that you love them.

▶ *Peer group:* Tell friends that you like them and want to continue being friends.

▶ *Community:* A good friend of your sister gave you a ride to a school event.

COMMENTS

This skill is difficult for many adults to carry out, and therefore students may have had the skill modeled for them quite infrequently. It is important for teachers to provide this type of modeling. Students may need to discuss how to express affection to persons in different roles: teachers, adult friends, peers. The way in which students display this affection will differ from one person to another.

Skillstreaming

From *Skillstreaming the Elementary School Child: Teaching Prosocial Skills* (3rd ed.), © 2012 by E. McGinnis, Champaign, IL: Research Press (www.researchpress.com, 800-519-2707).

Skill 33: Expressing Affection

Name _____ Date _____

SKILL STEPS

1. Decide if you have good feelings about the other person.

2. Decide if you think the other person would like to know you feel this way.

3. Decide what to say.

4. Choose a good time and place.

5. Tell the person in a friendly way.

FILL IN NOW

With whom will I try this? _____

When? _____

FILL IN AFTER YOU PRACTICE THE SKILL

What happened? _____

_____

_____

How did I do?   ☺   😐   ☹

Why did I circle this? _____

_____

From *Skillstreaming the Elementary School Child: Teaching Prosocial Skills* (3rd ed.), © 2012 by E. McGinnis, Champaign, IL: Research Press (www.researchpress.com, 800-519-2707).

Skill 33: Expressing Affection

Name _____ Date _____

SKILL STEPS

1. Decide if you have good feelings about the other person.

2. Decide if you think the other person would like to know you feel this way.

3. Decide what to say.

4. Choose a good time and place.

5. Tell the person in a friendly way.

When did I practice?   How did I do?

_____	☺	😐	☹
_____	☺	😐	☹
_____	☺	😐	☹
_____	☺	😐	☹

Skillstreaming

From *Skillstreaming the Elementary School Child: Teaching Prosocial Skills* (3rd ed.), © 2012 by E. McGinnis, Champaign, IL: Research Press (www.researchpress.com, 800-519-2707).

Skill 34: Dealing with Fear

SKILL STEPS

1. **Decide if you are feeling afraid.**

   Discuss bodily cues of fear (e.g., sweaty hands, nausea, pounding heart).

2. **Decide what you are afraid of.**

   Discuss real versus imagined threats. The student may need to check this out with another person.

3. **Think about your choices:**

   a. **Talk to someone about it.**

   Discuss choosing someone reassuring (teacher or parent).

   b. **Do a relaxation exercise.**

   Teach students Relaxing (Skill 56).

   c. **Try what you are afraid of doing anyway.**

   Discuss the feelings of accomplishment that can come from doing something difficult.

4. **Act out your best choice.**

   Discuss possible consequences of each choice. If one choice doesn't work, the student should try another one.

SUGGESTED MODELING SITUATIONS

► *School:* You are afraid to take a test, or you are afraid to go out to recess because someone said he/she would beat you up.

► *Home:* You are home alone at night.

► *Peer group:* Someone in the neighborhood challenges you to do something dangerous, or a peer threatens to say you did something that will get you into trouble.

► *Community:* You became separated from your friends or family.

COMMENTS

Encourage students to evaluate realistic versus unrealistic fears. When fears are realistic, talking to someone about them would be the best choice. Students may also need to problem solve ways to deal with realistic fears (see Skill 41: Problem Solving).

Skill 34: Dealing with Fear

Name _____ Date _____

SKILL STEPS

1. Decide if you are feeling afraid.

2. Decide what you are afraid of.

3. Think about your choices:

    a. Talk to someone about it.

    b. Do a relaxation exercise.

    c. Try what you are afraid of doing anyway.

4. Act out your best choice.

FILL IN NOW

With whom will I try this? _____

When? _____

FILL IN AFTER YOU PRACTICE THE SKILL

What happened? _____

_____

_____

How did I do?   ☺   😐   ☹

Why did I circle this? _____

_____

Skillstreaming

From *Skillstreaming the Elementary School Child: Teaching Prosocial Skills* (3rd ed.), © 2012 by E. McGinnis, Champaign, IL: Research Press (www.researchpress.com, 800-519-2707).

Skill 34: Dealing with Fear

Name_____ Date_____

SKILL STEPS

1. Decide if you are feeling afraid.

2. Decide what you are afraid of.

3. Think about your choices:

    a. Talk to someone about it.

    b. Do a relaxation exercise.

    c. Try what you are afraid of doing anyway.

4. Act out your best choice.

When did I practice?   How did I do?

Skillstreaming   From *Skillstreaming the Elementary School Child: Teaching Prosocial Skills* (3rd ed.), © 2012 by E. McGinnis, Champaign, IL: Research Press (www.researchpress.com, 800-519-2707).

Skill 35: Rewarding Yourself

SKILL STEPS

1. **Decide if you did a good job.**

   Discuss ways to evaluate your own performance.

2. **Say to yourself, "I did a good job."**

3. **Decide how else you will reward yourself.**

   Give examples of other self-rewards—take a break, do something you enjoy. Discuss.

4. **Do it.**

   Point out that students should reward themselves as soon after their performance as possible.

SUGGESTED MODELING SITUATIONS

- ► *School:* You completed all of your assignments.
- ► *Home:* You cleaned your room, you finished a difficult homework assignment, or you helped a neighbor who needed your help.
- ► *Peer group:* You helped a friend do his/her chores.
- ► *Community:* You helped a neighbor with a chore.

COMMENTS

Emphasize that people don't always have to depend on others to reward their actions.

Skillstreaming

From *Skillstreaming the Elementary School Child: Teaching Prosocial Skills* (3rd ed.), © 2012 by E. McGinnis, Champaign, IL: Research Press (www.researchpress.com, 800-519-2707).

Skill 35: Rewarding Yourself

Name _____ Date _____

SKILL STEPS

1. Decide if you did a good job.

2. Say to yourself, "I did a good job."

3. Decide how else you will reward yourself.

4. Do it.

FILL IN NOW

With whom will I try this? _____

When? _____

FILL IN AFTER YOU PRACTICE THE SKILL

What happened? _____

_____

_____

How did I do? ☺ 😐 ☹

Why did I circle this? _____

_____

From *Skillstreaming the Elementary School Child: Teaching Prosocial Skills* (3rd ed.), © 2012 by E. McGinnis, Champaign, IL: Research Press (www.researchpress.com, 800-519-2707).

Skill 35: Rewarding Yourself

Name _____ Date _____

SKILL STEPS

1. Decide if you did a good job.

2. Say to yourself, "I did a good job."

3. Decide how else you will reward yourself.

4. Do it.

When did I practice?   How did I do?

Skillstreaming

From *Skillstreaming the Elementary School Child: Teaching Prosocial Skills* (3rd ed.), © 2012 by E. McGinnis, Champaign, IL: Research Press (www.researchpress.com, 800-519-2707).

Group IV

Skill Alternatives to Aggression

Skills 36–44

Skill 36: Using Self-Control

SKILL STEPS

1. **Stop and count to 10.**

   Discuss the importance of allowing yourself time to cool off and think.

2. **Think of how your body feels.**

   Discuss how bodily cues may signal losing control (e.g., your hands become sweaty, you feel hot or weak).

3. **Think about your choices:**

   a. **Walk away for now.**

      Students should ask to leave the area for a few minutes, if necessary, until they regain control.

   b. **Do a relaxation exercise.**

      Teach students Relaxing (Skill 56).

   c. **Write about how you feel.**

   d. **Talk to someone about it.**

      Discuss choosing someone who would be likely to understand.

4. **Act out your best choice.**

   If one choice doesn't work, the student should try another one.

SUGGESTED MODELING SITUATIONS

- *School:* You are behind in your schoolwork and must stay after school to finish.
- *Home:* Your parents won't let you go to a friend's house.
- *Peer group:* A friend borrows something of yours and breaks it.
- *Community:* All your friends are buying treats at the game, but you don't have any money.

COMMENTS

Students should use this skill when they are too angry or upset to identify what they are feeling and need to gain control before dealing with the problem. Tell students that sometimes when people are very angry or upset, it is OK to delay dealing with the problem.

Skill 36: Using Self-Control

Name _____ Date _____

SKILL STEPS

1. Stop and count to 10.

2. Think of how your body feels.

3. Think about your choices:

   a. Walk away for now.

   b. Do a relaxation exercise.

   c. Write about how you feel.

   d. Talk to someone about it.

4. Act out your best choice.

FILL IN NOW

With whom will I try this? _____

When?_____

FILL IN AFTER YOU PRACTICE THE SKILL

What happened?_____

_____

_____

How did I do?   ☺   😐   ☹

Why did I circle this?_____

_____

Skillstreaming
From *Skillstreaming the Elementary School Child: Teaching Prosocial Skills* (3rd ed.), © 2012 by E. McGinnis, Champaign, IL: Research Press (www.researchpress.com, 800-519-2707).

Skill 36: Using Self-Control

Name _____ Date _____

SKILL STEPS

1. Stop and count to 10.

2. Think of how your body feels.

3. Think about your choices:

   a. Walk away for now.

   b. Do a relaxation exercise.

   c. Write about how you feel.

   d. Talk to someone about it.

4. Act out your best choice.

When did I practice?   How did I do?

Skill 37: Asking Permission

SKILL STEPS

1. **Decide what you want to do.**

   Remind students to be sure this activity won't be harmful to themselves or another person.

2. **Decide whom to ask.**

   This will usually be a parent or teacher.

3. **Plan what to say.**

   Discuss how to choose a good time: when the person isn't involved with another activity.

4. **Choose the right time and place.**

   The student may want to ask privately.

5. **Ask in a friendly way.**

   Discuss the body language and nonverbal communicators that show a friendly attitude.

SUGGESTED MODELING SITUATIONS

▶ *School:* Ask the teacher for a special privilege.

▶ *Home:* Ask your parents if you may go to a friend's house or if you may participate in a school activity.

▶ *Peer group:* Ask a friend if you may borrow something.

▶ *Community:* Ask a neighbor if you and your friends may play in his yard.

COMMENTS

We hope students' skill use will be successful most of the time. With this skill, however, many times permission may not be granted (e.g., parents can't afford it, the friend's house is too far away, or it's too late at night). It is therefore important to teach Rewarding Yourself (Skill 35) and/or Accepting No (Skill 54) immediately after this skill.

.Skillstreaming From *Skillstreaming the Elementary School Child: Teaching Prosocial Skills* (3rd ed.), © 2012 by E. McGinnis, Champaign, IL: Research Press (www.researchpress.com, 800-519-2707).

Skill 37: Asking Permission

Name _____ Date _____

SKILL STEPS

1. Decide what you want to do.

2. Decide whom to ask.

3. Plan what to say.

4. Choose the right time and place.

5. Ask in a friendly way.

FILL IN NOW

With whom will I try this? _____

When? _____

FILL IN AFTER YOU PRACTICE THE SKILL

What happened? _____

_____

_____

How did I do?   ☺   😐   ☹

Why did I circle this? _____

_____

From *Skillstreaming the Elementary School Child: Teaching Prosocial Skills* (3rd ed.), © 2012 by E. McGinnis, Champaign, IL: Research Press (www.researchpress.com, 800-519-2707).

Skill 37: Asking Permission

Name _____ Date _____

SKILL STEPS

1. Decide what you want to do.

2. Decide whom to ask.

3. Plan what to say.

4. Choose the right time and place.

5. Ask in a friendly way.

When did I practice?   How did I do?

Skillstreaming

From *Skillstreaming the Elementary School Child: Teaching Prosocial Skills* (3rd ed.), © 2012 by E. McGinnis, Champaign, IL: Research Press (www.researchpress.com, 800-519-2707).

Skill 38: Responding to Teasing

SKILL STEPS

1. **Stop and count to five.**

   Discuss how using this skill can prevent students from losing control.

2. **Think about your choices:**

   a. **Ignore the teasing.**

      Point out that ignoring for a short time doesn't always work; the student may need to ignore for a long time. Discuss ways to ignore (e.g., walk away).

   b. **Say how you feel.**

      Give an example of an "I feel" statement: "I feel _____ when _____."

   c. **Give a reason for the person to stop.**

      Suggest possible reasons: The student will talk to an adult about the problem or knows the teaser just wants to get someone upset. Emphasize giving the reason in a friendly tone of voice.

3. **Act out your best choice.**

   If one choice doesn't work, the student should try another one.

SUGGESTED MODELING SITUATIONS

► *School:* Someone is poking you or making faces at you in class.

► *Home:* Your brother or sister laughs at you.

► *Peer group:* Someone calls you a name or teases you about the way you look or the clothes you wear.

► *Community:* At the park, an older kid is teasing you about your basketball skills.

COMMENTS

Students may need practice in making appropriate, nonthreatening "I feel" statements.

From *Skillstreaming the Elementary School Child: Teaching Prosocial Skills* (3rd ed.), © 2012 by E. McGinnis, Champaign, IL: Research Press (www.researchpress.com, 800-519-2707).

Skill 38: Responding to Teasing

Name _____ Date _____

SKILL STEPS

1. Stop and count to five.

2. Think about your choices:

   a. Ignore the teasing.

   b. Say how you feel.

   c. Give a reason for the person to stop.

3. Act out your best choice.

FILL IN NOW

With whom will I try this? _____

When? _____

FILL IN AFTER YOU PRACTICE THE SKILL

What happened? _____

_____

_____

How did I do?   ☺   😐   ☹

Why did I circle this? _____

_____

Skillstreaming From *Skillstreaming the Elementary School Child: Teaching Prosocial Skills* (3rd ed.), © 2012 by E. McGinnis, Champaign, IL: Research Press (www.researchpress.com, 800-519-2707).

Skill 38: Responding to Teasing

Name _____ Date _____

SKILL STEPS

1. Stop and count to five.

2. Think about your choices:

   a. Ignore the teasing.

   b. Say how you feel.

   c. Give a reason for the person to stop.

3. Act out your best choice.

When did I practice?   How did I do?

_____   ☺   😐   ☹

_____   ☺   😐   ☹

_____   ☺   😐   ☹

_____   ☺   😐   ☹

From *Skillstreaming the Elementary School Child: Teaching Prosocial Skills* (3rd ed.), © 2012 by E. McGinnis, Champaign, IL: Research Press (www.researchpress.com, 800-519-2707).

Skill 39: Avoiding Trouble

SKILL STEPS

1. **Stop and think about what the consequences of an action might be.**

   With students, create a list of the possible consequences of particular actions.

2. **Decide if you want to stay out of trouble.**

   Discuss how to decide if it is important to avoid these consequences.

3. **Decide what to tell the other person.**

4. **Tell the person.**

   Discuss how to say no in a friendly but firm way.

SUGGESTED MODELING SITUATIONS

► *School:* Another student wants you to help him/her cheat on a test.

► *Home:* Your brother or sister wants you to take money from your parents.

► *Peer group:* A friend wants you to tease another friend.

► *Community:* A friend wants you to steal from the store.

COMMENTS

It is important to teach students to anticipate the consequences of their actions. They may still choose to accept the consequences.

Skillstreaming

From *Skillstreaming the Elementary School Child: Teaching Prosocial Skills* (3rd ed.), © 2012 by E. McGinnis, Champaign, IL: Research Press (www.researchpress.com, 800-519-2707).

Skill 39: Avoiding Trouble

Name _____ Date _____

SKILL STEPS

1. Stop and think about what the consequences of an action might be.

2. Decide if you want to stay out of trouble.

3. Decide what to tell the other person.

4. Tell the person.

FILL IN NOW

With whom will I try this? _____

When? _____

FILL IN AFTER YOU PRACTICE THE SKILL

What happened? _____

_____

_____

How did I do?   ☺   😐   ☹

Why did I circle this? _____

_____

From *Skillstreaming the Elementary School Child: Teaching Prosocial Skills* (3rd ed.), © 2012 by E. McGinnis, Champaign, IL: Research Press (www.researchpress.com, 800-519-2707).

Skill 39: Avoiding Trouble

Name _____ Date _____

SKILL STEPS

1. Stop and think about what the consequences of an action might be.

2. Decide if you want to stay out of trouble.

3. Decide what to tell the other person.

4. Tell the person.

When did I practice?   How did I do?

_____

_____

_____

_____

Skillstreaming From *Skillstreaming the Elementary School Child: Teaching Prosocial Skills* (3rd ed.), © 2012 by E. McGinnis, Champaign, IL: Research Press (www.researchpress.com, 800-519-2707).

Skill 40: Staying Out of Fights

SKILL STEPS

1. **Stop and count to 10.**

   Discuss how this can help the student to calm down.

2. **Decide what the problem is.**

   Discuss the consequences of fighting and whether fighting can solve a problem.

3. **Think about your choices:**

   a. **Walk away for now.**

   Students should ask to leave the area for a few minutes, if needed.

   b. **Talk to the person in a friendly way.**

   Discuss how to "read" the behavior of the other person (i.e., is he/she calm enough to talk with) and evaluate one's own degree of calmness and readiness to talk about the problem. Discuss ways to state the problem inoffensively.

   c. **Ask someone for help in solving the problem.**

   Discuss who can be the most help: teacher, parent, or friend.

4. **Act out your best choice.**

   If one choice doesn't work, the student should try another one.

SUGGESTED MODELING SITUATIONS

► *School:* Someone says that you did poorly on your schoolwork.

► *Home:* Your brother or sister tells your parents that you did something wrong.

► *Peer group:* Someone doesn't play fair in a game or calls you a name.

► *Community:* A neighbor kid says you cheated in a game at the park.

COMMENTS

This skill may not be supported at home or "on the streets." Nevertheless, students need to be taught the importance of handling conflict in a peaceful way.

From *Skillstreaming the Elementary School Child: Teaching Prosocial Skills* (3rd ed.), © 2012 by E. McGinnis, Champaign, IL: Research Press (www.researchpress.com, 800-519-2707).

Skill 40: Staying Out of Fights

Name _____ Date _____

SKILL STEPS

1. Stop and count to 10.

2. Decide what the problem is.

3. Think about your choices:

    a. Walk away for now.

    b. Talk to the person in a friendly way.

    c. Ask someone for help in solving the problem.

4. Act out your best choice.

FILL IN NOW

With whom will I try this? _____

When?_____

FILL IN AFTER YOU PRACTICE THE SKILL

What happened?_____

_____

_____

How did I do?   ☺   😐   ☹

Why did I circle this?_____

_____

Skillstreaming   From *Skillstreaming the Elementary School Child: Teaching Prosocial Skills* (3rd ed.), © 2012 by E. McGinnis, Champaign, IL: Research Press (www.researchpress.com, 800-519-2707).

Skill 40: Staying Out of Fights

Name_____ Date_____

SKILL STEPS

1. Stop and count to 10.

2. Decide what the problem is.

3. Think about your choices:

   a. Walk away for now.

   b. Talk to the person in a friendly way.

   c. Ask someone for help in solving the problem.

4. Act out your best choice.

When did I practice?   How did I do?

	☺	😐	☹
	☺	😐	☹
	☺	😐	☹
	☺	😐	☹

Skillstreaming　From *Skillstreaming the Elementary School Child: Teaching Prosocial Skills* (3rd ed.), © 2012 by E. McGinnis, Champaign, IL: Research Press (www.researchpress.com, 800-519-2707).

Skill 41: Problem Solving

SKILL STEPS

1. **Stop and say, "I have to calm down."**

   Discuss ways to calm down—for example, take three deep breaths, count to 10.

2. **Decide what the problem is.**

   Stress the importance of reflecting on the reason the student is upset.

3. **Think about different ways to solve the problem.**

   List and discuss a variety of alternatives and the consequences of each.

4. **Choose one way.**

   Discuss how to weigh alternatives to pick the best choice.

5. **Do it.**

6. **Ask yourself, "How did this work?"**

   If one alternative doesn't work, the student should try another.

SUGGESTED MODELING SITUATIONS

► *School:* You don't understand an assignment, or you forgot your lunch money.

► *Home:* You broke a window at your house.

► *Peer group:* You lost something you borrowed from a friend.

► *Community:* You can't find your bus ticket to get home from the mall.

COMMENTS

When a problem arises in the classroom, teachers may lead the class in discussing alternative ways to deal with the problem and the possible consequences of each alternative. Students can then choose the best alternative. Using this problem-solving technique when classroom problems arise will promote students' ability to use this skill and teach them when to use it. This is a good prerequisite skill for Accepting Consequences (Skill 42).

.■.Skillstreaming From *Skillstreaming the Elementary School Child: Teaching Prosocial Skills* (3rd ed.), © 2012 by E. McGinnis, Champaign, IL: Research Press (www.researchpress.com, 800-519-2707).

Skill 41: Problem Solving

Name_____ Date _____

SKILL STEPS

1. Stop and say, "I have to calm down."

2. Decide what the problem is.

3. Think about different ways to solve the problem.

4. Choose one way.

5. Do it.

6. Ask yourself, "How did this work?"

FILL IN NOW

With whom will I try this? _____

When?_____

FILL IN AFTER YOU PRACTICE THE SKILL

What happened?_____

_____

_____

How did I do?   ☺   😐   ☹

Why did I circle this?_____

_____

From *Skillstreaming the Elementary School Child: Teaching Prosocial Skills* (3rd ed.), © 2012 by E. McGinnis, Champaign, IL: Research Press (www.researchpress.com, 800-519-2707).

Skill 41: Problem Solving

Name _____ Date _____

SKILL STEPS

1. Stop and say, "I have to calm down."

2. Decide what the problem is.

3. Think about different ways to solve the problem.

4. Choose one way.

5. Do it.

6. Ask yourself, "How did this work?"

When did I practice?   How did I do?

_____   😊   😐   ☹️

_____   😊   😐   ☹️

_____   😊   😐   ☹️

_____   😊   😐   ☹️

Skillstreaming

From *Skillstreaming the Elementary School Child: Teaching Prosocial Skills* (3rd ed.), © 2012 by E. McGinnis, Champaign, IL: Research Press (www.researchpress.com, 800-519-2707).

Skill 42: Accepting Consequences

SKILL STEPS

1. **Decide if you were wrong.**

   Discuss that it is OK to be wrong: Everyone makes mistakes, and it's not the end of the world.

2. **If you were wrong, say to yourself, "I have to accept consequences."**

   Discuss the possible consequences of particular actions.

3. **Say to the person, "Yes, I did _____ (describe what you did)."**

   Discuss how to describe the behavior without making excuses.

4. **Say something else:**

   a. **How will you avoid this the next time?**

      Point out that this should be said in a friendly manner.

   b. **Apologize.**

      Emphasize sincerity.

SUGGESTED MODELING SITUATIONS

▶ *School:* You forgot your homework assignment.

▶ *Home:* Your parents tell you that you can't go to a movie because you didn't do your chores.

▶ *Peer group:* You lost the money your friend asked you to keep for him/her.

▶ *Community:* You were goofing off at the ballgame and were told to leave.

COMMENTS

Because this skill involves some problem solving, it is best to teach Problem Solving (Skill 41) first.

From *Skillstreaming the Elementary School Child: Teaching Prosocial Skills* (3rd ed.), © 2012 by E. McGinnis, Champaign, IL: Research Press (www.researchpress.com, 800-519-2707).

Skill 42: Accepting Consequences

Name _____ Date _____

SKILL STEPS

1. Decide if you were wrong.

2. If you were wrong, say to yourself, "I have to accept consequences."

3. Say to the person, "Yes, I did _____ (describe what you did)."

4. Say something else:

   a. How will you avoid this the next time?

   b. Apologize.

FILL IN NOW

With whom will I try this? _____

When? _____

FILL IN AFTER YOU PRACTICE THE SKILL

What happened? _____

_____

_____

How did I do?   ☺   😐   ☹

Why did I circle this? _____

_____

Skillstreaming

From *Skillstreaming the Elementary School Child: Teaching Prosocial Skills* (3rd ed.), © 2012 by E. McGinnis, Champaign, IL: Research Press (www.researchpress.com, 800-519-2707).

Skill 42: Accepting Consequences

Name_____ Date_____

SKILL STEPS

1. Decide if you were wrong.

2. If you were wrong, say to yourself, "I have to accept consequences."

3. Say to the person, "Yes, I did _____ (describe what you did)."

4. Say something else:

   a. How will you avoid this the next time?

   b. Apologize.

When did I practice?   How did I do?

_____

_____

_____

_____

From *Skillstreaming the Elementary School Child: Teaching Prosocial Skills* (3rd ed.), © 2012 by E. McGinnis, Champaign, IL: Research Press (www.researchpress.com, 800-519-2707).

Skill 43: Dealing with an Accusation

SKILL STEPS

1. **Stop and say, "I have to calm down."**

    Discuss ways to calm down—for example, take three deep breaths, count to 10.

2. **Think about what the person has accused you of.**

3. **Ask yourself, "Is this person right?"**

    If the person is correct, the student can use Accepting Consequences (Skill 42).

4. **Think about your choices:**

    a. **Explain, in a friendly way, that you didn't do it.**

        Discuss the body language and nonverbal communicators that show a friendly attitude.

    b. **Apologize.**

        Emphasize sincerity.

    c. **Offer to make up for what happened.**

        Discuss how to make amends: earning the money to pay for a lost or broken item, giving the person something of your own, or giving back a stolen item.

5. **Act out your best choice.**

    If one choice doesn't work, the student should try another one, but it should be an honest choice.

SUGGESTED MODELING SITUATIONS

► *School:* A teacher has accused you of cheating.

► *Home:* Your parents accuse you of breaking something.

► *Peer group:* A friend accuses you of taking something that isn't yours.

► *Community:* You are accused of breaking something at a store.

COMMENTS

It is helpful to reinforce that everyone makes mistakes at times but that it is important to learn from these mistakes and not continue to make the same ones. Such a discussion may help students admit a mistake when accused.

Skillstreaming

From *Skillstreaming the Elementary School Child: Teaching Prosocial Skills* (3rd ed.), © 2012 by E. McGinnis, Champaign, IL: Research Press (www.researchpress.com, 800-519-2707).

Skill 43: Dealing with an Accusation

Name _____ Date _____

SKILL STEPS

1. Stop and say, "I have to calm down."

2. Think about what the person has accused you of.

3. Ask yourself, "Is this person right?"

4. Think about your choices:

   a. Explain, in a friendly way, that you didn't do it.

   b. Apologize.

   c. Offer to make up for what happened.

5. Act out your best choice.

FILL IN NOW

With whom will I try this? _____

When? _____

FILL IN AFTER YOU PRACTICE THE SKILL

What happened? _____

_____

_____

How did I do?   ☺   😐   ☹

Why did I circle this? _____

_____

Skill 43: Dealing with an Accusation

Name _____ Date _____

SKILL STEPS

1. Stop and say, "I have to calm down."

2. Think about what the person has accused you of.

3. Ask yourself, "Is this person right?"

4. Think about your choices:

   a. Explain, in a friendly way, that you didn't do it.

   b. Apologize.

   c. Offer to make up for what happened.

5. Act out your best choice.

When did I practice?   How did I do?

Skillstreaming

From *Skillstreaming the Elementary School Child: Teaching Prosocial Skills* (3rd ed.), © 2012 by E. McGinnis, Champaign, IL: Research Press (www.researchpress.com, 800-519-2707).

Skill 44: Negotiating

SKILL STEPS

1. **Decide if you and the other person disagree.**

   Discuss signs of disagreement: Is the student getting angry? Is the other person getting angry?

2. **Tell how you feel about the problem.**

   Stress saying this in a friendly way so the other person does not become more angry.

3. **Ask the person how he/she feels about the problem.**

4. **Listen to the answer.**

   Discuss the importance of not interrupting. Remind students to use the skill of Listening (Skill 1).

5. **Suggest or ask for a compromise.**

   Discuss how to decide on something that will satisfy both the student and the other person.

SUGGESTED MODELING SITUATIONS

▶ *School:* Your teacher gives you work you feel you can't do.

▶ *Home:* Your parents want you to babysit, but you need to do your homework.

▶ *Peer group:* Your friend wants to play one game, but you want to play another.

▶ *Community:* You want to go to the ballgame with friends but you don't have a ride.

COMMENTS

This skill may be difficult for children younger than age eight. It is more appropriate for students in third through sixth grades.

Skill 44: Negotiating

Name _____ Date _____

SKILL STEPS

1. Decide if you and the other person disagree.

2. Tell how you feel about the problem.

3. Ask the person how he/she feels about the problem.

4. Listen to the answer.

5. Suggest or ask for a compromise.

FILL IN NOW

With whom will I try this? _____

When? _____

FILL IN AFTER YOU PRACTICE THE SKILL

What happened? _____

_____

_____

How did I do?   ☺   😐   ☹

Why did I circle this? _____

_____

Skillstreaming

From *Skillstreaming the Elementary School Child: Teaching Prosocial Skills* (3rd ed.), © 2012 by E. McGinnis, Champaign, IL: Research Press (www.researchpress.com, 800-519-2707).

Skill 44: Negotiating

Name _____ Date _____

SKILL STEPS

1. Decide if you and the other person disagree.

2. Tell how you feel about the problem.

3. Ask the person how he/she feels about the problem.

4. Listen to the answer.

5. Suggest or ask for a compromise.

When did I practice?   How did I do?

Group V

Skills for Dealing with Stress

Skills 45–60

Skill 45: Dealing with Boredom

SKILL STEPS

1. **Decide if you are feeling bored.**

   Discuss how to recognize signs of boredom (e.g., you don't know what to do or feel jittery inside).

2. **Think of things you like to do.**

   Encourage students to generate and discuss personal lists of acceptable activities.

3. **Decide on one thing to do.**

4. **Do it.**

5. **Say to yourself, "Good for me. I chose something to do."**

   Discuss ways of rewarding yourself.

SUGGESTED MODELING SITUATIONS

▶ *School:* There are no playground games that interest you.

▶ *Home:* It's a Saturday, and no one is around.

▶ *Peer group:* You and your friends can't think of anything to do.

▶ *Community:* You are with friends at the park.

COMMENTS

This skill, similar to Deciding on Something to Do (Skill 12), is geared for use outside the academic learning setting. It is helpful for students to generate lists of acceptable activities they may engage in on the playground, at home, and in the neighborhood. These lists can be included in an individual prosocial skills folder.

Rewarding Yourself (Skill 35) is a part of this skill (Step 5). Self-reinforcement may be necessary until the skill can be reinforced by teachers or parents.

From *Skillstreaming the Elementary School Child: Teaching Prosocial Skills* (3rd ed.), © 2012 by E. McGinnis, Champaign, IL: Research Press (www.researchpress.com, 800-519-2707).

Skill 45: Dealing with Boredom

Name _____ Date _____

SKILL STEPS

1. Decide if you are feeling bored.

2. Think of things you like to do.

3. Decide on one thing to do.

4. Do it.

5. Say to yourself, "Good for me. I chose something to do."

FILL IN NOW

With whom will I try this? _____

When? _____

FILL IN AFTER YOU PRACTICE THE SKILL

What happened? _____

_____

_____

How did I do?   ☺   😐   ☹

Why did I circle this? _____

_____

Skillstreaming From *Skillstreaming the Elementary School Child: Teaching Prosocial Skills* (3rd ed.), © 2012 by E. McGinnis, Champaign, IL: Research Press (www.researchpress.com, 800-519-2707).

Skill 45: Dealing with Boredom

Name _____ Date _____

SKILL STEPS

1. Decide if you are feeling bored.

2. Think of things you like to do.

3. Decide on one thing to do.

4. Do it.

5. Say to yourself, "Good for me. I chose something to do."

When did I practice?   How did I do?

Skill 46: Deciding What Caused a Problem

SKILL STEPS

1. **Decide what the problem is.**

   Discuss how students can recognize a problem: by the way they feel inside, by what someone said to them, or by how someone acted toward them.

2. **Think about what may have caused the problem.**

   Discuss how to evaluate possible causes of a problem: one's own behavior, someone else's behavior, or no one's fault.

3. **Decide what most likely caused the problem.**

   Discuss how to determine the most likely cause.

4. **Check it out.**

   Encourage students to ask someone, either the other person or an impartial judge.

SUGGESTED MODELING SITUATIONS

► *School:* The teacher seems angry with you.

► *Home:* Your parents have an argument, and you think it is about you.

► *Peer group:* You feel angry at a friend but don't know why, or you feel that someone doesn't like you.

► *Community:* Your parents won't let you play with friends at a community event.

COMMENTS

This skill is intended to help students distinguish between the problems that they are responsible for and those due to factors outside their control. This is a good skill for students who have difficulty accepting that their own behavior may have caused or contributed to a problem.

Skillstreaming From *Skillstreaming the Elementary School Child: Teaching Prosocial Skills* (3rd ed.), © 2012 by E. McGinnis, Champaign, IL: Research Press (www.researchpress.com, 800-519-2707).

Skill 46: Deciding What Caused a Problem

Name _____ Date _____

SKILL STEPS

1. Decide what the problem is.

2. Think about what may have caused the problem.

3. Decide what most likely caused the problem.

4. Check it out.

FILL IN NOW

With whom will I try this? _____

When? _____

FILL IN AFTER YOU PRACTICE THE SKILL

What happened? _____

_____

_____

How did I do? 😊 😐 ☹️

Why did I circle this? _____

_____

Skill 46: Deciding What Caused a Problem

Name _____ Date _____

SKILL STEPS

1. Decide what the problem is.

2. Think about what may have caused the problem.

3. Decide what most likely caused the problem.

4. Check it out.

When did I practice?   How did I do?

Skillstreaming

From *Skillstreaming the Elementary School Child: Teaching Prosocial Skills* (3rd ed.), © 2012 by E. McGinnis, Champaign, IL: Research Press (www.researchpress.com, 800-519-2707).

Skill 47: Making a Complaint

SKILL STEPS

1. **Decide what the problem is.**

   Discuss how students can recognize a problem: by the way they feel inside, by what someone said to them, or by how someone acted toward them.

2. **Decide whom to tell.**

   Talking about the problem with the other person is often the best way to begin finding a solution.

3. **Choose a good time and place.**

   Discuss how to choose a good time: when the person isn't involved with something else or when the person is alone.

4. **Tell the person your problem in a friendly way.**

   Tell students to wait until they are no longer angry or upset before talking about the problem. Discuss the body language and nonverbal communicators that show a friendly attitude.

SUGGESTED MODELING SITUATIONS

- *School:* The teacher gives you an assignment that you know how to do, but it seems far too long.
- *Home:* You feel your parents have been unfair because your brother is gone and you have to do his chores, too.
- *Peer group:* A friend usually chooses what the two of you will do.
- *Community:* Some older kids are being loud in the library, and the librarian tells you that you have to leave, too.

COMMENTS

Discuss the importance of stating the facts rather than blaming someone else. Students may also need instruction in distinguishing fact from opinion.

Skill 47: Making a Complaint

Name _____ Date _____

SKILL STEPS

1. Decide what the problem is.

2. Decide whom to tell.

3. Choose a good time and place.

4. Tell the person your problem in a friendly way.

FILL IN NOW

With whom will I try this? _____

When?_____

FILL IN AFTER YOU PRACTICE THE SKILL

What happened?_____

_____

_____

How did I do?   ☺   😐   ☹

Why did I circle this?_____

_____

Skillstreaming

From *Skillstreaming the Elementary School Child: Teaching Prosocial Skills* (3rd ed.), © 2012 by E. McGinnis, Champaign, IL: Research Press (www.researchpress.com, 800-519-2707).

Skill 47: Making a Complaint

Name _____ Date _____

SKILL STEPS

1. Decide what the problem is.

2. Decide whom to tell.

3. Choose a good time and place.

4. Tell the person your problem in a friendly way.

When did I practice?   How did I do?

From *Skillstreaming the Elementary School Child: Teaching Prosocial Skills* (3rd ed.), © 2012 by E. McGinnis, Champaign, IL: Research Press (www.researchpress.com, 800-519-2707).

Skill 48: Answering a Complaint

SKILL STEPS

1. **Listen to the complaint.**

   Discuss proper body language while listening (ways to show that you aren't defensive).

2. **Ask about anything you don't understand.**

   Discuss the body language and nonverbal communicators that show a friendly attitude.

3. **Decide if the complaint is justified.**

4. **Think about your choices:**

   a. **Apologize.**

      Emphasize sincerity.

   b. **Explain your behavior.**

      Even if a student did not intend to cause a problem, his/her behavior still might have caused difficulty. Sometimes giving a reason for acting a certain way will help others understand better. Discuss how to explain that an unjustified complaint is incorrect.

   c. **Suggest what to do now.**

   d. **Correct a mistake.**

5. **Act out your best choice.**

   If one choice doesn't work, the student should try another one.

SUGGESTED MODELING SITUATIONS

▶ *School:* The teacher complains that you are too loud or thinks you were the one who was making noises in class.

▶ *Home:* Your parents complain that you haven't helped at home.

▶ *Peer group:* A friend complains that you were teasing him/her.

▶ *Community:* The manager says you and your friends are too loud at a movie.

COMMENTS

Discuss the difference between making excuses and explaining your behavior.

.Skillstreaming

From *Skillstreaming the Elementary School Child: Teaching Prosocial Skills* (3rd ed.), © 2012 by E. McGinnis, Champaign, IL: Research Press (www.researchpress.com, 800-519-2707).

Skill 48: Answering a Complaint

Name _____ Date _____

SKILL STEPS

1. Listen to the complaint.

2. Ask about anything you don't understand.

3. Decide if the complaint is justified.

4. Think about your choices:

    a. Apologize.

    b. Explain your behavior.

    c. Suggest what to do now.

    d. Correct a mistake.

5. Act out your best choice.

FILL IN NOW

With whom will I try this? _____

When? _____

FILL IN AFTER YOU PRACTICE THE SKILL

What happened? _____

_____

_____

How did I do?   ☺   😐   ☹

Why did I circle this? _____

_____

From *Skillstreaming the Elementary School Child: Teaching Prosocial Skills* (3rd ed.), © 2012 by E. McGinnis, Champaign, IL: Research Press (www.researchpress.com, 800-519-2707).

Skill 48: Answering a Complaint

Name _____ Date _____

SKILL STEPS

1. Listen to the complaint.

2. Ask about anything you don't understand.

3. Decide if the complaint is justified.

4. Think about your choices:

   a. Apologize.

   b. Explain your behavior.

   c. Suggest what to do now.

   d. Correct a mistake.

5. Act out your best choice.

When did I practice?   How did I do?

Skillstreaming

From *Skillstreaming the Elementary School Child: Teaching Prosocial Skills* (3rd ed.), © 2012 by E. McGinnis, Champaign, IL: Research Press (www.researchpress.com, 800-519-2707).

Skill 49: Dealing with Losing

SKILL STEPS

1. **Say to yourself, "Everybody can't win. It's OK that I didn't win this time."**

    Memorizing this statement will help the student control his/her impulses.

2. **Think about your choices:**

    These choices will help the student get involved in another activity and not dwell on losing.

    a. **Ask to help someone.**

        Offer help to a teacher, your parents, or a friend.

    b. **Do an activity you like.**

        Students should generate and discuss personal lists of acceptable activities.

    c. **Do a relaxation exercise.**

        Teach the skill Relaxing (Skill 56).

3. **Act out your best choice.**

    If one choice doesn't work, the student should try another one.

SUGGESTED MODELING SITUATIONS

- ► *School:* You lose a contest or a raffle.
- ► *Home:* You lose at a game with your brother or sister.
- ► *Peer group:* Your team loses at basketball (or some other game).
- ► *Community:* You lose in a neighborhood game at the park.

COMMENTS

This is a good prerequisite skill for Being a Good Sport (Skill 50).

Skill 49: Dealing with Losing

Name _____ Date _____

SKILL STEPS

1. Say to yourself, "Everybody can't win. It's OK that I didn't win this time."

2. Think about your choices:

   a. Ask to help someone.

   b. Do an activity you like.

   c. Do a relaxation exercise.

3. Act out your best choice.

FILL IN NOW

With whom will I try this? _____

When? _____

FILL IN AFTER YOU PRACTICE THE SKILL

What happened? _____

_____

_____

How did I do?   ☺   😐   ☹

Why did I circle this? _____

_____

Skillstreaming

From *Skillstreaming the Elementary School Child: Teaching Prosocial Skills* (3rd ed.), © 2012 by E. McGinnis, Champaign, IL: Research Press (www.researchpress.com, 800-519-2707).

Skill 49: Dealing with Losing

Name _____ Date _____

SKILL STEPS

1. Say to yourself, "Everybody can't win. It's OK that I didn't win this time."

2. Think about your choices:

   a. Ask to help someone.

   b. Do an activity you like.

   c. Do a relaxation exercise.

3. Act out your best choice.

When did I practice?   How did I do?

From *Skillstreaming the Elementary School Child: Teaching Prosocial Skills* (3rd ed.), © 2012 by E. McGinnis, Champaign, IL: Research Press (www.researchpress.com, 800-519-2707).

Skill 50: Being a Good Sport

SKILL STEPS

1. **Decide how you and the other person played the game.**

   Discuss evaluating your own and an opponent's performance (e.g., level of skill or effort).

2. **Think of what you can honestly tell the other person:**

   Emphasize sincerity. Discuss the body language and nonverbal communicators that show a friendly, sincere attitude.

   a. **"Congratulations."**

   The student may also want to shake the person's hand.

   b. **"You played a good game."**

   c. **"You're getting a lot better at this game."**

   This is a way of encouraging another person. Students may want to comment on one thing the other person did particularly well.

3. **Act out your best choice.**

4. **Help the other person put equipment or materials away.**

SUGGESTED MODELING SITUATIONS

▶ *School:* Your team loses at a group game during recess, or your team wins.

▶ *Home:* You lose at a game with your brother or sister, or you win.

▶ *Peer group:* You lose at a game with a friend, or you win.

▶ *Community:* You win a prize at the carnival, or you don't win.

COMMENTS

Students should learn the skill Dealing with Losing (Skill 49) before learning the present skill.

Skillstreaming From *Skillstreaming the Elementary School Child: Teaching Prosocial Skills* (3rd ed.), © 2012 by E. McGinnis, Champaign, IL: Research Press (www.researchpress.com, 800-519-2707).

Skill 50: Being a Good Sport

Name_____ Date_____

SKILL STEPS

1. Decide how you and the other person played the game.

2. Think of what you can honestly tell the other person:

    a. "Congratulations."

    b. "You played a good game."

    c. "You're getting a lot better at this game."

3. Act out your best choice.

4. Help the other person put equipment or materials away.

FILL IN NOW

With whom will I try this?_____

When?_____

FILL IN AFTER YOU PRACTICE THE SKILL

What happened?_____

_____

_____

How did I do?

☺   😐   ☹

Why did I circle this?_____

_____

From *Skillstreaming the Elementary School Child: Teaching Prosocial Skills* (3rd ed.), © 2012 by E. McGinnis, Champaign, IL: Research Press (www.researchpress.com, 800-519-2707).

Skill 50: Being a Good Sport

Name _____ Date _____

SKILL STEPS

1. Decide how you and the other person played the game.

2. Think of what you can honestly tell the other person:

    a. "Congratulations."

    b. "You played a good game."

    c. "You're getting a lot better at this game."

3. Act out your best choice.

4. Help the other person put equipment or materials away.

When did I practice?   How did I do?

_____   ☺   😐   ☹

_____   ☺   😐   ☹

_____   ☺   😐   ☹

_____   ☺   😐   ☹

Skillstreaming   From *Skillstreaming the Elementary School Child: Teaching Prosocial Skills* (3rd ed.), © 2012 by E. McGinnis, Champaign, IL: Research Press (www.researchpress.com, 800-519-2707).

Skill 51: Dealing with Being Left Out

SKILL STEPS

1. **Decide what has happened to cause you to feel left out.**

   Discuss possible reasons a student may be ignored by peers.

2. **Think about your choices:**

   a. **Ask to join in.**

      Teach the skill Joining In (Skill 17).

   b. **Choose someone else with whom to play.**

      Choose someone who may also be feeling left out or someone who is not with the group.

   c. **Do an activity you enjoy.**

      Students should generate and discuss personal lists of acceptable activities.

3. **Act out your best choice.**

   If one choice doesn't work, the student should try another one.

SUGGESTED MODELING SITUATIONS

▶ *School:* You are left out of a group game at recess.

▶ *Home:* Your brother or sister is leaving you out of an activity with his or her friends.

▶ *Peer group:* A group of friends are going to a movie or a birthday party, but you weren't invited.

▶ *Community:* You want to play basketball with older kids at the park, but they won't include you.

COMMENTS

It is important to discuss the types of feelings that might result from being left out (feeling angry, hurt, or frustrated). Emphasize that it is better to deal with being left out by using the skill steps than to continue to feel angry or hurt.

Skill 51: Dealing with Being Left Out

Name _____ Date _____

SKILL STEPS

1. Decide what has happened to cause you to feel left out.

2. Think about your choices:

   a. Ask to join in.

   b. Choose someone else with whom to play.

   c. Do an activity you enjoy.

3. Act out your best choice.

FILL IN NOW

With whom will I try this? _____

When?_____

FILL IN AFTER YOU PRACTICE THE SKILL

What happened?_____

_____

_____

How did I do?   ☺   😐   ☹

Why did I circle this?_____

_____

Skillstreaming From *Skillstreaming the Elementary School Child: Teaching Prosocial Skills* (3rd ed.), © 2012 by E. McGinnis, Champaign, IL: Research Press (www.researchpress.com, 800-519-2707).

Skill 51: Dealing with Being Left Out

Name_____ Date _____

SKILL STEPS

1. Decide what has happened to cause you to feel left out.

2. Think about your choices:

   a. Ask to join in.

   b. Choose someone else with whom to play.

   c. Do an activity you enjoy.

3. Act out your best choice.

When did I practice?   How did I do?

When did I practice?	🙂	😐	☹️
	🙂	😐	☹️
	🙂	😐	☹️
	🙂	😐	☹️

From *Skillstreaming the Elementary School Child: Teaching Prosocial Skills* (3rd ed.), © 2012 by E. McGinnis, Champaign, IL: Research Press (www.researchpress.com, 800-519-2707).

Skill 52: Dealing with Embarrassment

SKILL STEPS

1. **Decide what happened to cause you to feel embarrassed.**

   Discuss how students can recognize signs of embarrassment (e.g., your face is flushed).

2. **Think of what you can do to feel less embarrassed:**

   Discuss the possible consequences of each choice.

   a. **Ignore it.**

   b. **Decide what to do next time.**

   c. **Say to yourself, "It's over. People will forget it."**

3. **Act out your best choice.**

   If one choice doesn't work, the student should try another one.

SUGGESTED MODELING SITUATIONS

- ▶ *School:* You give the wrong answer to a question in class.
- ▶ *Home:* You drop and break something belonging to your parents.
- ▶ *Peer group:* You fall down on the playground or make some mistake when playing a game.
- ▶ *Community:* You spill your food at a restaurant.

COMMENTS

It is important to let students know that everyone feels embarrassed at some time. Discussing when students (and group leaders!) are most likely to be embarrassed may lessen the intensity of real-life embarrassment.

Prior to teaching this skill, it is helpful to review Knowing Your Feelings (Skill 26).

Skillstreaming

From *Skillstreaming the Elementary School Child: Teaching Prosocial Skills* (3rd ed.), © 2012 by E. McGinnis, Champaign, IL: Research Press (www.researchpress.com, 800-519-2707).

Skill 52: Dealing with Embarrassment

Name _____ Date _____

SKILL STEPS

1. Decide what happened to cause you to feel embarrassed.

2. Think of what you can do to feel less embarrassed:

    a. Ignore it.

    b. Decide what to do next time.

    c. Say to yourself, "It's over. People will forget it."

3. Act out your best choice.

FILL IN NOW

With whom will I try this? _____

When? _____

FILL IN AFTER YOU PRACTICE THE SKILL

What happened? _____

_____

_____

How did I do?

Why did I circle this? _____

_____

From *Skillstreaming the Elementary School Child: Teaching Prosocial Skills* (3rd ed.), © 2012 by E. McGinnis, Champaign, IL: Research Press (www.researchpress.com, 800-519-2707).

Skill 52: Dealing with Embarrassment

Name _____ Date _____

SKILL STEPS

1. Decide what happened to cause you to feel embarrassed.

2. Think of what you can do to feel less embarrassed:

   a. Ignore it.

   b. Decide what to do next time.

   c. Say to yourself, "It's over. People will forget it."

3. Act out your best choice.

When did I practice?	How did I do?		
	☺	😐	☹
	☺	😐	☹
	☺	😐	☹
	☺	😐	☹

Skillstreaming

From *Skillstreaming the Elementary School Child: Teaching Prosocial Skills* (3rd ed.), © 2012 by E. McGinnis, Champaign, IL: Research Press (www.researchpress.com, 800-519-2707).

Skill 53: Reacting to Failure

SKILL STEPS

1. **Decide if you have failed.**

   Discuss the difference between failing and not doing as well as hoped.

2. **Think about why you failed.**

   Discuss reasons for failure: You didn't try as hard as you could have or weren't ready; it was a matter of chance.

3. **Think about what you could do next time.**

   Suggest practicing more, trying harder, or asking for help.

4. **Make your plan to do this.**

   This plan may be in written form, such as a contingency contract.

SUGGESTED MODELING SITUATIONS

- ► *School:* You failed a test.
- ► *Home:* You failed to complete your chores, so you couldn't do what you had planned.
- ► *Peer group:* You failed to get someone to join in the activity you wanted to do.
- ► *Community:* You didn't do well when you tried to help a neighbor.

COMMENTS

It is useful to discuss with students that human beings are not perfect and that everyone fails at something sometimes. Rather than dwell on the failure, it is more useful to think of ways to do better the next time.

From *Skillstreaming the Elementary School Child: Teaching Prosocial Skills* (3rd ed.), © 2012 by E. McGinnis, Champaign, IL: Research Press (www.researchpress.com, 800-519-2707).

Skill 53: Reacting to Failure

Name _____ Date _____

SKILL STEPS

1. Decide if you have failed.

2. Think about why you failed.

3. Think about what you could do next time.

4. Make your plan to do this.

FILL IN NOW

With whom will I try this? _____

When? _____

FILL IN AFTER YOU PRACTICE THE SKILL

What happened? _____

_____

_____

How did I do?　　　　　　　　　　　　☺　　　😐　　　☹

Why did I circle this? _____

_____

Skillstreaming

From *Skillstreaming the Elementary School Child: Teaching Prosocial Skills* (3rd ed.), © 2012 by E. McGinnis, Champaign, IL: Research Press (www.researchpress.com, 800-519-2707).

Skill 53: Reacting to Failure

Name _____ Date _____

SKILL STEPS

1. Decide if you have failed.

2. Think about why you failed.

3. Think about what you could do next time.

4. Make your plan to do this.

When did I practice?   How did I do?

☺   😐   ☹

_____

☺   😐   ☹

_____

☺   😐   ☹

_____

☺   😐   ☹

_____

Skillstreaming   From *Skillstreaming the Elementary School Child: Teaching Prosocial Skills* (3rd ed.), © 2012   **285**
by E. McGinnis, Champaign, IL: Research Press (www.researchpress.com, 800-519-2707).

Skill 54: Accepting No

SKILL STEPS

1. **Decide why you were told no.**

   Discuss the possible reasons for being told no in a particular situation.

2. **Think about your choices:**

   Discuss the possible consequences of each choice.

   a. **Do something else.**

   Students should generate and discuss personal lists of acceptable activities.

   b. **Say how you feel in a friendly way.**

   c. **Write about how you feel.**

   Practice "I feel" statements with students. Discuss the body language and nonverbal communicators that show a friendly attitude.

3. **Act out your best choice.**

   If one choice doesn't work, the student should try another one.

SUGGESTED MODELING SITUATIONS

► *School:* The teacher says that you can't do an activity.

► *Home:* Your parents say that you can't stay up late.

► *Peer group:* A friend tells you he/she won't come over to your house.

► *Community:* The store manager tells you you'll have to wait to come in the store because there are already too many kids.

COMMENTS

Writing about how you feel may not be appropriate for the child who does not have adequate writing skills or who is particularly frustrated with the writing process. Ask these students to generate other choices.

Skillstreaming

From *Skillstreaming the Elementary School Child: Teaching Prosocial Skills* (3rd ed.), © 2012 by E. McGinnis, Champaign, IL: Research Press (www.researchpress.com, 800-519-2707).

Skill 54: Accepting No

Name _____ Date _____

SKILL STEPS

1. Decide why you were told no.

2. Think about your choices:

    a. Do something else.

    b. Say how you feel in a friendly way.

    c. Write about how you feel.

3. Act out your best choice.

FILL IN NOW

With whom will I try this? _____

When? _____

FILL IN AFTER YOU PRACTICE THE SKILL

What happened? _____

_____

_____

How did I do?   ☺   😐   ☹

Why did I circle this? _____

_____

From *Skillstreaming the Elementary School Child: Teaching Prosocial Skills* (3rd ed.), © 2012 by E. McGinnis, Champaign, IL: Research Press (www.researchpress.com, 800-519-2707).

Skill 54: Accepting No

Name _____ Date _____

SKILL STEPS

1. Decide why you were told no.

2. Think about your choices:

   a. Do something else.

   b. Say how you feel in a friendly way.

   c. Write about how you feel.

3. Act out your best choice.

When did I practice?   How did I do?

☺	😐	☹
☺	😐	☹
☺	😐	☹
☺	😐	☹

Skillstreaming

From *Skillstreaming the Elementary School Child: Teaching Prosocial Skills* (3rd ed.), © 2012 by E. McGinnis, Champaign, IL: Research Press (www.researchpress.com, 800-519-2707).

Skill 55: Saying No

SKILL STEPS

1. **Decide whether or not you want to do what is being asked.**

   Discuss when and with whom saying no is appropriate.

2. **Think about why you don't want to do this.**

   Discuss reasons for saying no: You may get into trouble, or you may have something else you want to do.

3. **Tell the person no in a friendly way.**

   Students should practice saying no in a friendly but firm manner, paying attention to body language and nonverbal communicators.

4. **Give your reason.**

   Giving a reason may help the other person understand better.

SUGGESTED MODELING SITUATIONS

► *School:* A friend wants you to skip school.

► *Home:* Your brother or sister wants you to play a game, but you want to watch your favorite TV program.

► *Peer group:* A friend wants you to play when you have work to do, or he/she wants you to come over after school, but you'd rather play basketball.

► *Community:* A friend wants you to take a DVD from the library.

COMMENTS

Students need practice role-playing this skill with a variety of individuals assuming a variety of different roles. It should be emphasized that saying no to an adult who asks you to do something wrong or uncomfortable is very different from saying no to a parent who asks you to pick up your room or to a teacher who asks you to stop talking in class.

From *Skillstreaming the Elementary School Child: Teaching Prosocial Skills* (3rd ed.), © 2012 by E. McGinnis, Champaign, IL: Research Press (www.researchpress.com, 800-519-2707).

Skill 55: Saying No

Name _____ Date _____

SKILL STEPS

1. Decide whether or not you want to do what is being asked.

2. Think about why you don't want to do this.

3. Tell the person no in a friendly way.

4. Give your reason.

FILL IN NOW

With whom will I try this? _____

When? _____

FILL IN AFTER YOU PRACTICE THE SKILL

What happened? _____

_____

_____

How did I do?   ☺   😐   ☹

Why did I circle this? _____

_____

Skillstreaming

From *Skillstreaming the Elementary School Child: Teaching Prosocial Skills* (3rd ed.), © 2012 by E. McGinnis, Champaign, IL: Research Press (www.researchpress.com, 800-519-2707).

Skill 55: Saying No

Name_____ Date_____

SKILL STEPS

1. Decide whether or not you want to do what is being asked.

2. Think about why you don't want to do this.

3. Tell the person no in a friendly way.

4. Give your reason.

When did I practice?   How did I do?

Skill 56: Relaxing

SKILL STEPS

1. **Decide if you need to relax.**

   Discuss how to recognize bodily cues of tension (e.g., feeling tense, jittery, or queasy).

2. **Take three slow, deep breaths.**

   Teach students to breathe in through their noses and out through their mouths.

3. **Tighten one part of your body, count to three, and relax.**

   Instruct students about which parts of their bodies to tighten and then relax (jaw, shoulders, hands, stomach, legs, feet).

4. **Continue this for each part of your body.**

   Students will need to practice Step 3 before they can do this independently.

5. **Ask yourself how you feel.**

   Discuss how students feel physically before and after tightening muscles.

SUGGESTED MODELING SITUATIONS

- ► *School:* You feel nervous before a test.
- ► *Home:* Your grandparents are coming, and you're excited.
- ► *Peer group:* You are angry or upset with a friend, but you don't know why.
- ► *Community:* You're getting ready for a game against a top ranked team.

COMMENTS

Students may need a great deal of training in relaxation before they will be able to use this skill effectively.

.Skillstreaming

From *Skillstreaming the Elementary School Child: Teaching Prosocial Skills* (3rd ed.), © 2012 by E. McGinnis, Champaign, IL: Research Press (www.researchpress.com, 800-519-2707).

Skill 56: Relaxing

Name _____ Date _____

SKILL STEPS

1. Decide if you need to relax.

2. Take three slow, deep breaths.

3. Tighten one part of your body, count to three, and relax.

4. Continue this for each part of your body.

5. Ask yourself how you feel.

FILL IN NOW

With whom will I try this? _____

When? _____

FILL IN AFTER YOU PRACTICE THE SKILL

What happened? _____

_____

_____

How did I do?   ☺   😐   ☹

Why did I circle this? _____

_____

From *Skillstreaming the Elementary School Child: Teaching Prosocial Skills* (3rd ed.), © 2012 by E. McGinnis, Champaign, IL: Research Press (www.researchpress.com, 800-519-2707).

Skill 56: Relaxing

Name _____ Date _____

SKILL STEPS

1. Decide if you need to relax.

2. Take three slow, deep breaths.

3. Tighten one part of your body, count to three, and relax.

4. Continue this for each part of your body.

5. Ask yourself how you feel.

When did I practice?   How did I do?

_____   ☺   😐   ☹

_____   ☺   😐   ☹

_____   ☺   😐   ☹

_____   ☺   😐   ☹

Skillstreaming
From *Skillstreaming the Elementary School Child: Teaching Prosocial Skills* (3rd ed.), © 2012 by E. McGinnis, Champaign, IL: Research Press (www.researchpress.com, 800-519-2707).

Skill 57: Dealing with Group Pressure

SKILL STEPS

1. **Listen to what others want you to do.**

   Discuss possible reasons why the group may want someone to participate in particular actions.

2. **Think about what might happen.**

   Discuss possible consequences of particular actions: Someone may be hurt, or you may get into trouble.

3. **Decide what you want to do.**

   Discuss how difficult it is to resist pressure from a group of friends.

4. **If you decide not to go along with the group, say to them, "No, I can't because _____ (give the reason)."**

   Discuss how giving a reason for not going along may help the group to think about what they want to do.

5. **Suggest something else to do.**

   Help students generate and discuss a list of acceptable group activities.

SUGGESTED MODELING SITUATION

▶ *Peer group:* The group is teasing someone or planning on taking something that belongs to someone else, and they want you to go along with them.

COMMENTS

Students need to be aware that this is a difficult, but necessary, skill to master. This skill should be role-played in a variety of situations and reviewed periodically throughout Skillstreaming instruction.

Skill 57: Dealing with Group Pressure

Name _____ Date _____

SKILL SKILL STEPS

1. Listen to what others want you to do.

2. Think about what might happen.

3. Decide what you want to do.

4. If you decide not to go along with the group, say to them, "No, I can't because _____ (give the reason)."

5. Suggest something else to do.

FILL IN NOW

With whom will I try this? _____

When?_____

FILL IN AFTER YOU PRACTICE THE SKILL

What happened?_____

_____

_____

How did I do? ☺ 😐 ☹

Why did I circle this?_____

_____

Skillstreaming

From *Skillstreaming the Elementary School Child: Teaching Prosocial Skills* (3rd ed.), © 2012 by E. McGinnis, Champaign, IL: Research Press (www.researchpress.com, 800-519-2707).

Skill 57: Dealing with Group Pressure

Name _____ Date _____

SKILL SKILL STEPS

1. Listen to what others want you to do.

2. Think about what might happen.

3. Decide what you want to do.

4. If you decide not to go along with the group, say to them, "No, I can't because _____ (give the reason)."

5. Suggest something else to do.

When did I practice?   How did I do?

Skill 58: Dealing with Wanting Something That Isn't Yours

SKILL STEPS

1. **Say to yourself, "I want this, but I can't just take it."**

   Discuss how hard it may be to want something and not take it.

2. **Say, "It belongs to _____."**

   Discuss how the other person might feel if the item were gone.

3. **Think about your choices:**

   Discuss other alternatives, depending on the situation.

   a. **I could ask to borrow it.**

   b. **I could earn the money to buy it.**

   c. **I could ask the person to trade.**

   d. **I could do something else I like to do.**

      Help students generate and discuss personal lists of acceptable activities.

4. **Act out your best choice.**

   If temptation continues after the student tries one choice, he/she should try another one.

5. **Say, "Good for me. I didn't take it!"**

   Discuss ways of rewarding yourself.

SUGGESTED MODELING SITUATIONS

▶ *School:* You see a notebook you'd really like to have.

▶ *Home:* Your parents left money on the table.

▶ *Peer group:* A friend has a game you would like to have, or you see candy in the pocket of a coat hanging in a locker.

▶ *Community:* You really want the video game you see in the store.

COMMENTS

Self-reinforcement (Step 5) will be critical for many children. Because observers may not know that the student actually wanted to take something but succeeded in exerting self-control, outside reinforcement is unlikely.

From *Skillstreaming the Elementary School Child: Teaching Prosocial Skills* (3rd ed.), © 2012 by E. McGinnis, Champaign, IL: Research Press (www.researchpress.com, 800-519-2707).

Skill 58: Dealing with Wanting Something That Isn't Yours

Name_____ Date_____

SKILL STEPS

1. Say to yourself, "I want this, but I can't just take it."

2. Say, "It belongs to _____."

3. Think about your choices:

    a. I could ask to borrow it.

    b. I could earn the money to buy it.

    c. I could ask the person to trade.

    d. I could do something else I like to do.

4. Act out your best choice.

5. Say, "Good for me. I didn't take it!"

FILL IN NOW

With whom will I try this? _____

When?_____

FILL IN AFTER YOU PRACTICE THE SKILL

What happened?_____

_____

_____

How did I do?   ☺   😐   ☹

Why did I circle this?_____

_____

From *Skillstreaming the Elementary School Child: Teaching Prosocial Skills* (3rd ed.), © 2012 by E. McGinnis, Champaign, IL: Research Press (www.researchpress.com, 800-519-2707).

Skill 58: Dealing with Wanting Something That Isn't Yours

Name _____ Date _____

SKILL STEPS

1. Say to yourself, "I want this, but I can't just take it."

2. Say, "It belongs to _____."

3. Think about your choices:

    a. I could ask to borrow it.

    b. I could earn the money to buy it.

    c. I could ask the person to trade.

    d. I could do something else I like to do.

4. Act out your best choice.

5. Say, "Good for me. I didn't take it!"

When did I practice?   How did I do?

Skillstreaming From *Skillstreaming the Elementary School Child: Teaching Prosocial Skills* (3rd ed.), © 2012 by E. McGinnis, Champaign, IL: Research Press (www.researchpress.com, 800-519-2707).

Skill 59: Making a Decision

SKILL STEPS

1. **Think about the problem.**

   Discuss how students may want two conflicting things.

2. **Decide on your choices.**

   Have students make a list of alternatives.

3. **Think of the possible consequences of each choice.**

   Have students make a list of the consequences for each alternative, then discuss.

4. **Make the best choice.**

   Discuss how to evaluate competing alternatives to make the best choice.

SUGGESTED MODELING SITUATIONS

- ▶ *School:* Decide what group to play with.
- ▶ *Home:* Decide how to spend your money.
- ▶ *Peer group:* Decide whether to go to a movie or stay home and study for a test.
- ▶ *Community:* Decide whether to go along with a group to damage a car.

COMMENTS

Instruction should include generating alternatives and anticipating both short-term and long-term consequences.

Skill 59: Making a Decision

Name _____ Date _____

SKILL STEPS

1. Think about the problem.

2. Decide on your choices.

3. Think of the possible consequences of each choice.

4. Make the best choice.

FILL IN NOW

With whom will I try this? _____

When?_____

FILL IN AFTER YOU PRACTICE THE SKILL

What happened?_____

_____

_____

How did I do?

Why did I circle this?_____

_____

Skillstreaming From *Skillstreaming the Elementary School Child: Teaching Prosocial Skills* (3rd ed.), © 2012 by E. McGinnis, Champaign, IL: Research Press (www.researchpress.com, 800-519-2707).

Skill 59: Making a Decision

Name _____ Date _____

SKILL STEPS

1. Think about the problem.

2. Decide on your choices.

3. Think of the possible consequences of each choice.

4. Make the best choice.

When did I practice?   How did I do?

_____   ☺   😐   ☹

_____   ☺   😐   ☹

_____   ☺   😐   ☹

_____   ☺   😐   ☹

From *Skillstreaming the Elementary School Child: Teaching Prosocial Skills* (3rd ed.), © 2012 by E. McGinnis, Champaign, IL: Research Press (www.researchpress.com, 800-519-2707).   **303**

Skill 60: Being Honest

SKILL STEPS

1. **Decide what might happen if you are honest.**

   Discuss impoliteness versus honesty: Students should not be honest just to hurt someone, such as saying that they don't like a person's clothes. Also discuss how others may respect or trust the student more in the future if he/she is honest now.

2. **Decide what might happen if you aren't honest.**

   Discuss how punishing consequences are usually less severe if a person is honest in the beginning.

3. **Think of how to say what you have to say.**

   Give examples: "I'm sorry, but I did _____"; "Yes, I did it, but I didn't mean to."

4. **Say it.**

   Emphasize sincerity.

5. **Say to yourself, "Good for me. I told the truth."**

   Discuss ways of rewarding yourself.

SUGGESTED MODELING SITUATIONS

► *School:* You tore up your homework assignment or lost your reading book.

► *Home:* You broke a window, or you were throwing a basketball in the house and broke a picture hanging on the wall.

► *Peer group:* You borrowed someone's bike without asking permission.

► *Community:* You took a candy bar from the store and were caught.

COMMENTS

Rewarding Yourself (Skill 35) is a part of this skill (Step 5). Self-reinforcement may be necessary until the skill can be reinforced by teachers or parents.

Skillstreaming

From *Skillstreaming the Elementary School Child: Teaching Prosocial Skills* (3rd ed.), © 2012 by E. McGinnis, Champaign, IL: Research Press (www.researchpress.com, 800-519-2707).

Skill 60: Being Honest

Name_____ Date_____

SKILL STEPS

1. Decide what might happen if you are honest.

2. Decide what might happen if you aren't honest.

3. Think of how to say what you have to say.

4. Say it.

5. Say to yourself, "Good for me. I told the truth."

FILL IN NOW

With whom will I try this? _____

When?_____

FILL IN AFTER YOU PRACTICE THE SKILL

What happened?_____

_____

_____

How did I do? ☺ 😐 ☹

Why did I circle this?_____

_____

Skill 60: Being Honest

Name _____ Date _____

SKILL STEPS

1. Decide what might happen if you are honest.

2. Decide what might happen if you aren't honest.

3. Think of how to say what you have to say.

4. Say it.

5. Say to yourself, "Good for me. I told the truth."

When did I practice?   How did I do?

_____	☺	😐	☹
_____	☺	😐	☹
_____	☺	😐	☹
_____	☺	😐	☹

Skillstreaming

From *Skillstreaming the Elementary School Child: Teaching Prosocial Skills* (3rd ed.), © 2012 by E. McGinnis, Champaign, IL: Research Press (www.researchpress.com, 800-519-2707).

Program Forms

Parent Materials

TEACHER/STAFF CHECKLIST

Student _____ Class/age _____

Teacher/staff _____ Date _____

INSTRUCTIONS: Listed below are a number of skills that children are more or less proficient in using. This checklist will help you evaluate how well each child uses the various skills. For each child, rate his/her use of each skill, based on your observations of his/her behavior in various situations.

Circle 1 if the child is *almost never* good at using the skill.
Circle 2 if the child is *seldom* good at using the skill.
Circle 3 if the child is *sometimes* good at using the skill.
Circle 4 if the child is *often* good at using the skill.
Circle 5 if the child is *almost always* good at using the skill.

Please rate the child on all skills listed. If you know of a situation in which the child has particular difficulty using the skill well, please note it briefly in the space marked "Problem situation."

	almost never	seldom	sometimes	often	almost always

1. **Listening:** Does the student appear to listen when someone is speaking and make an effort to understand what is said?   1 2 3 4 5

   Problem situation:

2. **Asking for Help:** Does the student decide when he/she needs assistance and ask for this help in a pleasant manner?   1 2 3 4 5

   Problem situation:

3. **Saying Thank You:** Does the student tell others he/she appreciates help given, favors, and so forth?   1 2 3 4 5

   Problem situation:

4. **Bringing Materials to Class:** Does the student remember the books and materials he/she needs for class?   1 2 3 4 5

   Problem situation:

5. **Following Instructions:** Does the student understand instructions and follow them?   1 2 3 4 5

   Problem situation:

 From *Skillstreaming the Elementary School Child: Teaching Prosocial Skills* (3rd ed.), © 2012 by E. McGinnis, Champaign, IL: Research Press (www.researchpress.com, 800-519-2707).   **309**

6. **Completing Assignments:** Does the student complete assignments at his/her independent academic level?

    1   2   3   4   5

   Problem situation:

7. **Contributing to Discussions:** Does the student participate in class discussions in accordance with classroom rules?

    1   2   3   4   5

   Problem situation:

8. **Offering Help to an Adult:** Does the student offer to help you at appropriate times and in an appropriate manner?

    1   2   3   4   5

   Problem situation:

9. **Asking a Question:** Does the student know how and when to ask a question of another person?

    1   2   3   4   5

   Problem situation:

10. **Ignoring Distractions:** Does the student ignore classroom distractions?

    1   2   3   4   5

   Problem situation:

11. **Making Corrections:** Does the student make the necessary corrections on assignments without getting overly frustrated?

    1   2   3   4   5

   Problem situation:

12. **Deciding on Something to Do:** Does the student find something to do when he/she has free time?

    1   2   3   4   5

   Problem situation:

13. **Setting a Goal:** Does the student set realistic goals for himself/herself and take the necessary steps to meet these goals?

    1   2   3   4   5

   Problem situation:

14. **Introducing Yourself:** Does the student introduce himself/herself in an appropriate way to people he/she doesn't know?

          1   2   3   4   5

Problem situation:

15. **Beginning a Conversation:** Does the student know how and when to begin a conversation with another person?

          1   2   3   4   5

Problem situation:

16. **Ending a Conversation:** Does the student end a conversation when it is necessary and in an appropriate manner?

          1   2   3   4   5

Problem situation:

17. **Joining In:** Does the student know and practice acceptable ways of joining an ongoing activity or group?

          1   2   3   4   5

Problem situation:

18. **Playing a Game:** Does the student play games with classmates fairly?

          1   2   3   4   5

Problem situation:

19. **Asking a Favor:** Does the student know how to ask a favor of another person?

          1   2   3   4   5

Problem situation:

20. **Offering Help to a Classmate:** Can the student recognize when someone needs or wants assistance and offer this help?

          1   2   3   4   5

Problem situation:

21. **Giving a Compliment:** Does the student tell others that he/she likes something about them or something they have done?

          1   2   3   4   5

Problem situation:

22. **Accepting a Compliment:** Does the student accept these comments given by adults or his/her peers in a friendly way?
    1   2   3   4   5

Problem situation:

23. **Suggesting an Activity:** Does the student suggest appropriate activities to others?
    1   2   3   4   5

Problem situation:

24. **Sharing:** Is the student agreeable to sharing things with others and, if not, does he/she offer acceptable reasons for not sharing?
    1   2   3   4   5

Problem situation:

25. **Apologizing:** Does the student tell others sincerely that he/she is sorry for doing something?
    1   2   3   4   5

Problem situation:

26. **Knowing Your Feelings:** Does the student identify feelings he/she is experiencing?
    1   2   3   4   5

Problem situation:

27. **Expressing Your Feelings:** Does the student express his/her feelings in acceptable ways?
    1   2   3   4   5

Problem situation:

28. **Recognizing Another's Feelings:** Does the student try to figure out in acceptable ways how others are feeling?
    1   2   3   4   5

Problem situation:

29. **Showing Understanding of Another's Feelings:** Does the student show understanding of others' feelings in acceptable ways?
    1   2   3   4   5

Problem situation:

30. **Expressing Concern for Another:** Does the student express concern for others in acceptable ways?

    Problem situation:

<table>
<tr><td>almost never</td><td>seldom</td><td>sometimes</td><td>often</td><td>almost always</td></tr>
<tr><td>1</td><td>2</td><td>3</td><td>4</td><td>5</td></tr>
</table>

31. **Dealing with Your Anger:** Does the student use acceptable ways to express his/her anger?

    Problem situation:

1   2   3   4   5

32. **Dealing with Another's Anger:** Does the student try to understand another's anger without getting angry himself/herself?

    Problem situation:

1   2   3   4   5

33. **Expressing Affection:** Does the student let others know in acceptable ways that he/she cares about them?

    Problem situation:

1   2   3   4   5

34. **Dealing with Fear:** Does the student know why he/she is afraid and practice strategies to reduce this fear?

    Problem situation:

1   2   3   4   5

35. **Rewarding Yourself:** Does the student say and do nice things for himself/herself when a reward is deserved?

    Problem situation:

1   2   3   4   5

36. **Using Self-Control:** Does the student know and practice strategies to control his/her temper or excitement?

    Problem situation:

1   2   3   4   5

37. **Asking Permission:** Does the student know when and how to ask whether he/she may do something?

    Problem situation:

1   2   3   4   5

38. **Responding to Teasing:** Does the student deal with being teased in ways that allow him/her to remain in control?

     1   2   3   4   5

   Problem situation:

39. **Avoiding Trouble:** Does the student stay away from situations that may get him/her into trouble?

     1   2   3   4   5

   Problem situation:

40. **Staying Out of Fights:** Does the student know of and practice socially appropriate ways of handling potential fights?

     1   2   3   4   5

   Problem situation:

41. **Problem Solving:** When a problem occurs, does the student think of alternatives, choose an alternative, then evaluate how well this solved the problem?

     1   2   3   4   5

   Problem situation:

42. **Accepting Consequences:** Does the student accept the consequences for his/her behavior without becoming defensive or upset?

     1   2   3   4   5

   Problem situation:

43. **Dealing with an Accusation:** Does the student know of and practice ways to deal with being accused of something?

     1   2   3   4   5

   Problem situation:

44. **Negotiating:** Is the student willing to give and take in order to reach a compromise?

     1   2   3   4   5

   Problem situation:

45. **Dealing with Boredom:** Does the student select acceptable activities when he/she is bored?

     1   2   3   4   5

   Problem situation:

	almost never	seldom	sometimes	often	almost always

46. **Deciding What Caused a Problem:** Does the student assess what caused a problem and accept responsibility if appropriate?   1 2 3 4 5

Problem situation:

47. **Making a Complaint:** Does the student know how to express disagreement in acceptable ways?   1 2 3 4 5

Problem situation:

48. **Answering a Complaint:** Is the student willing to arrive at a fair solution to someone's justified complaint?   1 2 3 4 5

Problem situation:

49. **Dealing with Losing:** Does the student accept losing at a game or activity without becoming upset or angry?   1 2 3 4 5

Problem situation:

50. **Being a Good Sport:** Does the student give a sincere compliment to others about how they played a game?   1 2 3 4 5

Problem situation:

51. **Dealing with Being Left Out:** Does the student deal with being left out of an activity without losing control?   1 2 3 4 5

Problem situation:

52. **Dealing with Embarrassment:** Does the student know of things to do that help him/her feel less embarrassed or self-conscious?   1 2 3 4 5

Problem situation:

53. **Reacting to Failure:** Does the student figure out reason(s) for his/her failure and ways to be more successful the next time?   1 2 3 4 5

Problem situation:

54. **Accepting No:** Does the student accept being told no
without becoming unduly upset or angry?

	almost never	seldom	sometimes	often	almost always
	1	2	3	4	5

Problem situation:

55. **Saying No:** Does the student say no in acceptable ways to
things he/she doesn't want to do or to things that may get
him/her into trouble?

	1	2	3	4	5

Problem situation:

56. **Relaxing:** Is the student able to relax when tense or upset?

	1	2	3	4	5

Problem situation:

57. **Dealing with Group Pressure:** Does the student decide
what he/she wants to do when others pressure him/her
to do something else?

	1	2	3	4	5

Problem situation:

58. **Dealing with Wanting Something That Isn't Yours:** Does
the student refrain from taking things that don't belong to
him/her?

	1	2	3	4	5

Problem situation:

59. **Making a Decision:** Does the student make thoughtful
choices?

	1	2	3	4	5

Problem situation:

60. **Being Honest:** Is the student honest when confronted
with a negative action?

	1	2	3	4	5

Problem situation:

PARENT CHECKLIST

Name _____ Date _____

Child's name _____ Birth date _____

INSTRUCTIONS: Based on your observations in various situations, rate your child's use of the following skills.

Circle 1 if the child is *almost never* good at using the skill.
Circle 2 if the child is *seldom* good at using the skill.
Circle 3 if the child is *sometimes* good at using the skill.
Circle 4 if the child is *often* good at using the skill.
Circle 5 if the child is *almost always* good at using the skill.

	almost never	seldom	sometimes	often	almost always
1. **Listening:** Does your child listen when you or others talk to him/her?	1	2	3	4	5
Comments:					
2. **Asking for Help:** Does your child decide when he/she needs assistance and ask for this help in a pleasant manner?	1	2	3	4	5
Comments:					
3. **Saying Thank You:** Does your child tell others he/she appreciates help given, favors, and so forth?	1	2	3	4	5
Comments:					
4. **Bringing Materials to Class:** Does your child remember the books and materials he/she needs for school?	1	2	3	4	5
Comments:					
5. **Following Instructions:** Does your child understand instructions and follow them?	1	2	3	4	5
Comments:					
6. **Completing Assignments:** Does your child complete his/her homework assignments?	1	2	3	4	5
Comments:					

From *Skillstreaming the Elementary School Child: Teaching Prosocial Skills* (3rd ed.), © 2012 by E. McGinnis, Champaign, IL: Research Press (www.researchpress.com, 800-519-2707).

7. **Contributing to Discussions:** Does your child participate in class discussions in accordance with classroom rules?

    1   2   3   4   5

Comments:

8. **Offering Help to an Adult:** Does your child offer to help you at appropriate times and in an appropriate manner?

    1   2   3   4   5

Comments:

9. **Asking a Question:** Does your child know how and when to ask a question of another person?

    1   2   3   4   5

Comments:

10. **Ignoring Distractions:** Does your child ignore distractions in order to get his/her work done?

    1   2   3   4   5

Comments:

11. **Making Corrections:** Does your child make the necessary corrections on assignments without getting overly frustrated?

    1   2   3   4   5

Comments:

12. **Deciding on Something to Do:** Does your child find something to do when he/she has free time?

    1   2   3   4   5

Comments:

13. **Setting a Goal:** Does your child set realistic goals for himself/herself and take the necessary steps to meet these goals?

    1   2   3   4   5

Comments:

14. **Introducing Yourself:** Does your child introduce himself/herself in an appropriate way to people he/she doesn't know?

    1   2   3   4   5

Comments:

15. **Beginning a Conversation:** Does your child know how and when to begin a conversation with another person?   1 2 3 4 5

Comments:

16. **Ending a Conversation:** Does your child end a conversation when it is necessary and in an appropriate manner?   1 2 3 4 5

Comments:

17. **Joining In:** Does your child know and practice acceptable ways of joining an ongoing activity or group?   1 2 3 4 5

Comments:

18. **Playing a Game:** Does your child play games with friends fairly?   1 2 3 4 5

Comments:

19. **Asking a Favor:** Does your child know how to ask a favor of another person in an appropriate way?   1 2 3 4 5

Comments:

20. **Offering Help to a Classmate:** Does your child recognize when someone needs or wants assistance and offer this help?   1 2 3 4 5

Comments:

21. **Giving a Compliment:** Does your child tell others that he/she likes something about them or something they have done?   1 2 3 4 5

Comments:

22. **Accepting a Compliment:** Does your child accept compliments given by adults or his/her peers in a friendly way?   1 2 3 4 5

Comments:

23. **Suggesting an Activity:** Does your child suggest appropriate activities to others?

        1 2 3 4 5

Comments:

24. **Sharing:** Is your child agreeable to sharing things with others and, if not, does he/she offer acceptable reasons for not sharing?

        1 2 3 4 5

Comments:

25. **Apologizing:** Does your child tell others sincerely that he/she is sorry for doing something?

        1 2 3 4 5

Comments:

26. **Knowing Your Feelings:** Does your child identify feelings he/she is experiencing?

        1 2 3 4 5

Comments:

27. **Expressing Your Feelings:** Does your child express his/her feelings in acceptable ways?

        1 2 3 4 5

Comments:

28. **Recognizing Another's Feelings:** Does your child try to figure out in acceptable ways how others are feeling?

        1 2 3 4 5

Comments:

29. **Showing Understanding of Another's Feelings:** Does your child show understanding of others' feelings in acceptable ways?

        1 2 3 4 5

Comments:

30. **Expressing Concern for Another:** Does your child express concern for others in acceptable ways?

        1 2 3 4 5

Comments:

		almost never	seldom	sometimes	often	almost always

31. **Dealing with Your Anger:** Does your child use acceptable ways to express his/her anger?

    Comments:

    1 2 3 4 5

32. **Dealing with Another's Anger:** Does your child try to understand another's anger without getting angry himself/herself?

    Comments:

    1 2 3 4 5

33. **Expressing Affection:** Does your child let others know in acceptable ways that he/she cares about them?

    Comments:

    1 2 3 4 5

34. **Dealing with Fear:** Does your child know why he/she is afraid and do positive things to reduce this fear?

    Comments:

    1 2 3 4 5

35. **Rewarding Yourself:** Does your child say and do nice things for himself/herself when a reward is deserved?

    Comments:

    1 2 3 4 5

36. **Using Self-Control:** Does your child know and use positive ways to control his/her temper or excitement?

    Comments:

    1 2 3 4 5

37. **Asking Permission:** Does your child know when and how to ask whether he/she may do something?

    Comments:

    1 2 3 4 5

38. **Responding to Teasing:** Does your child deal with being teased without losing control?

    Comments:

    1 2 3 4 5

	almost never	seldom	sometimes	often	almost always

39. **Avoiding Trouble:** Does your child stay away from situations that may get him/her into trouble?

1 2 3 4 5

Comments:

40. **Staying Out of Fights:** Does your child know of and practice socially appropriate ways of handling potential fights?

1 2 3 4 5

Comments:

41. **Problem Solving:** When a problem occurs, does your child think of alternatives, choose an alternative, then evaluate how well this solved the problem?

1 2 3 4 5

Comments:

42. **Accepting Consequences:** Does your child accept the consequences for his/her behavior without becoming defensive or upset?

1 2 3 4 5

Comments:

43. **Dealing with an Accusation:** Does your child deal in positive ways with being accused of something?

1 2 3 4 5

Comments:

44. **Negotiating:** Is your child willing to give and take in order to reach a compromise?

1 2 3 4 5

Comments:

45. **Dealing with Boredom:** Does your child select acceptable activities when he/she is bored?

1 2 3 4 5

Comments:

46. **Deciding What Caused a Problem:** Does your child assess what caused a problem and accept responsibility if appropriate?

1 2 3 4 5

Comments:

47. **Making a Complaint:** Does your child know how to express disagreement in acceptable ways?

Comments:

almost never   seldom   sometimes   often   almost always

1   2   3   4   5

48. **Answering a Complaint:** Is your child willing to arrive at a fair solution to someone's justified complaint?

Comments:

1   2   3   4   5

49. **Dealing with Losing:** Does your child accept losing at a game or activity without becoming upset or angry?

Comments:

1   2   3   4   5

50. **Being a Good Sport:** Does your child give a sincere compliment to others about how they played a game?

Comments:

1   2   3   4   5

51. **Dealing with Being Left Out:** Does your child deal with being left out of an activity without losing control?

Comments:

1   2   3   4   5

52. **Dealing with Embarrassment:** Does your child know of things to do that help him/her feel less embarrassed or self-conscious?

Comments:

1   2   3   4   5

53. **Reacting to Failure:** Does your child figure out the reason(s) for his/her failure and ways he/she can be more successful the next time?

Comments:

1   2   3   4   5

54. **Accepting No:** Does your child accept being told no without becoming unduly upset or angry?

Comments:

1   2   3   4   5

55. **Saying No:** Does your child say no in acceptable ways to things he/she doesn't want to do or to things that may get him/her into trouble?

almost never / seldom / sometimes / often / almost always

1   2   3   4   5

Comments:

56. **Relaxing:** Is your child able to relax when tense or upset?

1   2   3   4   5

Comments:

57. **Dealing with Group Pressure:** Does your child decide what he/she wants to do when others pressure him/her to do something else?

1   2   3   4   5

Comments:

58. **Dealing with Wanting Something That Isn't Yours:** Does your child refrain from taking things that don't belong to him/her?

1   2   3   4   5

Comments:

59. **Making a Decision:** Does your child make thoughtful choices?

1   2   3   4   5

Comments:

60. **Being Honest:** Is your child honest when confronted with a negative action?

1   2   3   4   5

Comments:

STUDENT CHECKLIST

INSTRUCTIONS: Each of the questions will ask you about how well you do something. Next to each question is a number.

Circle number 1 if you *almost never* do what the question asks.
Circle number 2 if you *seldom* do it.
Circle number 3 if you *sometimes* do it.
Circle number 4 if you do it *often*.
Circle number 5 if you *almost always* do it.

There are no right or wrong answers to these questions. Answer the way you really feel about each question.

	almost never	seldom	sometimes	often	almost always
1. Is it easy for me to listen to someone who is talking to me?	1	2	3	4	5
2. Do I ask for help in a friendly way when I need help?	1	2	3	4	5
3. Do I tell people thank you for something they have done for me?	1	2	3	4	5
4. Do I have the materials I need for my classes (like books, pencils, paper)?	1	2	3	4	5
5. Do I understand what to do when directions are given, and do I follow these directions?	1	2	3	4	5
6. Do I finish my schoolwork?	1	2	3	4	5
7. Do I join in on class talks or discussions?	1	2	3	4	5
8. Do I try to help an adult when I think he/she could use the help?	1	2	3	4	5
9. Do I decide what I don't understand about my schoolwork and ask my teacher questions in a friendly way?	1	2	3	4	5
10. Is it easy for me to keep doing my schoolwork when people are noisy?	1	2	3	4	5
11. Do I fix mistakes on my work without getting upset?	1	2	3	4	5

 From *Skillstreaming the Elementary School Child: Teaching Prosocial Skills* (3rd ed.), © 2012 by E. McGinnis, Champaign, IL: Research Press (www.researchpress.com, 800-519-2707).

325

	almost never	seldom	sometimes	often	almost always

12. Do I choose something to do when I have free time?   1 2 3 4 5

13. Do I decide on something I want to work for and keep working until I get it?   1 2 3 4 5

14. Is it easy for me to take the first step to meet somebody I don't know?   1 2 3 4 5

15. Is it easy for me to start a conversation with someone?   1 2 3 4 5

16. When I have something else I have to do, do I end a conversation with someone in a nice way?   1 2 3 4 5

17. Do I ask to join in a game or activity in a friendly way?   1 2 3 4 5

18. Do I follow the rules when I play a game?   1 2 3 4 5

19. Is it easy for me to ask a favor of someone?   1 2 3 4 5

20. Do I notice when somebody needs help and try to help the person?   1 2 3 4 5

21. Do I tell others that I like something nice about them or something nice they have done for me or for somebody else?   1 2 3 4 5

22. When someone says something nice about me, do I accept what the person says?   1 2 3 4 5

23. Do I suggest things to do with my friends?   1 2 3 4 5

24. Am I willing to share my things with others?   1 2 3 4 5

25. Do I tell others I'm sorry after I do something wrong?   1 2 3 4 5

26. Do I know how I feel about different things that happen?   1 2 3 4 5

27. Do I let others know what I am feeling and do it in a good way?   1 2 3 4 5

28. Do I try to tell how other people are feeling?   1 2 3 4 5

29. Do I show others that I understand how they feel?   1 2 3 4 5

30. When someone has a problem, do I let the person know that I care?   1 2 3 4 5

	almost never	seldom	sometimes	often	almost always

31. When I am angry, do I deal with it in ways that won't hurt other people?   1   2   3   4   5

32. Do I try to understand other people's angry feelings?   1   2   3   4   5

33. Do I let others know I care about them?   1   2   3   4   5

34. Do I know what makes me afraid, and do I think of things to do so I don't stay afraid?   1   2   3   4   5

35. Do I say and do nice things for myself when I have earned it?   1   2   3   4   5

36. Do I keep my temper when I am upset?   1   2   3   4   5

37. Do I know when I have to ask to do something I want to do, and do I ask in a friendly way?   1   2   3   4   5

38. When somebody teases me, do I stay in control?   1   2   3   4   5

39. Do I try to stay away from things that may get me into trouble?   1   2   3   4   5

40. Do I think of ways other than fighting to take care of problems?   1   2   3   4   5

41. Do I think of ways to deal with a problem and what might happen if I use these ways?   1   2   3   4   5

42. When I do something I shouldn't have done, do I accept what happens then?   1   2   3   4   5

43. Do I decide what I have been accused of and why, then think of a good way to handle the situation?   1   2   3   4   5

44. When I don't agree with somebody, do I help think of a plan to make both of us happy?   1   2   3   4   5

45. When I feel bored, do I think of good things to do and then do them?   1   2   3   4   5

46. Do I know when a problem happened because of something I did?   1   2   3   4   5

47. Do I tell others without getting mad or yelling when they have caused a problem for me?   1   2   3   4   5

48. Do I help think of a fair way to take care of a complaint against me?   1   2   3   4   5

49. When I lose at a game, do I keep from getting upset?   1   2   3   4   5

50. Do I tell others something good about the way they played a game?   1   2   3   4   5

51. Do I decide if I have been left out, then do things in a good way to make me feel better?   1   2   3   4   5

52. Do I do things that will help me feel less embarrassed?   1   2   3   4   5

53. When I don't do well on something (on a test, doing my chores), do I decide ways I could do better next time?   1   2   3   4   5

54. When I am told no, can I keep from becoming upset?   1   2   3   4   5

55. Do I say no to things that might get me into trouble or that I don't want to do, and do I say it in a friendly way?   1   2   3   4   5

56. Can I keep my body from getting tight and tense when I am angry or upset?   1   2   3   4   5

57. When a group of kids wants me to do something that might get me into trouble or that is wrong, do I say no?   1   2   3   4   5

58. Do I keep from taking things that aren't mine?   1   2   3   4   5

59. Is it easy for me to decide what to do when I'm given a choice?   1   2   3   4   5

60. Do I tell the truth about what I have done, even if I might get into trouble?   1   2   3   4   5

GROUPING CHART

	student names													
GROUP I: Classroom Survival Skills														
1. Listening														
2. Asking for Help														
3. Saying Thank You														
4. Bringing Materials to Class														
5. Following Instructions														
6. Completing Assignments														
7. Contributing to Discussions														
8. Offering Help to an Adult														
9. Asking a Question														
10. Ignoring Distractions														
11. Making Corrections														
12. Deciding on Something to Do														
13. Setting a Goal														
GROUP II: Friendship-Making Skills														
14. Introducing Yourself														
15. Beginning a Conversation														
16. Ending a Conversation														
17. Joining In														
18. Playing a Game														
19. Asking a Favor														
20. Offering Help to a Classmate														
21. Giving a Compliment														
22. Accepting a Compliment														
23. Suggesting an Activity														
24. Sharing														
25. Apologizing														

 **Skillstreaming** From *Skillstreaming the Elementary School Child: Teaching Prosocial Skills* (3rd ed.), © 2012 by E. McGinnis, Champaign, IL: Research Press (www.researchpress.com, 800-519-2707).

	student names														
GROUP III: **Skills for Dealing with Feelings**															
26. Knowing Your Feelings															
27. Expressing Your Feelings															
28. Recognizing Another's Feelings															
29. Showing Understanding of Another's Feelings															
30. Expressing Concern for Another															
31. Dealing with Your Anger															
32. Dealing with Another's Anger															
33. Expressing Affection															
34. Dealing with Fear															
35. Rewarding Yourself															
GROUP IV: **Skill Alternatives to Aggression**															
36. Using Self-Control															
37. Asking Permission															
38. Responding to Teasing															
39. Avoiding Trouble															
40. Staying Out of Fights															
41. Problem Solving															
42. Accepting Consequences															
43. Dealing with an Accusation															
44. Negotiating															
GROUP V: **Skills for Dealing with Stress**															
45. Dealing with Boredom															
46. Deciding What Caused a Problem															
47. Making a Complaint															
48. Answering a Complaint															
49. Dealing with Losing															
50. Being a Good Sport															

	student names																

(Group V, continued)

	student names																
51. Dealing with Being Left Out																	
52. Dealing with Embarrassment																	
53. Reacting to Failure																	
54. Accepting No																	
55. Saying No																	
56. Relaxing																	
57. Dealing with Group Pressure																	
58. Dealing with Wanting Something That Isn't Yours																	
59. Making a Decision																	
60. Being Honest																	

Name _____ Date _____

Skill _____

SKILL STEPS

FILL IN NOW

With whom will I try this? _____

When? _____

FILL IN AFTER YOU PRACTICE THE SKILL

What happened? _____

_____

_____

How did I do?　　　　　　　　　☺　　　😐　　　☹

Why did I circle this? _____

_____

  From *Skillstreaming the Elementary School Child: Teaching Prosocial Skills* (3rd ed.), © 2012 by E. McGinnis, Champaign, IL: Research Press (www.researchpress.com, 800-519-2707).

Name _____ Date _____

Skill _____

SKILL STEPS

When did I practice?   How did I do?

😊   😐   ☹️

_____

😊   😐   ☹️

_____

😊   😐   ☹️

_____

😊   😐   ☹️

_____

GROUP SELF-REPORT CHART

Skills

student names

Skillstreaming

From *Skillstreaming the Elementary School Child: Teaching Prosocial Skills* (3rd ed.), © 2012 by E. McGinnis, Champaign, IL: Research Press (www.researchpress.com, 800-519-2707).

I will practice _____

_____
                    Student

If I do, then _____

_____

_____
                    Teacher

_____
                     Date

To be reevaluated on or before

_____
                     Date

From *Skillstreaming the Elementary School Child: Teaching Prosocial Skills* (3rd ed.), © 2012
by E. McGinnis, Champaign, IL: Research Press (www.researchpress.com, 800-519-2707).

My goal is to practice the skill of

_____

from _____ to _____
                    (dates)

If I do this, I will have earned

_____

_____

_____

Student _____

Teacher _____

Date _____

Skillstreaming

From *Skillstreaming the Elementary School Child: Teaching Prosocial Skills* (3rd ed.), © 2012 by E. McGinnis, Champaign, IL: Research Press (www.researchpress.com, 800-519-2707).

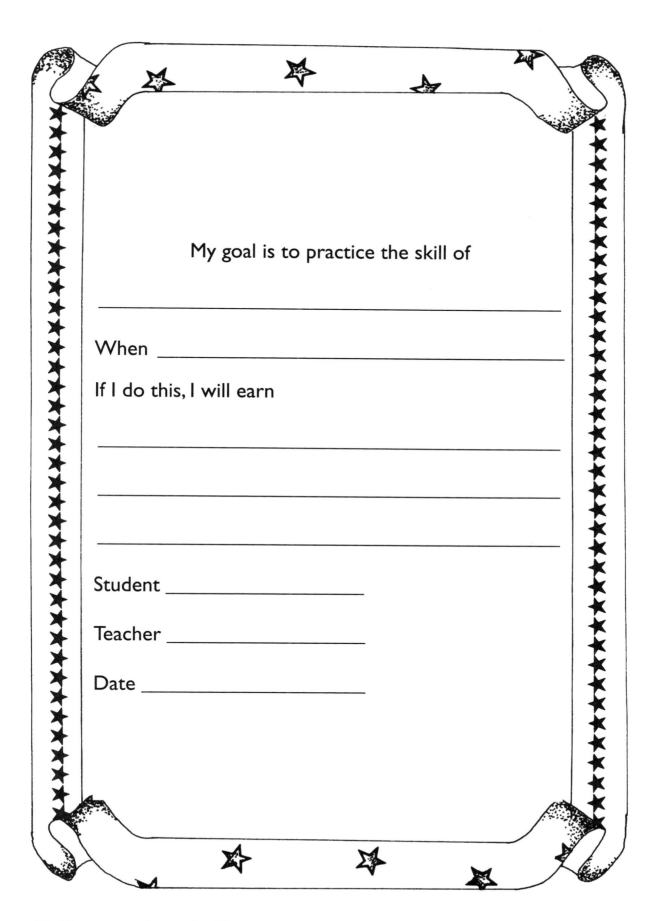

My goal is to practice the skill of

_____

When _____

If I do this, I will earn

_____

_____

_____

Student _____

Teacher _____

Date _____

From *Skillstreaming the Elementary School Child: Teaching Prosocial Skills* (3rd ed.), © 2012 by E. McGinnis, Champaign, IL: Research Press (www.researchpress.com, 800-519-2707).

Student _____

Date _____

Color in a space each time you use the skill of

_____

Skillstreaming

From *Skillstreaming the Elementary School Child: Teaching Prosocial Skills* (3rd ed.), © 2012 by E. McGinnis, Champaign, IL: Research Press (www.researchpress.com, 800-519-2707).

Student _____

Date _____

Color in a balloon each time you use the skill of

_____

Student _____

Date _____

Color a number each time you practice the skill of

_____

Skillstreaming

From *Skillstreaming the Elementary School Child: Teaching Prosocial Skills* (3rd ed.), © 2012 by E. McGinnis, Champaign, IL: Research Press (www.researchpress.com, 800-519-2707).

Classroom Survival Award

to

_____

for using the skill of

_____

Date _____

From *Skillstreaming the Elementary School Child: Teaching Prosocial Skills* (3rd ed.), © 2012 by E. McGinnis, Champaign, IL: Research Press (www.researchpress.com, 800-519-2707).

Friendship Award

to

_____

for using the skill of

_____

Date _____

Skillstreaming

From *Skillstreaming the Elementary School Child: Teaching Prosocial Skills* (3rd ed.), © 2012 by E. McGinnis, Champaign, IL: Research Press (www.researchpress.com, 800-519-2707).

Dealing with Feelings Award

to

_____

for using the skill of

_____

Date _____

From *Skillstreaming the Elementary School Child: Teaching Prosocial Skills* (3rd ed.), © 2012
by E. McGinnis, Champaign, IL: Research Press (www.researchpress.com, 800-519-2707).

Stop and Think Award

to

_____

for using the skill of

_____

Date _____

Skillstreaming

From *Skillstreaming the Elementary School Child: Teaching Prosocial Skills* (3rd ed.), © 2012 by E. McGinnis, Champaign, IL: Research Press (www.researchpress.com, 800-519-2707).

Dealing with Stress Award

to

_____

for using the skill of

_____

Date _____

Skillstreaming From *Skillstreaming the Elementary School Child: Teaching Prosocial Skills* (3rd ed.), © 2012 by E. McGinnis, Champaign, IL: Research Press (www.researchpress.com, 800-519-2707).

PARENT ORIENTATION NOTE

Date _____

Dear Parent or Guardian:

Your child and his or her classmates are learning to handle a variety of day-to-day concerns in positive ways. Sharing, taking turns, handling teasing and anger, and following directions are some of the concerns we are working on. We are all learning specific steps to social skills in order to handle these problems in acceptable ways.

The process we are using to learn these skills is called Skillstreaming. First, your child is watching someone else use the skill. Then he or she will try out the skill and receive feedback about how well he or she performed the skill from both peers and adults. Finally, your child will be asked to practice the skill in real-life situations.

Each week we will be sending home a note describing the skill and its steps. We hope that you review this note with your child and help your child practice the skill at home. Please feel free to call me or e-mail me if you have any questions.

Sincerely,

_____

Phone _____

E-mail _____

.Skillstreaming

From *Skillstreaming the Elementary School Child: Teaching Prosocial Skills* (3rd ed.), © 2012 by E. McGinnis, Champaign, IL: Research Press (www.researchpress.com, 800-519-2707).

SCHOOL-HOME NOTE

Student _____ Date _____

DESCRIPTION OF LESSON

Skill name _____

Skill steps:

Skill purpose, use, value _____

_____

DESCRIPTION OF SKILL HOMEWORK

_____

_____

REQUEST TO PARENTS

1. Provide skill homework recognition and reward.
2. Respond positively to your child's skill use.
3. Return this school-home note with your comments (on the back) about quality of homework done and questions/suggestions for the teacher.
4. Please sign and return this form to _____

   by _____

Signature _____ Date _____

PARENT/STAFF SKILL RATING FORM

Date _____

_____ is learning
(student's name)

the skill of _____

The steps involved in this skill are:

1. Did he or she demonstrate this skill in your presence?   ☐ yes   ☐ no

2. How would you rate his or her skill demonstration? *(check one)*

   ☐ poor   ☐ below average   ☐ average   ☐ above average   ☐ excellent

3. How sincere was he or she in performing the skill? *(check one)*

   ☐ not sincere   ☐ somewhat sincere   ☐ very sincere

Comments:

_____

_____

_____

Please sign and return this form to _____

by _____

Signature _____ Date _____

Skillstreaming   From *Skillstreaming the Elementary School Child: Teaching Prosocial Skills* (3rd ed.), © 2012 by E. McGinnis, Champaign, IL: Research Press (www.researchpress.com, 800-519-2707).

Program Integrity Checklists

LEADER'S CHECKLIST

INSTRUCTIONS: Leader(s) may complete this checklist at the conclusion of the Skillstreaming group by marking "yes" or "no" relative to each procedure implemented.

Group leader(s) _____

Date of group _____ Time of group _____

	Yes	No
Step 1: Define the skill		
1. The skill to be taught was defined, and the group understood its meaning.	☐	☐
2. Skill steps were presented and discussed (via poster or skill cards).	☐	☐
(For all sessions after the first)		
3. Group members' skill homework was discussed.	☐	☐
4. Appropriate reinforcement was provided for group members who completed homework.	☐	☐
Step 2: Model the skill		
5. Two examples of the skill were modeled.	☐	☐
6. Each skill step was identified as the modeling unfolded.	☐	☐
7. Modeling displays were relevant to group members' real-life circumstances.	☐	☐
8. Group members were directed to watch for the steps being modeled.	☐	☐
9. The model was friendly and helpful.	☐	☐
10. A coping model was presented if indicated.	☐	☐
11. The model used self-talk to illustrate the steps and thinking about skill performance.	☐	☐
12. The modeling display depicted positive outcomes.	☐	☐
13. The model was rewarded for skill performance (following the skill steps).	☐	☐
Step 3: Establish student skill need		
14. Each group member's need for skill use was defined (when, where, and with whom) and listed.	☐	☐
Step 4: Select the first role-player		
15. The main actor was selected for role-play (e.g., "Who would like to go first?")	☐	☐
Step 5: Set up the role-play		
16. Main actor selected a coactor who reminded him/her most of the real-life person with whom he/she has the skill need.	☐	☐
17. Main actor described the physical setting, events preceding the problem, mood/manner of the person, and any other relevant information.	☐	☐

From *Skillstreaming the Elementary School Child: Teaching Prosocial Skills* (3rd ed.), © 2012 by E. McGinnis, Champaign, IL: Research Press (www.researchpress.com, 800-519-2707).

		Yes	No
Step 6: Conduct the role-play			
18.	Group members were assigned specific step(s) to observe.	☐	☐
19.	Main actor was instructed to follow the behavioral steps.	☐	☐
20.	Main actor was reminded to "think aloud."	☐	☐
21.	Coactor was reminded to stay in the role of the other person.	☐	☐
22.	Group leader assisted the main actor as needed (pointed to skill steps, coached).	☐	☐
Step 7: Provide performance feedback			
23.	Coactor was asked to provide feedback (e.g., how he/she felt, how well the main actor enacted the steps).	☐	☐
24.	Group members were asked if the main actor followed each step.	☐	☐
25.	Leaders provided appropriate feedback (praise, approval, encouragement), identifying specific aspects of the main actor's performance.	☐	☐
26.	Reinforcement in an amount consistent with the quality of role-play was provided.	☐	☐
27.	Main actor was invited to give comments.	☐	☐
Step 8: Select the next role-player			
28.	Volunteer participant asked to act as the main actor in the next role-play and coached in Steps 5 through 7.	☐	☐
29.	All group members were given a chance to role-play, or plans were made to role-play for those who did not have a chance.	☐	☐
Step 9: Assign skill homework			
30.	Skill homework was assigned to each main actor.	☐	☐
31.	Assistance was provided as needed in identifying the day, place, with whom the skill will be used, and so forth.	☐	☐

TOTAL YES _____   **TOTAL NO** _____

OBSERVER'S CHECKLIST

INSTRUCTIONS: A highly skilled observer may complete this observation checklist as the Skillstreaming group is taking place. The observer will note whether leader(s) completed each procedure with a low level of competence (score 1), medium proficiency (score 2), or a high level of skill (score 3). At the conclusion of the observation, the observer may provide leader(s) with recommendations for specific steps needing improvement.

Group leader(s) _____ Observers _____

Date of group _____ Time of group _____

	Proficiency Level		
	1	2	3
Step 1: Define the skill			
1. The skill to be taught was defined and the group understood its meaning.	☐	☐	☐
2. Skill steps are presented and discussed (via poster or skill cards).	☐	☐	☐
(For all sessions after the first)			
3. Group members' skill homework was discussed.	☐	☐	☐
4. Appropriate reinforcement was provided for group members who completed homework.	☐	☐	☐
Step 2: Model the skill			
5. Two examples of the skill were modeled.	☐	☐	☐
6. Each skill step was identified as the modeling unfolded.	☐	☐	☐
7. Modeling displays were relevant to group members' real-life circumstances.	☐	☐	☐
8. Group members were directed to watch for the steps being modeled.	☐	☐	☐
9. The model was friendly and helpful.	☐	☐	☐
10. A coping model was presented if indicated.	☐	☐	☐
11. The model used self-talk to illustrate the steps and thinking about skill performance.	☐	☐	☐
12. The modeling display depicted positive outcomes.	☐	☐	☐
13. The model was rewarded for skill performance (following the skill steps).	☐	☐	☐
Step 3: Establish student skill need			
14. Each group member's need for skill use was defined (when, where, and with whom) and listed.	☐	☐	☐
Step 4: Select the first role-player			
15. The main actor was selected for role-play (e.g., "Who would like to go first?")	☐	☐	☐

From *Skillstreaming the Elementary School Child: Teaching Prosocial Skills* (3rd ed.), © 2012 by E. McGinnis, Champaign, IL: Research Press (www.researchpress.com, 800-519-2707).

Step 5: Set up the role-play

16. Main actor selected a coactor who reminded him/her most of the real-life person with whom he/she has the skill need.   ☐ ☐ ☐

17. Main actor described the physical setting, events preceding the problem, mood/manner of the person, and any other relevant information.   ☐ ☐ ☐

Step 6: Conduct the role-play

18. Group members were assigned specific step(s) to observe.   ☐ ☐ ☐

19. Main actor was instructed to follow the behavioral steps.   ☐ ☐ ☐

20. Main actor was reminded to "think aloud."   ☐ ☐ ☐

21. Coactor was reminded to stay in the role of the other person.   ☐ ☐ ☐

22. Group leader assisted the main actor as needed (pointed to skill steps, coached).   ☐ ☐ ☐

Step 7: Provide performance feedback

23. Coactor was asked to provide feedback (e.g., how he/she felt, how well the main actor enacted the steps).   ☐ ☐ ☐

24. Group members were asked if the main actor followed each step.   ☐ ☐ ☐

25. Leaders provided appropriate feedback (praise, approval, encouragement), identifying specific aspects of the main actor's performance.   ☐ ☐ ☐

26. Reinforcement in an amount consistent with the quality of role-play was provided.   ☐ ☐ ☐

27. Main actor was invited to give comments.   ☐ ☐ ☐

Step 8: Select the next role-player

28. Volunteer participant asked to act as the main actor in the next role-play. Repeated Steps 5 through 7.   ☐ ☐ ☐

29. All group members were given a chance to role-play, or plans were made to role-play for those who did not have a chance.   ☐ ☐ ☐

Step 9: Assign skill homework

30. Skill homework was assigned to each main actor.   ☐ ☐ ☐

31. Assistance was provided as needed in identifying the day, place, with whom the skill will be used, and so forth.   ☐ ☐ ☐

TOTAL _____

59 points or below	Group leader intervention needed.
60–74 points	Continued monitoring of instruction necessary.
75–83 points	Consultation with master leader available.
84–93 points	Mastery of intervention demonstrated.

Comments:

Recommendations for improvement:

GENERALIZATION INTEGRITY CHECKLIST

Leader(s) _____

Group _____ Date(s) of review _____

INSTRUCTIONS: This self-rating checklist is designed to assist group leader(s) in enhancing generalization of student skill learning. While a numerical score is not computed, leader(s) may use this checklist to both plan instruction and evaluate the emphasis placed on generalization following instruction.

	Minimal	Average	Strong
Before session			
1. Instruction is provided to the same peers with whom the target students interact outside of the group.	☐	☐	☐
2. One instructor has ongoing, regular contact with the students.	☐	☐	☐
3. Skills likely to provide natural reinforcement are included.	☐	☐	☐
During session			
4. Students know the specific behavioral skill steps and can perform them well.	☐	☐	☐
5. Attempts made to create similarities between the instructional and real-life situations and settings.	☐	☐	☐
6. Numerous trials of correct skill performance provided.	☐	☐	☐
7. Variability of situations (range of settings, various people, variety of reasons for skill use, various cues) provided.	☐	☐	☐
8. When possible, instruction occured in the real-life environment where the skill is to be used.	☐	☐	☐
9. Some flexibility allowed in order to meet individual student needs and settings.	☐	☐	☐
After session			
10. Homework assignments provided after students competently performed the role-plays.	☐	☐	☐
11. Skill use prompted or coached when daily situations suggest skill use.	☐	☐	☐
12. Skill use reinforced with gradual thinning and delaying of reinforcement.	☐	☐	☐
13. Prompts and reminders gradually faded.	☐	☐	☐
14. Instruction in self-mediated generalization (e.g., self-recording, self-reinforcement) provided as appropriate to student need.	☐	☐	☐
15. Booster or coaching sessions are provided as needed.	☐	☐	☐
16. Plan for addressing competing behaviors developed and implemented as needed.	☐	☐	☐
17. Strategies for parent involvement implemented.	☐	☐	☐

Skillstreaming

From *Skillstreaming the Elementary School Child: Teaching Prosocial Skills* (3rd ed.), © 2012 by E. McGinnis, Champaign, IL: Research Press (www.researchpress.com, 800-519-2707).

APPENDIX C

Behavior Management Techniques

Behaviors that both promote and inhibit skill learning can be influenced by behavior management techniques based on the principles of behavior modification. The effectiveness of behavior modification rests on a firm experimental foundation. Although not all of the techniques described in this appendix are equally valid for all age groups, a basic understanding of them is critical to managing the Skillstreaming group and to developing individual behavior intervention plans for those children and adolescents who need them. The techniques described are grouped under the behavioral principles of reinforcement and punishment.

Behavior modification techniques are derived from formal learning theory, systematically applied in an effort to change observable behavior and rigorously evaluated by experimental research. These procedures are based on the core premise that behavior is largely determined by its environmental consequences (Ferster & Skinner, 1957; Skinner, 1938, 1953). Operationally, this premise has been employed in techniques that contingently present or withdraw rewards or punishments (i.e., environmental consequences) to alter the behavior preceding these consequences. It is this contingent quality that has led to the use of the term *contingency management* to describe most of these activities.

REINFORCEMENT

Reinforcement can be of two types: positive or negative. Positive reinforcement is central to promoting enduring change in Skillstreaming and other learning efforts and is therefore discussed here at length. Negative reinforcement is far less common but does play a role in the classroom and Skillstreaming group.

Positive Reinforcement

A *positive reinforcer* is any event that increases the subsequent frequency of a behavior it follows. Presenting positive reinforcement to the student following and contingent on the occurrence of appropriate behavior is an effective way to substitute appropriate for inappropriate behaviors. Teachers and other school-based staff have worked successfully with four types of positive reinforcers: material, social, activity, and token. (For a list of commonly used reinforcers, see Table 5 in chapter 6.)

Material reinforcers (sometimes called *tangible reinforcers*) are actual goods or objects presented to the individual contingent on enactment of appropriate behaviors. Skill awards and skill tickets, discussed in chapters 2 and 3, are examples of specific types of material reinforcers. An important subcategory of material reinforcement, *primary reinforcement,* occurs when the contingent event presented satisfies a basic biological need. Food is one such primary reinforcer.

Social reinforcers—most often expressed in the form of attention, praise, or approval—are particularly powerful and are frequently used in the Skillstreaming group. Both teacher experience and extensive experimental research testify to the potency of teacher-dispensed social reinforcement in influencing personal, interpersonal, and academic student behaviors.

Activity reinforcers are events a child or adolescent freely chooses when an opportunity exists to engage in several different activities. Given freedom to choose, many youth will watch television or spend time on the computer rather than complete their homework. The parent wishing to use this type of activity reinforcer may specify that the youth may watch television or use the computer for a given time period contingent upon the prior completion of the homework. Stated otherwise, the opportunity to perform a higher probability behavior (given free choice) can be used as a reinforcer for a lower probability behavior.

Token reinforcers, usually employed when more easily implemented social reinforcers prove insufficient, are symbolic items (chips, stars, points, etc.) provided contingent upon the performance of appropriate or desirable behaviors. Tokens are then exchangeable for a wide range of material or activity reinforcers. A *token economy* is a system by which specific numbers of tokens are contingently gained and exchanged for the backup material or activity reinforcers.

In making decisions about which type of reinforcer to use with a given youth, the teacher should keep in mind that social reinforcement (e.g., attention, praise, approval) is easiest to implement on a continuing basis and is most likely to lead to enduring behavior change. Therefore, it is the type of reinforcement the teacher will wish to use most frequently. Unfortunately, in the initial stages of a behavior change effort—especially when aggressive, disruptive, and other inappropriate behaviors are probably being richly rewarded by teacher and peer attention, as well as by tangible reinforcers, the teacher will likely need to rely more on material and activity reinforcers.

A token reinforcement system may prove effective as the initial reinforcement strategy. Reinforcement preferences change over time, and teacher views of the appropriate reward value of desirable behaviors also change over time. Both variables are easily reflected in token-level adjustments. Some issues to be considered prior to implementing a token system (Kaplan & Carter, 2005) and are summarized as follows:

1. Identify what the student needs to do, the specific behaviors, to earn tokens.

2. Post a list of these contingent behaviors (e.g., somewhere in the classroom, on the student's desk) to remind him or her of the expectations.

3. Decide what the tokens will be. Tokens should be age appropriate and might include check marks, play money, stickers, tickets, and so forth. Provisions need to be made to prevent students from having tokens that they have not earned (e.g., accept only tokens validated with the teacher's signature).

4. Determine how many tokens the students will earn for given behaviors and how much students will be charged (in tokens) for the reinforcers.

5. Determine the backup reinforcers—for example, prizes, entitlements (privileges students normally receive without having to earn them), other privileges.

6. Decide who will give the tokens (typically the teacher, associate, peer tutor).

7. Determine when the tokens will be given. Typically, tokens should be given as soon after the behavior is demonstrated as possible and according to the reinforcement schedule that is being followed with a particular student.

8. Determine how the tokens will be given (e.g., Given directly to the student? Marked

on a card? Placed in a bank?). This system should be kept simple.

9. Determine when the tokens will be redeemed. The primary consideration should be the student's needs (i.e., how long the student is able to wait before receiving the reinforcer). Activities or privileges that may be disruptive to the instructional setting will require additional consideration.

Tokens, as well as other tangible rewards, should be combined with social reinforcers. It is critical to remember that, with few exceptions, reliance on material, activity, or token reinforcement eventually should give way to reliance on more "real-life" social reinforcement.

The potency of many reinforcers is increased when the reward, in addition to being inherently desirable, also brings reinforcement from peers and others (e.g., ordering a DVD to watch as a group, earning extra gym or recess time for the class). A further benefit of certain activity reinforcers (e.g., playing a game with peers, helping in the principal's office) is the degree to which the activity, while serving as a reward, also helps the student practice one or more Skillstreaming skills.

Identifying Reinforcers

Identifying positive reinforcers for a given child or adolescent is often necessary prior to presenting such events contingently upon the occurrence of desirable behaviors. Given that almost any event may serve as a reinforcer for one individual but not another, how can the teacher decide which reinforcers may best be used? Simply, the youth may be asked straightforwardly which items he or she would like to earn. This direct approach may be insufficient because youth are unaware of the full range of reinforcers available to them or may discount in advance the possibility that a reinforcer will actually be given. When this is the case, other identification procedures must be employed. Carr (1981) and others have reported three procedures typically used for this purpose.

First, the teacher can often make an accurate determination of whether a given event is functioning as a reinforcer by carefully *observing effects* on the youth. The event probably is reinforcing if the youth (a) asks that the event be repeated, (b) seems happy during the event's occurrence, (c) seems unhappy when the event ends, or (d) will work to earn the event. If one or more of these reactions are observed, chances are good that the event is a positive reinforcer and that it can be contingently provided to strengthen appropriate, nonaggressive, or interactive behaviors. Second, *observing choices* can be helpful. As noted earlier in connection with activity reinforcers, when a youth is free to choose from among several equally available activities, which one the youth chooses and how long he or she engages in it are clues to whether an event is reinforcing. Finally, *questionnaires* have been effectively used to identify positive reinforcers.

As noted earlier, which objects or activities will in fact be reinforcing for a given youth will vary from individual to individual and from time to time. In addition, the strength of selected reinforcers often decreases the more frequently they are used. Some teachers therefore find it useful to create a "reinforcement menu," or a list of rewards from which the student can choose. Such a menu may be in the form of an actual list, or it may be in the form of "coupons" for tangible and activity rewards. Each coupon may be a voucher for a particular amount of a given reinforcer (e.g., five minutes of computer time, five minutes playing with the gerbil). Using a reinforcement menu prevents students from becoming satiated with one reward when it is offered over a period of time and also allows them to make their own reinforcement choices.

Presenting Positive Reinforcers

As noted, a basic principle of contingency management is that the presentation of a reinforcing event contingent upon the occurrence of a given behavior will function to increase the likelihood of the reoccurrence of that behavior. A number of considerations influence the success of the reinforcement effort and should be reflected in the actual presentation of reinforcers.

Contingency

The connection between the desirable behavior and the subsequent reward should be made explicit. As is true for all contingency management efforts, this description should be behaviorally specific—that is, the connection between particular behavioral acts and reinforcement should be emphasized over behaviorally ambiguous concepts like "good behavior" or "being well behaved." Instead, comments like "Good job taking turns" and "Good listening" will help the student understand what has gained him or her the desired reinforcement.

Immediacy

The more immediately the reinforcer follows the desirable behavior, the more likely it is to be effective. Rapid reinforcement augments the message that the immediately preceding behavior is desirable, whereas delayed reinforcement increases the risk that an inappropriate behavior will occur between the positive behavior and the reinforcement. In other words, the following sequence occurs: A (desirable behavior), B (undesirable behavior), and C (reinforcement intended for A that in actuality reinforces B).

Consistency

The effects of positive reinforcement on behavior are usually gradual, not dramatic, working slowly to strengthen behavior over a period of time. Thus, it is important that positive reinforcement be presented consistently. Consistency means not only that the teacher must be consistent but also that the teacher must attempt to match his or her reinforcement efforts with similar efforts from as many other important persons in the student's life as possible. This means, ideally, that when the student enacts the behavior to be reinforced—in school in the presence of other teachers, at home in the presence of parents or siblings, or at play in the presence of peers—such reinforcement will be forthcoming.

Frequency

When first trying to establish a new appropriate behavior, the teacher reinforces all or almost all instances of that behavior. This high frequency of reinforcement is necessary to establish the behavior in the individual's behavioral repertoire. Once it seems clear that the behavior has actually been acquired, the teacher thins the reinforcement schedule, decreasing presentation so that only some of the student's desirable behaviors are followed by the reinforcement. This schedule, known as *partial reinforcement,* contributes to the continuation of the appropriate behavior because it parallels the sometimes reinforced/sometimes not reaction the appropriate behavior will elicit in other settings from other people. Partial reinforcement of the appropriate behaviors may be on a fixed-time schedule (e.g., at the end of each Skillstreaming session), on a fixed-number-of-response schedule (e.g., every fifth instance of the appropriate behavior), or on variable-time or number-of-response schedules. In any event, the basic strategy for reinforcement frequency remains a rich level for initial learning and partial reinforcement to sustain performance.

Amount

Learning (i.e., acquiring knowledge about how to perform new behaviors) and performance (i.e., overtly using these behaviors) are different aspects of behavior. The amount of reinforcement provided influences performance much more than it does learning. Children and adolescents will learn new appropriate behaviors just about as fast for a small reward as for a large reward, but they are more likely to perform the behaviors on a continuing basis when large rewards are involved. Yet rewards can be too large, causing a *satiation effect* in which youth lose interest in seeking the reinforcement because it is "too much of a good thing." Or rewards can be too small: too little time on the playground, too few tokens, too thin a social reinforcement schedule. The optimal amount can be determined empirically. If a youth has in the past worked energetically to obtain a particular reinforcer but gradually slacks off and seems to lose interest in obtaining it, a satiation effect has probably occurred, and the amount of reinforcement should be reduced. On the other hand, if a youth seems unwilling to work for a reinforcer believed desirable, it can be given once or twice for free—that is, not contingent on a specific desirable behavior. If the youth seems to enjoy the reinforcer or wants more, the amount used may have been too little. The amount can be increased and made contingent; observations will then show whether it is yielding the desired effect. If so, the amount of reinforcement offered is appropriate.

Variety

A type of reinforcement satiation parallel to a satiation effect due to excessive reinforcement occurs when the teacher uses the same approving phrase or other reward over and over again. Students may perceive such reinforcement as mechanical, and they may lose interest in or decrease responsiveness to it. By varying the content of the reinforcer, the teacher can maintain its potency. Thus, instead of repeating "Nice job" four or five times, using a mix of comments (e.g., "Well done," "Good work," "You really listened") is more likely to yield a sustained effect.

Pairing with Praise

As noted previously, social reinforcement is most germane to enduring behavior change, although there are circumstances under which material, activity, or token reinforcers are at least initially more appropriate. To move toward social reinforcement, the teacher pairs all presentations of material, activity, or token rewards with some expression of social reinforcement: an approving comment, a pat on the back, a wink, a smile, and so forth. Walker (1979) has noted a major benefit of this tactic:

> By virtue of being consistently paired with reinforcement delivery, praise can take on the reinforcing properties of the actual reinforcer(s) used. This is especially important since teacher praise is not always initially effective.... By systematically increasing the incentive value of praise through pairing, the teacher is in a position to gradually reduce the frequency of (material, activity, or token) reinforcement and to substitute praise. After systematic pairing, the teacher's praise may be much more effective in maintaining the child's appropriate behavior. (p. 108)

Shaping

The first time a student practices an unfamiliar behavior, the performance may be rough or imperfect. This is true for classroom behaviors such as participating or paying attention, which a particular student may not have exhibited often. Therefore, even a partial or flawed performance should be reinforced early on. As the student becomes more confident and skilled in performing the behavior, rewards are given for the improved skill behaviors and eliminated for the earlier and less adequate approximations. Gradually, the rewarded performance will come to approximate the target behavior. The student's performance is thus "shaped" by the teacher. Social behavior can be shaped according to the following guidelines, developed by Sloane (1976):

1. Find some behavior in which the student is currently engaging that is a better approximation of your goal than the student's usual behavior and reinforce this approximation each time it occurs.

2. When an approximation has become more frequent for several days, select a slightly better one for reinforcement and stop reinforcing the first.

3. Ensure that each approximation is only slightly different from the last one.

4. Let a new approximation receive many reinforcements before moving on to another approximation.

5. Reinforce any behavior that is better than that currently required.

Behavior Contracting

Behavior contracting, sometimes known as contingency contracting, does not rely on the management of contingencies, but it can be effectiveness in helping children and adolescents understand and change problem behaviors. A behavior contract is a written agreement between a leader and group member. It is a document each signs that specifies desirable behaviors and their contingent positive consequences, as well as undesirable behaviors and their contingent undesirable consequences. As Homme et al. (1969) specify in their early description of this procedure, such contracts will more reliably lead to desirable behaviors when the contract payoff is immediate; approximations to the desirable behavior are rewarded; the contract rewards accomplishment rather than obedience; accomplishment precedes reward; and the contract is fair, clear, honest, positive, and systematically implemented.

Group Reinforcement

Children and adolescents are very responsive to the influence of their peers. This phenomenon can be used to encourage the performance of infrequent but desirable behaviors. In using group reinforcement, the teacher provides a reward (e.g., privilege, activity) to the entire group contingent upon the cooperative behavior of individual group members. If the reward is meaningful and desirable to the entire group, group members are likely to put pressure on one another to behave appropriately. For example:

> For the last three sessions, Tammy has made statements about how "stupid and dumb" she thought the Skillstreaming group was. When Tammy made these remarks, other students joined in by adding their own derogatory comments. The group leader decided to deal with this problem by telling the students that if, for the next three sessions, they encouraged one another's participation in the activities, they would earn an additional recess. The teacher prepared a small chart on which he wrote the dates of the next three sessions and a space for marking how frequently encouraging statements were offered. The extra recess was a desirable enough group reinforcer that when Tammy began her usual comments, the other students insisted that she stop disrupting the group.

Removing Positive Reinforcement

The teacher's behavior management goal with students who display aggressive or other problem behaviors is, in a general sense, twofold. Both sides of the behavioral coin—appropriate and inappropriate, prosocial and antisocial, desirable and undesirable—must be attended to. In a proper behavior change effort, procedures are simultaneously or sequentially employed to reduce and eliminate the inappropriate, antisocial, or undesirable components of the students' behavioral repertoires and to increase the quality and frequency of appropriate, prosocial, or desirable components. This latter task is served primarily by the direct teaching of prosocial behaviors via Skillstreaming participation and by the contingent presentation of positive reinforcement following skill use. Conversely, the contingent removal of positive reinforcement in response to aggressive, disruptive, or other negative behaviors is the major behavior management strategy for reducing or eliminating such behaviors. Therefore, in conjunction with the procedures discussed previously for presenting positive reinforcement, the teacher should also simultaneously or consecutively employ one or both of the following techniques for removing positive reinforcement.

Negative Reinforcement

Negative reinforcement is the removal of aversive stimuli contingent upon the occurrence of desirable behaviors. Negative reinforcement has seldom been used to modify behavior in a classroom context. The major exception to this rule is the contingent release of youth from time-out (an aversive environment), depending on such desirable behaviors as quietness and calmness.

Such release serves as negative reinforcement for these behaviors. Unfortunately, negative reinforcement often proves important in a classroom context in a less constructive way. Consider a teacher-student interaction in which the student behaves disruptively (shouts, swears, fights), the teacher responds with anger and punishment, and the punishment brings about a temporary suppression of the youth's disruptiveness. The decrease in the student's disruptiveness may also be viewed by the teacher as a decrease in aversive stimulation, which functions to negatively reinforce the immediately preceding teacher behavior (in this case, punishment). The net effect of this sequence is to increase the likelihood that the teacher will use punishment in the future. Analogous sequences may occur and function to increase the likelihood of other ineffective or inappropriate teacher behaviors.

PUNISHMENT

Formally, punishment is the presentation of an aversive or negative stimulus contingent upon the performance of a given behavior, intended to decrease the future occurrences of that behavior. Two common forms are verbal punishment (e.g., reprimands) and physical punishment (e.g., paddling, spanking). Corporal punishment is no longer allowed in most schools, nor is it recommended in any setting, including the home.

In fact, it is a common finding that, when verbal and physical punishment does succeed in altering behavior, such effects are often temporary. A number of clinicians and researchers have assumed an antipunishment stance, seeing little place for punishment, especially in the classroom. This view corresponds to punishment research demonstrating such undesirable side effects as withdrawal from social contact, counteraggression toward the punisher, violence, vandalism, modeling of punishing behavior, disruption of social relationships, failure of effects to generalize, selective avoidance (refraining from inappropriate behaviors only when under surveillance), and stigmatizing labeling effects (Azrin & Holz, 1966; Bandura, 1973; Mayer, 2001). Nelson, Lott, and Glenn (1993) state:

> Most teachers mean well when they administer punishment. They believe punishment is the best way to motivate students to behave properly. If the misbehavior stops for a while because of punishment, they may have been fooled into thinking they were right. However, when they become aware of the long-range effects of punishment on students, they naturally want to learn more respectful methods of motivating students to behave properly. (p. 78)

Because they are intended to reduce the frequency of behavior, extinction and time-out are, strictly speaking, also forms of punishment. These two techniques can be helpful in effecting behavior change in the Skillstreaming group if proper guidelines for their use are followed. Response cost and logical consequences can also have a place in helping children and adolescents decrease undesirable behavior.

Extinction

Extinction is the withdrawal or removal of positive reinforcement for aggressive or other undesirable behaviors that have been either deliberately or inadvertently reinforced in the past. This technique is the procedure of choice with milder forms of aggression (e.g., sarcasm, put-downs, or other low-level forms of verbal aggression).

Knowing When to Use Extinction

Determining when to use extinction is, of course, in part a function of each teacher's guiding group management philosophy and tolerance for deviant behavior. Each teacher will have to decide individually the range of undesirable behaviors that can be safely ignored. Taking a rather conservative stance, Walker (1979) suggests that extinction "should be applied only to those inappropriate behaviors that are minimally disruptive to classroom atmosphere" (p. 40). In any event, it is clear that the first step in applying extinction is knowing when to use it.

Providing Positive Reinforcement for Appropriate Behaviors

As noted earlier, attempts to reduce inappropriate behavior by reinforcement withdrawal should always be accompanied by efforts to increase appropriate behaviors by reinforcement provision. This combination of efforts will succeed especially well when the appropriate and inappropriate behaviors involved are opposite from, or at least incompatible with, each other (e.g., reward in-seat behavior, ignore out-of-seat behavior; reward talking at a conversational level, ignore talking loudly).

Identifying Positive Reinforcers Maintaining Inappropriate Behaviors

The reinforcers maintaining inappropriate behaviors are the ones to be withheld. The teacher should discern what the student is working for; what payoffs are involved; and what reinforcers are being sought or earned by aggression, disruptiveness, and similar behaviors. Very often, the answer will be attention. Looking, staring, yelling at, talking to, or turning toward are common teacher and peer reactions to a student's inappropriate behaviors. The withdrawal of such positive social reinforcement by ignoring the behaviors (by turning away and not yelling, talking, or looking at the perpetrator) is the teacher and peer behavior that will effect extinction.

Ignoring Low-Level Aggressive Behaviors

Carr (1981) has suggested guidelines for ignoring low-level aggressive behaviors (e.g., verbal comments). First, do not comment to the youth that you are ignoring. Long (or even short) explanations about why teachers, peers, or others are going to avoid attending to given behaviors provide precisely the type of social reinforcement that extinction is designed to withdraw. Ignoring behavior should simply occur with no forewarning, introduction, or explanation. Second, do not look away suddenly when the youth behaves inappropriately. Doing so may communicate the message that "I really noticed and was impelled to action by your behavior," the exact opposite of an extinction message. As Carr recommends, "It is best to ignore the behavior by reacting to it in a matter of fact way by continuing natural ongoing activities" (p. 38).

These guidelines should be followed only with behaviors that are not harmful to others. Observed incidents of verbal and physical aggression (or harassment) must be dealt with quickly and consistently to maintain a safe school environment. Thus, extinction is not supported as a method for dealing with behaviors that could cause harm to the student or others.

Using Extinction Consistently

As is true for the provision of reinforcement, removal of reinforcement must be consistent. Within a given Skillstreaming group, this rule of consistency means that the teacher and students must act in concert and that the teacher must be consistent across time. Within a given school, consistency means that, to the degree possible, all teachers having significant contact with a given student must strive to ignore the same inappropriate behaviors. In addition, to avoid the student's making the discrimination "I can't act up here, but I can out there," parent conferences should be held to bring parents, siblings, and other significant real-world figures in the student's life into the extinction effort.

Using Extinction Long Enough

Disruptive behaviors often have a long history of positive reinforcement. Especially if much of that history is one of intermittent reinforcement, efforts to undo these behaviors must be sustained. Teacher persistence in this regard will usually succeed. There are, however, two types of events to keep in mind when judging the effectiveness of extinction efforts. The first is what is known as the *extinction burst*. When extinction is first introduced, it is not uncommon for the rate or intensity of the aggressive behavior to increase sharply before it begins its more gradual decline toward zero. It is important that the teacher not be discouraged during this short detour. In fact, the meaning of the increase is that extinction is beginning to work. Second, inappropriate behaviors that have been successfully extinguished will reappear occasionally for reasons that are difficult to determine. Like the extinction burst, this *spontaneous recovery* is transitory and will disappear if the teacher persists in the extinction effort.

Time-Out

In time-out, a child or adolescent who engages in aggressive or other inappropriate behavior is removed from all sources of reinforcement for a specified time period. As with extinction, the purpose of time-out is to reduce the undesirable behavior. It differs from extinction in that extinction involves removing reinforcement from the person, whereas time-out usually involves removing the person from the reinforcing situation.

In school-based practice, time-out has typically taken three forms. *Isolation* or *seclusion time-out* requires that the youth be removed from the classroom to a time-out room. Because isolation or seclusion time-out is now considered to be a type of restraint, individuals considering this type of intervention should consult their state and district policies and procedures.

Exclusion time-out is somewhat less restrictive but also involves removing the youth from sources of reinforcement; it is perhaps the most common form of time-out used in elementary school classrooms. Here the youth is required to go to an area of the classroom and perhaps to sit in a "quiet chair," which is sometimes behind a screen. The youth is not removed from the classroom but is excluded from classroom activities for a specified time period. *Nonexclusion time-out* (also called *contingent observation*), the least restrictive time-out variant, requires the youth to sit and watch on the periphery of classroom

activities, to observe the appropriate behaviors of other students. This variant combines time-out with modeling opportunities and thus is the preferred approach for Skillstreaming group use. The implementation of time-out in any of its forms optimally employs the procedures next described.

Knowing When to Use Time-Out

As noted, extinction is the recommended procedure for undesirable behaviors that can be safely ignored. Behaviors potentially injurious to others require a more active teacher response, possibly time-out. Exclusion or nonexclusion time-out is also the procedure to use for less severe forms of problematic behavior when the combination of extinction and positive reinforcement for more positive behaviors has been attempted and failed.

Whenever possible, the student should be verbally directed to use the time-out area. If he or she refuses to go, the rest of the class or group may be removed instead of the student causing the problem. This will leave the student with the same response—time-out from positive reinforcement. In certain situations where student safety is at risk, it may be necessary to move a student physically to time-out. This may be the case for children age 2 to 12 who display high rates of potentially dangerous or aggressive behaviors. Such physical intervention should be used only as a last resort to protect the safety of the student or others—and only after attempts have been made to deescalate the student's behavior. Many times, after deescalation the student will move to the time-out area independently.

Providing Positive Reinforcement for Appropriate Behaviors

As is the case for extinction, positive reinforcement for appropriate behaviors should accompany any extinction procedure, including time-out. When possible, the behaviors positively reinforced should be opposite to, or at least incompatible with, those for which the time-out procedure is used. Carr (1981) recommends an additional basis combining these two techniques:

> Although one important reason for using positive reinforcement is to strengthen non-aggressive behaviors to the point where they replace aggressive behaviors, there is a second reason for using reinforcement procedures. If extensive use of positive reinforcement is made, then time-out will become all the more aversive since it would involve the temporary termination of a rich diversity of positive reinforcers. In this sense, then, the use of positive reinforcement helps to enhance the effectiveness of the time-out procedure. (pp. 41–42)

Arranging an Effective Time-Out Setting

Time-out must be a boring environment, with all reinforcers removed. With exclusionary time-out, there should be no attractive or distracting objects or opportunities—no toys, books, posters, people, windows to look out, sounds to overhear, or other obvious or not-so-obvious potential reinforcers. When contingent observation is used, the youth will still hear the ongoing activity.

Sending a Student to Time-Out

The teacher can take a number of actions when initiating time-out to increase the likelihood of its effectiveness. As for positive reinforcement, immediacy is an issue. Time-out is best instituted immediately following the aggressive or other behavior to be modified. Having earlier explained to the student the nature of time-out, as well as when and why it will be used, the teacher should initiate the procedure in a more or less automatic manner following the undesirable behavior—that is, in a way that minimizes social reinforcement. This means sending the student to time-out without a lengthy explanation but with a brief description of the precipitating behavior. This process is best conducted in a calm and matter-of-fact manner. In addition, the effectiveness of time-out is further enhanced by its consistent application, when appropriate, by

the same teacher on other occasions, as well as by other teachers.

Maintaining a Student in Time-Out

Two questions arise during a student's period in time-out: What is he or she doing? and How long should time-out last? Answering the first question by monitoring the student makes certain that the time-out experience is not in fact pleasant or positively reinforcing. For example, rather than being a removal from positive reinforcement, time-out may in reality help a youth avoid an aversive situation from which he or she would prefer to escape. Similarly, if monitoring reveals that the youth is singing or playing, time-out will be less effective. Unless the situation can be made essentially nonreinforcing, a different behavioral intervention may be required.

With regard to duration, most successful time-out implementations have been from 2 to 10 minutes long (2 to 3 minutes for preschoolers and kindergartners, 3 to 5 minutes for the elementary-age student, and 5 to 10 minutes for an adolescent) with clear preference for the shorter time spans in this range. If time-out periods are longer than necessary, the student may calm down and then act up again out of boredom or frustration. When experimenting to find the optimal duration for any given youth, it is best to begin with a shorter duration and to lengthen the time until an effective span is identified rather than to shorten an initially longer span. This latter approach would, again, risk the danger of introducing an event the student experiences as positive reinforcement when the teacher's intention is quite the opposite.

Excusing a Student from Time-Out

As noted earlier in connection with extinction, withdrawal of positive reinforcement frequently leads to an extinction burst in which more intense or more frequent problem behaviors appear before they begin to subside. This same pattern is evident with withdrawal from positive reinforcement—that is, time-out. The first few times a student is directed to use time-out, what might be termed a *time-out burst* of heightened aggression or other problem behaviors may occur. These outbursts will usually subside, especially if the teacher requires the time-out to be served and the outburst does not result in the suspension of the time-out.

The student's release from time-out should be conducted in a matter-of-fact manner, and the student should be quickly returned to regular Skillstreaming activities. Lengthy teacher explanations or moralizing are, once again, tactically erroneous provisions of positive reinforcement that communicate to the student that acting out in the classroom will bring a short period of removal from reinforcement and then a (probably longer) period of undivided teacher attention.

It is important once the student returns to ongoing activities that the teacher quickly reinforce the student for subsequent positive behaviors. The Skillstreaming group must be a positive place—a place where the student wants to be—or time-out will be perceived as a reward instead of a negative consequence.

Providing Prosocial Alternatives

The responsible group leader will plan instruction in specific skills that could serve as prosocial ways of dealing with the problem that led to the use of time-out. For example, the student could be guided through the steps of Using Self-Control (Skill 36) or Dealing with Your Anger (Skill 31) to reduce the likelihood that the event will reoccur. In addition, the leader must attempt to deescalate future occurrences of such behavior through techniques like prompting.

Response Cost

Response cost involves the removal of previously acquired reinforcers contingent upon and in order to reduce future instances of inappropriate behavior. The previously acquired reinforcers may have been earned, as when response-cost procedures are a component of a token economy, or they may have simply been provided, as is the case with a freestanding response-cost system. In

either instance, reinforcers are removed (the cost) whenever the undesirable behaviors occur (the response). Response-cost procedures can be effective, especially when combined with the provision of positive reinforcement via a token-economy system, for increasing prosocial behaviors. However, response-cost systems should never be a first choice in dealing with problem behaviors. Although the cost can be framed as a fine for breaking the rules or engaging in other actions for adolescents, this procedure has frequently shown to elicit aggressive responses on its own. Response cost is not appropriate for use with preschool or children in the early elementary grades.

Logical Consequences

An encouraging environment teaches students to respect themselves and others and treats all students with dignity. Rarely are students exposed to reprimands or other forms of harsh punishment; however, clear and consistent limits on unacceptable behavior are set and enforced so all students have the opportunity to learn. Logical consequences to reduce the frequency of undesirable behavior are most often recommended. Logical consequences are related to the individual's action, and they make sense (i.e., there is a cause-effect relationship; McLeod, Fisher, & Hoover, 2003). Consequences hold the student accountable yet maintain the student's dignity. As McLeod et al. (2003) state:

> Punishment does not teach alternative acceptable behaviors; in fact, it models just the opposite. Teachers use punishment out of anger, frustration, or lack of other strategies. Consequences, however, teach students the connection between how they choose to behave and the outcomes of that behavior. (p. 114)

These authors suggest using restitution (fixing or replacing damaged, lost, or stolen items), restoration (giving the student a respite by being away from the group for a brief period of time), restriction (limiting privileges for a length of time), and reflection (reflecting on a problem and developing a plan through problem solving).

Dreikurs and Cassel (1972) further define logical consequences. Such consequences are related to the misbehavior; are planned, explained, and agreed on by students in advance; are administered in a neutral way; and are given consistently. In addition, consequences are reasonable and demonstrate respect by giving students a choice (i.e., to engage in the inappropriate behavior and receive an unpleasant consequence or to engage in the appropriate behavior and receive positive reinforcement).

When planning logical consequences, teachers will need to keep in mind that these consequences must be reasonable, related to the misbehavior, and respectful to the student (Nelson et al., 1993). Examples of logical consequences include the following:

- For choosing to talk instead of completing a class assignment, the student must complete the work during an enjoyable activity.

- For choosing to fight when provoked at recess, the student must stay on a specific area of the playground where there is increased supervision.

- For choosing to take a notebook belonging to someone else, the student must make restitution.

Overcorrection

Overcorrection is a behavior modification approach developed by Foxx and Azrin (1973) for circumstances in which other behavioral strategies have failed and when few alternative appropriate behaviors are available to reinforce. Overcorrection is a two-part procedure, having restitution and positive practice as components. Restitution requires that the individual return the behavioral setting (e.g., the classroom) to its status prior to disruption or better. Thus, objects broken by an angry youth must be repaired, classmates struck in anger apologized to, papers scattered across the room picked up. The positive practice component of overcorrection requires that the youth then be made to repair objects broken by others, apologize to classmates who witnessed the classmate being struck, or clean up the rest of the classroom (including areas not disturbed by the youth). It is clear that the restitution and positive practice requirements serve both punitive and instructional functions.

References

Adams, M. B., Womack, S. A., Shatzer, R. H., & Caldarella, P. (2010). Parent involvement in school-wide social skills instruction: Perceptions of a home note program. *Education, 130*(3), 513–528.

Advancement Project/Civil Rights Project. (2000, February). *Education denied: The negative impact of zero tolerance policies.* Testimony before the U.S. Commission on Civil Rights, Washington, DC.

Ahmad, Y., & Smith, P. K. (1994). Bullying in schools and the issue of sex differences. In John Archer (Ed.), *Male violence.* London: Routledge.

Alberto, P. S., & Troutman, A. C. (2006). *Applied behavior analysis for teachers: Influencing student performance.* Upper Saddle River, NJ: Merrill/Prentice Hall.

Andrews, S. P., Taylor, P. B., Martin, E. P., & Slate, J. R. (1998). *Evaluation of an alternative discipline program.* Chapel Hill: The University of North Carolina Press.

Applied Research Center. (1999). *Making the grade: A racial justice report card.* Washington, DC: Author.

Asarnow, J. R., & Callan, J. W. (1985). Boys with peer adjustment problems: Social cognitive processes. *Journal of Consulting and Clinical Psychology, 53,* 80–87.

Ascher, C. (1994). *Gaining control of violence in the schools: A view from the field* (ERIC Digest No. 100). New York: ERIC Clearinghouse on Urban Education.

Ayllon, T., & Azrin, N. H. (1968). *The token economy: A motivational system for therapy rehabilitation.* New York: Appleton-Century-Crofts.

Azrin, N. H., & Holz, W. C. (1966). Punishment. In W. K. Honig (Ed.), *Operant behavior: Areas of research and application.* New York: Appleton-Century-Crofts.

Bandura, A. (1973). *Aggression: A social learning analysis.* Englewood Cliffs, NJ: Prentice Hall.

Bandura, A. (1977). *Social learning theory.* Englewood Cliffs, NJ: Prentice Hall.

Beane, A. (1999). *The bully-free classroom.* Minneapolis: Free Spirit.

Bender, W. N. (2009). Beyond the RTI pyramid: Solutions for the first years of implementation. Bloomington, IN: Solution Tree Press.

Blair, K. C., Fox, L., & Lentini, R. (2010). Use of positive behavior support to address the challenging behavior of young children within a community early childhood program. *Topics in Early Childhood Special Education, 30*(2), 68–79.

Blood, E., & Neel, R. S. (2007). From FBA to implementation: A look at what is actually being delivered. *Education and Treatment of Children, 30*(4), 67–80.

Bock, S. J., Tapscott, K. E., & Savner, J. L. (1998). Suspension and expulsion: Effective management for students? *Intervention in School and Clinic, 34*(1), 50–52.

Bourland, E. (1995). *RRFC Links 2*(3). (Available from Federal Resource Center for Special Education, Academy for Educational Development, 1875 Connecticut Ave., NW, Washington, DC 20009–1202)

Boyajian, A. E., DuPaul, G. J., Handler, M. W., Eckert, T. L., & McGoey, K. E. (2001). The use of classroom-based brief functional analyses with preschoolers at-risk for attention deficit hyperactivity disorder. *School Psychology Review, 30*(2), 278–293.

Brannon, D. (2008). Character education: A joint responsibility. *Kappa Delta Pi Record, 44* (Winter), 62–65.

Brendtro, L. K., Brokenleg, M., & Van Bockern, S. (2002). *Reclaiming youth at risk: Our hope for the future.* Bloomington, IN: National Educational Service.

Brownstein, R. (2010). Pushed out. *Teaching Tolerance,* March, 23–27.

Bruder, M. B. (2010). Early childhood intervention: A promise to children and families for their future. *Exceptional Children, 76*(3), 339–355.

Buhremester, D. (1982). *Children's Concerns Inventory manual.* Los Angeles: University of California, Department of Psychiatry.

Caldarella, P., & Merrell, K. W. (1977). Common dimensions of social skills of children and adolescents: A taxonomy of positive behaviors. *School Psychology Review, 26*(2), 264–279.

Camodeca, M., Goossens, F. A., Schuengel, C., & Terwogt, M. M. (2003). Links between social information processing in middle childhood and involvement in bullying. *Aggressive Behavior, 29,* 116–127.

Camp, B. W., & Bash, M. A. S. (1981). *Think Aloud: Increasing social and cognitive skills—A problem-solving program for children* (Primary Level). Champaign, IL: Research Press.

Camp, B. W., & Bash, M. A. S. (1985). *Think Aloud: Increasing social and cognitive skills—A problem-solving program for children* (Classroom Program, Grades 1–2). Champaign, IL: Research Press.

Caprara, G. V., Barbaranelli, C., Pastorelli, C., Bandura, A., & Zimbardo, P. (2000). Prosocial foundations of children's academic achievement. *Psychological Science, 11,* 301–306.

Carr, E. G. (1981). Contingency management. In A. P. Goldstein, E. G. Carr, W. Davidson, & P. Wehr (Eds.), *In response to aggression.* New York: Pergamon.

Carr, E. G., Dunlap, G., Horner, R. H., Koegel, R. L., Turnbull, A. P., Sailor, W., Anderson, J. L., Albin, R. W., Koegel, L. K., & Fox, L. (2002). Positive behavior support: Evolution of an applied science. *Journal of Positive Behavior Interventions, 4*(1), 4–16.

Carter, D. A., & Horner, R. H. (2007). Adding functional behavioral assessment to First Step to Success: A case study. *Journal of Positive Behavior Interventions, 9*(4), 229–238.

Cartledge, G. (2003, February 20). *Discipline, diversity and behavioral disorders: Issues and interventions.* Presentation made at the Midwest Symposium for Leadership in Behavioral Disorders, Kansas City, MO.

Cartledge, G., & Feng, H. (1996). The relationship of culture and social behavior. In G. Cartledge (Ed.), *Cultural diversity and social skills instruction: Understanding ethnic and gender differences.* Champaign, IL: Research Press.

Cartledge, G., & Johnson, S. (1997). Cultural sensitivity. In A. P. Goldstein & J. C. Conoley (Eds.), *School violence intervention: A practical handbook.* New York: Guilford.

Cartledge, G., & Kourea, L. (2008). Culturally responsive classrooms for culturally diverse students with and at risk for disabilities. *Exceptional Children, 74*(3), 351–371.

Cartledge, G., & Lo, Y. (2006). *Teaching urban learners: Culturally responsive strategies for developing academic and behavioral competence.* Champaign, IL: Research Press.

Cartledge, G., & Milburn, J. F. (1980). *Teaching social skills to children.* New York: Pergamon.

Cartledge, G., & Milburn, J. F. (1995). *Teaching social skills to children and youth: Innovative approaches* (3rd ed.). Needham Heights, MA: Allyn and Bacon.

Cartledge, G., & Milburn, J. F. (1996). A model for teaching social skills. In G. Cartledge (Ed.), *Cultural diversity and social skills instruction: Understanding ethnic and gender differences.* Champaign, IL: Research Press.

Chapman, W. E. (1977). *Roots of character education.* Schenectady, NY: Character Research Press.

Chen, K. (2006). Social skills intervention for students with emotional/behavioral disorders: A literature review from the American perspective. *Educational Research and Reviews, 1*(3), 143–149.

Cochrane, W. S., & Laux, J. M. (2007). Investigating school psychologists' perceptions of treatment integrity in school-based interventions for children with academic and behavior concerns. *Preventing School Failure, 51*(4), 29–34.

Cohen, J., Pickeral, T., & McCloskey, M. (2009, April). Assessing school climate. *Education Digest, 74*(8) 45–48.

Coie, J. D., & Kupersmidt, J. B. (1983). A behavioral analysis of emerging social status in boys' groups. *Child Development, 54,* 1400–1416.

Cook, C. R., Crews, S. D., Wright, D. B., Mayer, G. R., Gale, B., Kramer, B., & Gresham, F. M. (2007). Establishing and evaluating the substantive adequacy of Positive Behavioral Support Plans. *Journal of Behavioral Education, 16,* 191–206.

Cook, C. R., Gresham, F. M., Kern, L., Barreras, R. B., & Crews, S. D. (2008). Social skills training for secondary students with emotional and/or behavioral disorders: A review and analysis of the meta-analytic literature. *Journal of Emotional and Behavioral Disorders, 16*(3), 131–144.

Costenbader, V., & Markson, S. (1998). School suspension: A study with secondary school students. *Journal of School Psychology, 36,* 59–82.

Crick, N. R., & Dodge, K. A. (1994). A review and reformulation of social information processing mechanisms in children's social adjustment. *Psychological Bulletin, 115,* 74–101.

Crick, N. R., & Dodge, K. A. (1996). Social information-processing mechanisms in reactive and proactive aggression. *Child Development, 67,* 993–1002.

Crone, D. A., Hawken, L. S., & Bergstrom, M. (2007). A demonstration of training, implementing, and using functional behavioral assessment in 10 elementary and middle school settings. *Journal of Positive Behavior Interventions, 9*(1), 15–29.

Crone, D. A., & Horner, R. H. (2003). *Building positive behavior support systems in schools: Functional behavioral assessment.* New York: Guilford Press.

Denham, S. A. (1998). *Emotional development in young children.* New York: Guilford.

Denham, A., Hatfield, S., Smethurst, J., Tan, E., & Tribe, C. (2006). The effect of social skills interventions in the primary school. *Educational Psychology in Practice, 22*(1), 33–51.

Dewey, J. (1938). *Experience and education.* New York: Collier.

Docksai, R. (2010). Teaching social skills. *Futurist, 44*(3), 12–13.

Dodge, K. A. (1983). Behavioral antecedents of peer social status. *Child Development, 54,* 1385–1399.

Dodge, K. A. (1985). Facets of social interaction and the assessment of social competence in children. In B. H. Schneider, K. H. Rubin, & J. E. Ledingham (Eds.), *Children's peer relations: Issues in assessment and intervention.* New York: Springer-Verlag.

Dodge, K. A., Coie, J. D., & Bralke, N. P. (1982). Behavior patterns of socially rejected and neglected preadolescents: The roles of social approach and aggression. *Journal of Abnormal Child Psychology, 10,* 389–410.

Dodge, K. A., Lockman, J. E., Harnish, J. D., Bates, J. E., & Pettit, G. S. (1997). Reactive and proactive aggression in school children and psychiatrically impaired chronically assaultive youth. *Journal of Abnormal Psychology, 106*(1), 37–51.

Dodge, K. A., Murphy, R. R., & Birchsbaum, K. C. (1984). The assessment of intention-cue detection skills in children: Implications for developmental psychology. *Child Development, 55,* 163–173.

Donovan, M. S., & Cross, C. T. (Eds.). (2002). *Minority students in special and gifted education.* Washington, DC: National Academy Press.

Dreikurs, R., & Cassel, P. (1972). *Discipline without tears.* New York: Hawthorne.

Dupper, D. R., & Bosch, L. A. (1996). Reasons for school suspensions. *Journal for a Just and Caring Education, 2*(2), 140–150.

Dykeman, B. F. (2003). School-based interventions for treating social adjustment difficulties in children with traumatic brain injury. *Journal of Instructional Psychology, 30*(3), 225–230.

Elksnin, L. K., & Elksnin, N. (2000). Teaching parents to teach their children to be prosocial. *Intervention in School and Clinic, 36*(1), 27–35.

Elliott, S. N., & Gresham, F. M. (1991). *Social skills intervention guide: Practical strategies for social skills training.* Circle Pines, MN: American Guidance Service.

Ellis, H. (1965). *The transfer of learning.* New York: Macmillan.

Epps, S., Thompson, F. J., & Lane, M. P. (1985). *Procedures for incorporating generalization programming into interventions for behaviorally disordered students.* Unpublished manuscript, Iowa State University, Ames.

Evertson, C. M., Emmer, E. T., Worsham, M. E. (2003). *Classroom management for elementary teachers* (6th ed.). Needham, MA: Allyn & Bacon.

Farmer, T. W., Farmer, E. M. Z., Estell, D. B., & Hutchins, B. C. (2007). The developmental dynamics of aggression and the prevention of school violence. *Journal of Emotional and Behavioral Disorders 15*(4), 197–208.

Feindler, E. L. (1979). *Cognitive and behavioral approaches to anger control training in explosive adolescents.* Unpublished doctoral dissertation, West Virginia University, Morgantown.

Feindler, E. L. (1995). An ideal treatment package for children and adolescents with anger disorders. In H. Kassinove (Ed.), *Anger disorders: Definition, diagnosis, and treatment.* New York: Taylor & Francis.

Feindler, E. L., & Ecton, R. B. (1986). *Adolescent anger control: Cognitive-behavioral techniques.* New York: Pergamon.

Ferster, C. B., & Skinner, B. F. (1957). *Schedules of reinforcement.* New York: Appleton-Century-Crofts.

Fialka, J., & Mikus, K. C. (1999). *Do you hear what I hear?* Ann Arbor, MI: Proctor.

Fox, C. L., & Boulton, J. J. (2003). Evaluating the effectiveness of a social skills training (SST) programme for victims of bullying. *Educational Research, 45*(3), 231–247.

Foxx, R. M., & Azrin, N. H. (1973). A method of eliminating aggressive-disruptive behavior for retarded and brain-damaged patients. *Behaviour Research and Therapy, 10,* 15–27.

Friesen, B. J., & Stephens, B. (1998). Expanding family roles in the system of care: Research and practice. In M. H. Epstein, K. Kutash, & A. Duchnowski (Eds.), *Outcomes for children and youth with behavioral and emotional disorders and their families.* Austin, TX: PRO-ED.

Fullerton, E. K., Conroy, M. A., & Correa, V. I. (2009). Early childhood teacher's use of specific praise statements with young children at risk for behavioral disorders. *Behavioral Disorders, 34*(3), 118–135.

Galassi, J. P., & Galassi, M. D. (1984). Promoting transfer and maintenance of counseling outcomes. In S. D. Brown & R. W. Lent (Eds.), *Handbook of counseling psychology.* New York: Wiley.

Gemelli, R. J. (1996). Understanding and helping children who do not talk in school. In N. J. Long & W. C. Morse (Eds.), *Conflict in the classroom: The education of at-risk and troubled students.* Austin, TX: PRO-ED.

Gibbs, J. C., Potter, G. B., & Goldstein, A. P. (1995). *The EQUIP program: Teaching youth to think and act responsibly through a peer-helping approach.* Champaign, IL: Research Press.

Gilliam, W. S. (2005). Prekindergarteners left behind: Expulsion rates in state prekindergarten systems. Retrieved May 22, 2011 from www.hartfordinfo.org/ issues/wsd/education/NationalPreKExpulsionPaper

Glick, B., & Gibbs, J. C. (2010). *Aggression Replacement Training: A comprehensive intervention for aggressive youth* (3rd ed.). Champaign, IL: Research Press.

Goldstein, A. P. (1973). *Structured Learning Therapy: Toward a psychotherapy for the poor.* New York: Academic.

Goldstein, A. P. (1989). *The Prepare Curriculum: Teaching prosocial competencies.* Champaign, IL: Research Press.

Goldstein, A. P. (1999a). *Low-level aggression: First steps on the ladder to violence.* Champaign, IL: Research Press.

Goldstein, A. P. (1999b). *The Prepare Curriculum: Teaching prosocial competencies* (Rev. ed.). Champaign, IL: Research Press.

Goldstein, A. P., Gershaw, N. J., Klein, P., & Sprafkin, R. P. (1980). *Skillstreaming the adolescent: A structured learning approach to teaching prosocial skills.* Champaign, IL: Research Press.

Goldstein, A. P., & Glick, B. (1987). *Aggression Replacement Training: A comprehensive program for aggressive youth.* Champaign, IL: Research Press.

Goldstein, A. P., Glick, B., Carthan, W., & Blancero, D. (1994). *The prosocial gang.* New York: Pergamon.

Goldstein, A. P., Glick, B., & Gibbs, J. C. (1998). *Aggression Replacement Training: A comprehensive intervention for aggressive youth* (Rev. ed.). Champaign, IL: Research Press.

Goldstein, A. P., Glick, B., Irwin, J. J., Pask-McCartney, C., & Rubama, I. (1989). *Reducing delinquency: Intervention in the community.* New York: Pergamon.

Goldstein, A. P., & Kanfer, F. H. (1979). *Maximizing treatment gains.* New York: Academic.

Goldstein, A. P., & McGinnis, E. (1988). *The Skillstreaming video: How to teach students prosocial skills.* Champaign, IL: Research Press.

Goldstein, A. P., & McGinnis, E. (1997). *Skillstreaming the adolescent: New strategies and perspectives for teaching prosocial skills* (Rev. ed.). Champaign, IL: Research Press.

Goldstein, A. P., & Michaels, G. Y. (1985). *Empathy: Development, training and consequences.* Hillsdale, NJ: Erlbaum.

Goldstein, S. E., Young, A., & Boyd, C. (2008). Relational aggression at school: Associations with school safety and social climate. *Journal of Youth Adolescence, 37,* 641–654.

Grayson, M. C., Kiraly, J., Jr., & McKinnon, A. J. (1996). Using time-out procedures with disruptive students. In N. J. Long & W. C. Morse (Eds.), *Conflict in the classroom: The education of at-risk and troubled students.* Austin, TX: PRO-ED.

Greene, R. W. (2010). Calling all frequent flyers. *Educational Leadership, 68*(2), 28–34.

Greenbaum, S., Turner, B., & Stephens, R. D. (1989). *Set straight on bullies.* Malibu, CA: National School Safety Center.

Greenwood, C. R., Hops, H., Delquadri, J., & Guild, J. (1974). Group contingencies for group consequences in classroom management: A further analysis. *Journal of Applied Behavior Analysis, 7,* 413–425.

Greenwood, C. R., Todd, N. M., Hops, H., & Walker, H. M. (1978). *Description of withdrawn children's behavior in preschool settings* (Report No. 40). Eugene: University of Oregon, Center at Oregon for Research in the Behavioral Education of the Handicapped.

Gresham, F. M. (1998a). Social skills training: Should we raze, remodel, or rebuild? *Behavioral Disorders, 24*(1), 19–25.

Gresham, F. M. (1998b). Social skills training with children: Social learning and applied behavioral analytic approaches. In T. S. Watson & F. M. Gresham (Eds.), *Handbook of child behavior therapy.* New York: Plenum Press.

Gresham, F. M. (2002). Social skills assessment and instruction for students with emotional and behavioral disorders. In K. L. Lane, F. M. Gresham, & T. E. O'Shaughnessy (Eds.), *Interventions for children with or at risk for emotional and behavioral disorders.* Boston: Allyn and Bacon.

Gresham, F. M. (2005). Methodological issues in evaluating cognitive-behavioral treatments for students with behavioral disorders. *Behavioral Disorders, 30*(3), 213–215.

Gresham, F. M. (2009). Evolution of the treatment integrity concept: Current status and future directions. *School Psychology Review, 38*(4), 533–540.

Gresham, F. M., Cook, C. R., Crews, S. L., & Kern, L. (2004). Social skills training for children and youth with emotional and behavioral disorders: Validity considerations and future directions. *Behavioral Disorders, 30*(1), 32–46.

Gresham, F. M., & Elliott, S. N. (1990). *Social Skills Rating System.* Circle Pines, MN: American Guidance Service.

Gresham, F. M., & Gansle, K. A. (1993). Treatment integrity of school-based behavioral intervention studies: 1980–1990. *School Psychology Review, 22*(2), 254–272.

Gresham, F. M., MacMillan, M. E., Beebe-Frankenberger, M. E., & Bocian, K. M. (2000). Treatment integrity in learning disabilities intervention research: Do we really know how treatments are implemented? *Learning Disabilities Research and Practice, 15*(4), 198–205.

Gresham, F. M., Sugai, G., & Horner, R. H. (2001). Interpreting outcomes of social skills training for students with high-incidence disabilities. *Exceptional Children, 67,* 331–344.

Gresham, F. M., Van, M. B., & Cook, C. R. (2006). Social skills training for teaching replacement behaviors: Remediating acquisition deficits in at-risk students. *Behavioral Disorders, 31*(4), 363–377.

Gresham, F. M., Watson, T. S., & Skinner, C. H. (2001). Functional behavioral assessment: Principles, procedures, and future directions. *School Psychology Review, 30*(2), 156–172.

Grizenko, J., Zappitelli, M., Langevin, J. P., Hrychko, S., El-Messidi, A., Kaminester, D., Pawliuk, N., & Stepanian, M. T. (2000). Effectiveness of a social skills training program using self/other perspective-taking: A nine month follow-up. *American Journal of Orthopsychiatry, 70*(4), 501–509.

Guerra, N. G., Boxer, P., & Kim, T. E. (2005). A cognitive-ecological approach to serving students with emotional and behavioral disorders: Application to aggressive behavior. *Behavioral Disorders, 30*(3), 277–288.

Guerra, N. G., & Slaby, R. G. (1989). Evaluative factors in social problem solving by aggressive boys. *Journal of Abnormal Child Psychology, 17,* 277–289.

Guzzetta, R. A. (1974). *Acquisition and transfer of empathy by the parents of early adolescents through Structured Learning training.* Unpublished doctoral dissertation, Syracuse University.

Hickman, G. P., Bartholomew, M., Mathwig, J., & Heinrichs, R. S. (2008). Differential developmental pathways of high school dropouts and graduates. *Journal of Educational Research, 102*(1), 3–14.

Homme, L., Csanyi, A. P., Gonzales, M. A., & Rechs, J. R. (1969). *How to use contingency contracting in the classroom.* Champaign, IL: Research Press.

Hoover, J. H., & Oliver, R. (1996). *The bullying prevention handbook: A guide for principals, teachers, and counselors.* Bloomington, IN: National Education Service.

Horner, R. H., & Carr, E. G. (1997). Behavioral support for students with severe disabilities: Functional assessment and comprehensive intervention. *The Journal of Special Education, 31*(1), 84–104.

Hubbard, J. A., Dodge, K. A., Cillessen, A. H., Coie, J. D., & Schwartz, D. (2001). The dyadic nature of social information processing in boys' reactive and proactive aggression. *Journal of Personality and Social Psychology, 80*(2), 268–280.

Individuals with Disabilities Education Act (IDEA) Amendments of 1997, Pub. L. 105–17.

Individuals with Disabilities Education Act (IDEA) Amendments of 2004, Pub. L. 180–446.

Ingram, K., Lewis-Palmer, T., & Sugai, G. (2005). Function-based intervention planning: Comparing the effectiveness of FBA function-based and non-function based intervention plans. *Journal of Positive Behavior Interventions, 7*(4), 224–236.

Jewett, J. (1992). *Aggression and cooperation: Helping young children develop constructive strategies.* (ERIC Document Reproduction Service No. ED351147)

Johns, B. H., Carr, V. G., & Hoots, C. W. (1995). *Reduction of school violence: Alternatives to suspension.* Horsham, PA: LRP.

Johnson, S. L. (2009). Improving the school environment to reduce school violence: A review of the literature. *Journal of School Health, 79*(10), 451–465.

Jolivette, K., Scott, T. M., & Nelson, C. M. (2000). *The link between Functional Behavioral Assessments*

(FBAs) and Behavioral Intervention Plans (BIPs) (ERIC Digest E592). Reston, VA: Council for Exceptional Children.

Jones, K. M., Young, M. M., & Friman, P. C. (2000). Increasing peer praise of socially rejected delinquent youth: Effects on cooperation and acceptance. *School Psychology Review, 15,* 30–39.

Jones, V. F., & Jones, L. S. (2008). *Comprehensive classroom management* (9th ed.). Needham, MA: Allyn & Bacon.

Jung, L. A., Gomez, C., Baird, S. M., & Keramidas, C. L. G. (2008). Designing intervention plans: Bridging the gap between individualized education programs and implementation. *Teaching Exceptional Children, 41*(1), 26–33.

Kame'enui, E. J., & Simmons, D. C. (1990). *Designing instructional strategies: The prevention of academic learning problems.* Columbus, OH: Merrill.

Kaplan, J. S., & Carter, J. (2005). *Beyond behavior modification: A cognitive behavioral approach to behavior management in the school* (3rd ed.). Austin, TX: PRO-ED.

Karoly, P., & Steffen, J. J. (1980). Operant methods. In F. H. Kanfer & A. P. Goldstein (Eds.), *Helping people change.* New York: Pergamon.

Kauffman, J. M. (2005). *Characteristics of emotional and behavioral disorders of children and youth* (9th ed.). Upper Saddle River, NJ: Pearson.

Kauffman, J. M., Mostert, M. P., Trent, S. C., & Hallahan, D. P. (1998). *Managing classroom behavior: A reflective case-based approach* (2nd ed.). Boston: Allyn and Bacon.

Kavale, K. A., & Forness, S. R. (1996). Learning disability grows up: Rehabilitation issues for individuals with learning disabilities. *Journal of Rehabilitation, 62*(1), 34–42.

Kazdin, A. E. (1975). *Behavior modification in applied settings.* Homewood, IL: Dorsey.

Keeley, S. M., Shemberg, K. M., & Carbonell, J. (1976). Operant clinical intervention: Behavior management or beyond? Where are the data? *Behavior Therapy, 7,* 292–305.

Kendall, P. C., & Braswell, L. (1985). *Cognitive behavioral therapy for children.* New York: Guilford.

Kern, L., Hilt, A. M., & Gresham, F. (2004). An evaluation of the functional behavioral assessment process used with students with or at-risk for emotional and behavioral disorders. *Education and Treatment of Children, 27*(4), 440–452.

Knight, B. J., & West, D. J. (1975). Temporary and continuing delinquency. *British Journal of Criminology, 15,* 43–50.

Kohlberg, L. (1969). Stage and sequence: The cognitive-developmental approach to socialization. In D. A. Goslin (Ed.), *Handbook of socialization theory and research.* Chicago: Rand McNally.

Kohlberg, L. (Ed.). (1973). *Collected papers on moral development and moral education.* Cambridge, MA: Harvard University, Center for Moral Education.

Kounin, J. (1970). *Discipline and group management in classrooms.* New York: Holt, Rinehart and Winston.

Kulli, K. (2008). Developing effective behavior intervention plans: Suggestions for school personnel. *Intervention in School and Clinic, 43*(3), 140–149.

Kurtz, M. M., & Mueser, K. T. (2008). A meta-analysis of controlled research on social skills training for schizophrenia. *Journal of Consulting and Clinical Psychology, 76*(3), 491–504.

Ladd, G. W., & Mize, J. (1983). A cognitive-social learning model of social skill training. *Psychological Review, 90,* 127–157.

Lane, K. L., Givner, C. C., & Pierson, M. R. (2004). Teacher expectations of student behavior: Social skills necessary for success in elementary school classrooms. *Journal of Special Education, 38,* 104–110.

Lane, K. L., Menzies, H. M., Barton-Arwood, S. M., Doukas, G. L., & Munton, S. M. (2005). Designing, implementing, and evaluating social skills interventions for elementary students: Step-by-step procedures based on actual school-based investigations. *Preventing School Failure, 49*(2), 18–26.

Lane, K. L., Wehby, J. H., & Cooley, C. (2006). Teacher expectations of students' classroom behavior across the grade span: Which social skills are necessary for success? *Exceptional Children, 72*(2), 153–167.

LaRue, Jr., R. H., Weiss, M. J., & Ferraioli, S. J. (2008). State of the art procedures for assessment and treatment of learners with behavioral problems. *International Journal of Behavioral Consultation and Therapy, 4*(2), 250–263.

Lassen, S. R., Steele, M. M., & Sailor, W. (2006). The relationship of school-wide positive behavior support to academic achievement in an urban middle school. *Psychology in the Schools, 43*(6), 701–712.

Lo, Y., Loe, S. A., & Cartledge, G. (2002). The effects of social skills instruction on the social behaviors of students at risk for emotional or behavioral disorders. *Behavioral Disorders, 27*(4), 371–385.

Loeber, R., & Dishion, T. (1983). Early predictors of male delinquency: A review. *Psychological Bulletin, 94,* 68–99.

Lopata, C., Thomeer, M. L., Bolker, M. A., & Nida, R. E. (2006). Effectiveness of a cognitive-behavioral treatment on the social behaviors of children with Asperger Disorder. *Focus on Autism and Other Developmental Disabilities, 21*(4), 237–244.

Maag, J. W. (2006). Social skills training for students with emotional and behavioral disorders: A review of reviews. *Behavioral Disorders, 32*(1), 5–17.

Maag, J. W., & Swearer, S. M. (2005). Cognitive-behavioral interventions for depression: Review and implications for school personnel. *Behavioral Disorders, 30*(3), 259–276.

MacNeil, A. J., Prater, D. L., & Busch, S. (2009). The effects of school culture and climate on student achievement. *International Journal of Leadership in Education, 12*(1), 73–84.

Maddern, L., Franey, J., McLaughlin, V., & Cox, S. (2004). An evaluation of the impact of an interagency programme to promote social skills in primary school children. *Educational Psychology in Practice, 20*(2), 135–155.

Mann, J. H. (1956). Experimental evaluations of role playing. *Psychological Bulletin, 53,* 227–234.

Manning, M., Heron, J., & Marshall, T. (1978). Styles of hostility and of social interactions at nursery, at school and at home: An extended study of children. In L. A. Hersov & M. Berger (Eds.), *Aggression and anti-social behavior in childhood and adolescence.* Oxford, UK: Pergamon.

Marx, G. (2006). *An overview of sixteen trends: Their profound impact on our future: Implications for students, education, communities, and whole of society.* Alexandria, VA: Educational Research Service.

Marzano, R. J., & Haystead, M. W. (2008). *Making standards useful in the classroom.* Alexandria, VA: Association for Supervision and Curriculum Development.

Mayer, G. R. (2001). Antisocial behavior: Its causes and prevention within our schools. *Education and Treatment of Children, 245*(4), 414–429.

McConnell, S. R. (1987). Entrapment effects and the generalization and maintenance of social skills training for elementary school students with behavioral disorders. *Behavioral Disorders, 12,* 252–263.

McGinnis, E. (2005). *Skillstreaming the elementary school child: Lesson plans and activities.* Champaign, IL: Research Press.

McGinnis, E., & Goldstein, A. P. (1990). *Skillstreaming in early childhood: Teaching prosocial skills to the preschool and kindergarten child.* Champaign, IL: Research Press.

McGinnis, E., & Goldstein, A. P. (1997). *Skillstreaming the elementary school child: New strategies and perpectives for teaching prosocial skills* (Rev. ed.). Champaign, IL: Research Press.

McGinnis, E., & Goldstein, A. P. (2003). *Skillstreaming in early childhood: New strategies and perpectives for teaching prosocial skills* (Rev. ed.). Champaign, IL: Research Press.

McIntosh, K., Borgmeier, C., Anderson, C. M., Horner, R. H., Rodriguez, B. J., & Tobin, T. (2008). Technical adequacy of the functional assessment checklist: Teacher and staff (FACTS) FBA interview measure. *Journal of Positive Behavior Interventions, 10*(1), 33–45.

McIntosh, K., & MacKay, L. D. (2008). Enhancing generalization of social skills: Making social skills curricula effective after the lesson. *Beyond Behavior, Fall,* 18–25.

McIntosh, R., Vaughn, S., & Zaragoza, N. (1991). A review of social interventions for students with learning disabilities. *Journal of Learning Disabilities, 24,* 451–458.

McLaren, E. M., & Nelson, C. M. (2009). Using functional behavior assessment to develop behavior interventions for students in Head Start. *Journal of Positive Behavior Interventions, 11*(1), 3–21.

McLeod, J., Fisher, J., & Hoover, G. (2003). *The key elements of classroom management: Managing time and space, student behavior, and instructional strategies.* Alexandria, VA: Association for Supervision and Curriculum Development.

Meichenbaum, D. H. (1977). *Cognitive-behavior modification: An integrative approach.* New York: Plenum.

Meier, C. R., DiPerna, J. C., & Oster, M. M. (2006). Importance of social skills in the elementary grades. *Education and Treatment of Children, 29,* 409–419.

Mendler, A. N., & Curwin, R. L. (1999). *Discipline with dignity for challenging youth.* Bloomington, IN: National Educational Service.

Mercer, C. D., & Pullen, P. C. (2005). *Students with learning disabilities.* Upper Saddle River, NJ: Pearson Education.

Miller, J. P. (1976). *Humanizing the classroom.* New York: Praeger.

Modro, M. (1995). *Safekeeping: Adult responsibility, children's right.* Providence: Behavioral Health Resource.

Moroz, K. B., & Jones, K. M. (2002). The effects of positive peer reporting on children's social involvement. *School Psychology Review, 31*(2) 235–245.

Morrison, R. L., & Bellack, A. S. (1981). The role of social perception in social skills. *Behavior Therapy, 12,* 69–70.

Mruzek, D. W., Cohen, C., & Smith, T. (2007). Contingency contracting with students on the autism spectrum. *Journal of Developmental and Physical Disabilities, 19,* 103–114.

National Association for the Education of Young Children. (1993). NAEYC position statement on violence in the lives of children. *Young Children, 48*(6), 80–84.

Neilans, T. H., & Israel, A. C. (1981). Towards maintenance and generalization of behavior change: Teaching children self-regulation and self-instructional skills. *Cognitive Therapy and Research, 5,* 189–196.

Nelson, J., Lott, L., & Glenn, H. S. (1993). *Positive discipline in the classroom: How to effectively use class meetings and other positive discipline strategies.* Rocklin, CA: Prima.

Newman, D. A., Horne, A. M., & Bartolomucci, C. L. (2000). *Bully busters: A teacher's manual for helping bullies, victims, and bystanders.* Champaign, IL: Research Press.

Nickerson, A. B., & Martens, M. P. (2008). School violence: Associations with control, security/enforcement, educational/therapeutic approaches, and demographic factors. *School Psychology Review, 37*(2), 228–241.

Nowicki, S., Jr., & Duke, M. P. (1992). *Helping the child who doesn't fit in.* Atlanta, GA: Peachtree.

Olweus, D. (1991). Bully/victim problems among school children: Basic facts and effects of a school-based intervention program. In D. Pepler & K. H. Rubin (Eds.), *The development and treatment of childhood aggression.* Hillsdale, NJ: Erlbaum.

Olweus, D. (1993). *Bullying at school: What we know and what we can do.* Oxford, UK: Blackwell.

Osgood, C. E. (1953). *Method and theory in experimental psychology.* New York: Oxford University Press.

Partnership for 21st Century Skills. (2008). 21st Century skills, education, and competitiveness: A resource and policy guide. Retrieved May 22, 2011, from www.p21.org/documents/21st_century_skills_ education_and_competitiveness_guide.pdf

Patterson, G. R. (1982). *Coercive family process.* Eugene, OR: Castalia.

Patterson, G. R., Reid, J. B., Jones, R. R., & Conger, R. E. (1975). *A social learning approach to family intervention* (Vol. 1). Eugene, OR: Castalia.

Pelco, L. E., & Reed-Victor, E. (2007). Self-regulation and learning-related social skills: Intervention ideas for elementary school students. *Preventing School Failure, 51*(3), 36–41.

Perea, S. (2004). *The new America: The America of the moo-shoo burrito.* Denver, CO: HIS Ministries Publications.

Perry, P. G., Perry, L. C., & Rasmussen, P. (1986). Cognitive social learning mediators of aggression. *Child Development, 57,* 700–711.

Pettit, G. S., Bates, J. E., & Dodge, K. A. (2000). Supportive parenting, ecological context, and children's adjustment: A seven-year longitudinal study. In W. Craig (Ed.), *Childhood social development: The essential readings.* Malden, MS: Blackwell.

Quinn, M. M., Osher, D., Warger, C. L., Hanley, T. V., Bader, B. D., & Hoffman, C. C. (2000). *Teaching and working with children who have emotional and behavioral challenges.* Longmont, CO: Sopris West.

Raine, A., Dodge, K., Loeber, R., Gatzke-Kopp, L. M., Lynam, D., Reynolds, C., Stouthamer-Loeber, M., & Liu, J. (2006). The Reactive-Proactive Aggression Questionnaire: Differential correlates of reactive and proactive aggression in adolescent boys. *Aggressive Behavior, 32,* 159–171.

Redl, F., & Wineman, D. (1957). *The aggressive child.* New York: Free Press.

Reid, M. J., Webster-Stratton, C., & Hammond, M. (2007). Enhancing a classroom social competence and problem-solving curriculum by offering parent training to families of moderate-to high-risk elementary school children. *Journal of Clinical Child and Adolescent Psychology, 36*(4), 605–620.

Robins, K. N., Lindsey, R. B., Lindsey, D. B., & Terrell, R. D. (2006). *Culturally proficient instruction: A guide for people who teach* (2nd ed.). Thousand Oaks, CA: Corwin Press.

Robins, L. N., West, P. A., & Herjanic, B. L. (1975). Arrests and delinquency in two generations: A study of black urban families and their children. *Journal of Child Psychology and Psychiatry, 16,* 125–140.

Rock, E. E., Fessler, M. A., & Church, R. P. (1997). The concomitance of learning disabilities and emotional/behavioral disorders: A conceptual model. *Journal of Learning Disabilities, 30,* 245–263.

Rose, L. C., & Gallup, A. M. (2004). *The 36th Annual Phi Delta Kappa/Gallup poll of the public's attitude toward public schools.* Bloomington, IN: Phi Delta Kappa International.

Sanetti, L. M., & Kratochwill, T. R. (2009). Toward developing a science of treatment integrity: Introduction to a special series. *School Psychology Review, 38*(4), 445–459.

Sarason, I. G., Glaser, M., & Fargo, G. A. (1972). *Reinforcing productive classroom behavior.* New York: Behavioral Publications.

Schoenfeld, N. A., Rutherford, R. B., Jr., Gable, R. A., & Rock, M. L. (2008). *ENGAGE: A blueprint for incorporating social skills training into daily academic instruction.* Birmingham, AL: Heldref.

Scott, T. M., Anderson, C. M., & Spaulding, S. A. (2008). Strategies for developing and carrying out functional assessment and behavior intervention planning. *Preventing School Failure, 52*(3), 39–49.

Scott, T. M., & Nelson, C. M. (1998). Confusion and failure in facilitating generalized social responding in the school setting: Sometimes 2 + 2 = 5. *Behavioral Disorders, 23*(4), 264–275.

Simon, S. G., Howe, L. W., & Kirschenbaum, H. (1972). *Values clarification.* New York: Hart.

Skiba, R. J., Peterson, R. L., & Williams, T. (1997). Office referrals and suspension: Disciplinary intervention in middle schools. *Education and Treatment of Children, 20*(3), 295–315.

Skiba, R. J., & Sprague, J. (2008). Safety without suspension. *Educational Leadership, 66*(1), 38–43.

Skinner, B. F. (1938). *The behavior of organisms: An experimental analysis.* New York: Appleton-Century-Crofts.

Skinner, B. F. (1953). *Science and human behavior.* New York: Macmillan.

Skinner, C. H., Cashwell, T. H., & Skinner, A. L. (2000). Increasing tooling: Effects of a peer-monitored group contingency program on students' reports of peers' prosocial behaviors. *Psychology in the Schools, 37,* 263–270.

Slavin, R. E. (1980). *Using student team learning* (Rev. ed.). Baltimore: Johns Hopkins University, Center for Social Organization of Schools.

Slim, L., Whiteside, S. P., Dittner, C. A., & Mellon, M. (2006). Effectiveness of a social skills training program with school age children: Transition to clinical setting. *Journal of Child and Family Studies, 15,* 409–418.

Sloane, H. N. (1976). *Classroom management: Remediation and prevention.* New York: Wiley.

Smith, P. K., & Levan, S. (1995). Perceptions and experiences of bullying in younger pupils. *British Journal of Educational Psychology, 65,* 489–500.

Smith, S. W., & Gilles, D. L. (2003). Using key instructional elements to systematically promote social skill generalization for students with challenging behavior. *Intervention in School and Clinic, 39*(1), 30–37.

Smith, S. W., Lochman, J. E., & Daunic, A. P. (2005). Managing aggression using cognitive-behavioral interventions: State of practice and future directions. *Behavioral Disorders, 30*(3), 227–240.

Spivack, G. E., & Shure, M. B. (1974). *Social adjustment of young children.* San Francisco: Jossey-Bass.

Sprague, J., & Walker, H. (2000). Early identification and intervention for youth with antisocial and violent behavior. *Exceptional Children, 66*(3), 367–379.

Stokes, T. F., & Baer, D. M. (1977). An implicit technology of generalization. *Journal of Applied Behavior Analysis, 10,* 349–367.

Stormont, M., & Reinke, W. (2009). The importance of precorrective statements and behavior-specific praise and strategies to increase their use. *Beyond Behavior, 18*(3), 26–32.

Strain, P. S., & Timm, M. A. (2001). Remediation and prevention of aggression: An evaluation of the regional intervention program over a quarter century. *Behavioral Disorders, 26*(4), 297–313.

Sugai, G., Guardino, D., & Lathrop, M. (2007). Response to intervention: Examining classroom behavior support in second grade. *Exceptional Children, 73*(3), 288–310.

Sulzer-Azaroff, B., & Mayer, G. R. (1991). *Behavior analysis for lasting change.* San Francisco: Holt, Rinehart and Winston.

Thorndike, E. L., & Woodworth, R. S. (1901). The influence of improvement in one mental function upon the efficiency of other functions. *Psychological Review, 8,* 247–261.

Trussell, R. P., Lewis, T. J., & Stichter, J. P. (2008). The impact of targeted classroom interventions and function-based behavior interventions on problem behaviors of students with emotional/behavioral disorders. *Behavioral Disorders, 33*(3), 153–166.

Trzesniewski, K. H., Moffit, T. E., Caspi, A., Taylor, A., & Maughan, B. (2006). Revisiting the association between reading and antisocial behavior: New evidence of an environmental explanation from a twin study. *Child Development, 77,* 72–88.

Tse, J., Strulovitch, J., Tagalakis, V., Linyan, M., & Fombonne, E. (2007). Social skills training for adolescents with Asperger Syndrome and High Functioning Autism. *Journal of Autism and Developmental Disorders, 37,* 1960–1968.

Turner, N. D. (2003). Preparing preservice teachers for inclusion in secondary classrooms. *Education, 123*(3), 491–495.

Voltz, D. L., Sims, M. J., & Nelson, B. (2010). *Connecting teachers, students and standards: Strategies for success in diverse and inclusive classrooms.* Alexandria, VA: Association for Supervision and Curriculum Development.

Walker, H. M. (1979). *The acting-out child: Coping with classroom disruption.* Boston: Allyn & Bacon.

Walker, H. M., Colvin, G., & Ramsey, E. (1995). *Antisocial behaviors in schools: Strategies and best practices.* Pacific Grove, CA: Brooks/Cole.

Walker, H. M., Ramsey, E., & Gresham, F. M. (2004). *Antisocial behavior in school: Evidence-based practices* (2nd ed.). Belmont, CA: Wadsworth/Thomson Learning.

Warden, D., & MacKinnon, S. (2003). Prosocial children, bullies, and victims: An investigation of their sociometric status, empathy, and social-problem-solving strategies. *British Journal of Developmental Psychology, 21,* 367–385.

Werner, E. E., & Smith, R. S. (1982). *Vulnerable but invincible.* New York: McGraw-Hill.

Wood, B. K., Umbreit, J., Liaupsin, C. J., & Gresham, F. M. (2007). A treatment integrity analysis of function-based intervention. *Education and Treatment of Children, 30*(4), 105–120.

Zahn-Waxler, C., & Radke-Yarrow, M. (1982). The development of altruism: Alternative research strategies. In N. Eisenberg (Ed.), *The development of prosocial behavior.* New York: Academic.

Zahn-Waxler, C., & Radke-Yarrow, M. (1990). The origins of empathic concern. *Motivation and Emotion, 14,* 107–130.

Zins, J. E., Bloodworth, M. R., Weissberg, R. P., & Walberg, H. J. (2004). The scientific base linking social and emotional learning to school success. In J. Zins, M. Bloodworth, R. Weissberg, & G. Walberg (Eds.). *Building academic success on social and emotional learning: What does the research say?* New York: Teachers College Press.

About the Author

Ellen McGinnis earned her Ph.D. from the University of Iowa in 1986. She holds degrees in elementary education, special education, and school administration. She has taught elementary and secondary students in the public schools in Minnesota, Iowa, and Arizona. In addition, she has served as a special education consultant in both public and hospital schools and as assistant professor of special education at the University of Wisconsin–Eau Claire. Dr. McGinnis also served with the Des Moines Public Schools as the principal of the education program at Orchard Place, a residential and day treatment facility for children and adolescents with emotional/behavioral disorders. She has been an executive director of student support services in both Iowa and Colorado and is currently a private consultant. The author of numerous articles on identifying and teaching youth with emotional/behavioral disorders, Dr. McGinnis collaborated with Dr. Arnold P. Goldstein on earlier Skillstreaming books and is author of the newly released third editions of *Skillstreaming in Early Childhood* and *Skillstreaming the Adolescent*.

Skillstreaming

The widely acclaimed and evidence-based social skills teaching method developed by Dr. Arnold P. Goldstein and colleagues

FOR PRESCHOOL AND KINDERGARTEN

SKILLSTREAMING IN EARLY CHILDHOOD

A Guide for Teaching Prosocial Skills

Dr. Ellen McGinnis

PROGRAM BOOK

A complete description of the *Skillstreaming* program, with instructions for teaching 40 prosocial skills.

Skill Areas

- Beginning Social Skills
- School-Related Skills
- Friendship-Making Skills
- Dealing with Stress
- Alternatives to Aggression
- Dealing with Feelings

8 ½ × 11, 352 pages (CD included)

SKILL CARDS

Convenient 3 × 5 cards, illustrated for nonreaders, listing the behavioral steps for each of the 40 early childhood skills. Eight cards provided for each skill—a total of 320 cards.

SKILL POSTERS

A set of 40 12 × 18 posters, illustrated for nonreaders and displaying the behavioral steps in each of the skills for preschool and kindergarten.

FOR ELEMENTARY SCHOOL STUDENTS

SKILLSTREAMING THE ELEMENTARY SCHOOL CHILD

A Guide for Teaching Prosocial Skills

Dr. Ellen McGinnis

PROGRAM BOOK

Instructions for teaching 60 prosocial skills, plus complete guidelines for running the *Skillstreaming* program.

Skill Areas

- Classroom Survival Skills
- Friendship-Making Skills
- Skills for Dealing with Feelings
- Skill Alternatives to Aggression
- Skills for Dealing with Stress

8 ½ × 11, 408 pages (CD included)

SKILLSTREAMING IN THE ELEMENTARY SCHOOL

Lesson Plans and Activities

Make *Skillstreaming* even more fun! This book provides supplementary activities for at least one week of additional instruction for each of the 60 elementary skills. Features 600 easy-to-use lesson plans and a CD including over 200 printable forms necessary to implement the lesson plans.

8½ × 11, 312 pages (CD included)

STUDENT MANUAL

Written for the elementary-age student, a concise guide describing the program, designed to promote active involvement in the *Skillstreaming* group. A useful reference and organizer.

8½ × 11, 80 pages

SKILL CARDS

In a convenient 3 × 5 format, cards list the behavioral steps for each of the 60 elementary *Skillstreaming* skills. Eight cards provided for each skill—480 cards total.

POSTERS

A set of 60 18 × 12 posters displaying the behavioral steps in each of the skills for elementary-age students.

DVD—For Student Viewing
PEOPLE SKILLS: DOING 'EM RIGHT!

A quick and easy way to show your students what *Skillstreaming* is all about. Illustrates the process of teacher modeling, student role-playing, and feedback to clarify the benefits of using skills and motivate students to participate.

Elementary DVD, 17 minutes (closed captioned)

FOR ADOLESCENTS

SKILLSTREAMING THE ADOLESCENT

A Guide for Teaching Prosocial Skills

Dr. Ellen McGinnis with Dr. Robert P. Sprafkin, Dr. N. Jane Gershaw, and Paul Klein

PROGRAM BOOK

A complete description of the *Skillstreaming* program, with detailed instructions for teaching 50 prosocial skills.

Skill Areas

- ◆ Beginning Social Skills
- ◆ Advanced Social Skills
- ◆ Skills for Dealing with Feelings
- ◆ Skill Alternatives to Aggression
- ◆ Skills for Dealing with Stress
- ◆ Planning Skills

8½ × 11, 360 pages (CD included)

SKILL CARDS

Convenient 3 × 5 cards listing the behavioral steps for each of the 50 adolescent Skillstreaming skills. Eight cards provided for each skill—400 cards total.

ALSO FROM RESEARCH PRESS . . .

AGGRESSION REPLACEMENT TRAINING®

A Comprehensive Intervention for Aggressive Youth

Third Edition

Dr. Barry Glick and Dr. John C. Gibbs

Identified as a promising or model program by the Office of Juvenile Justice and Delinquency Prevention, Office of Safe and Drug-Free Schools, and National Center for Mental Health Promotion and Youth Violence Prevention

A new edition of the groundbreaking ART approach originally developed by Dr. Arnold P. Goldstein and Dr. Barry Glick, employing social skills training, anger control training, and moral reasoning. Updated and reorganized, with session-by-session instructions. Completely new moral reasoning problem situations, along with photocopiable skill cards, participant handouts, parent materials, and evaluation forms.

8½ × 11, 426 pages (CD included)

STUDENT MANUAL

A concise description of the program written in language adolescents can understand. Promotes active involvement in the *Skillstreaming* group and serves as a useful reference and organizer.

8½ × 11, 64 pages

POSTERS

A set of 50 18 × 12 posters displaying the behavioral steps for each of the adolescent skills.

DVD—For Student Viewing
PEOPLE SKILLS: DOING 'EM RIGHT!

A quick and easy way to show your students what *Skillstreaming* is all about. Illustrates the process of teacher modeling, student role-playing, and feedback to clarify the benefits of using skills and motivate students to participate.

Adolescent DVD, 17 minutes (closed captioned)

FOR TEACHER AND STAFF TRAINING

THE SKILLSTREAMING DVD

How to Teach Students Prosocial Skills

Shows Drs. Arnold P. Goldstein and Ellen McGinnis in actual training sessions with educators and small groups of adolescents and elementary-age children. Clearly demonstrates the *Skillstreaming* teaching model and procedures. Purchase includes a copy of the *Skillstreaming the Adolescent* and *Skillstreaming the Elementary School Child* program books.

26 minutes (closed captioned)

Contact Research Press for current prices and ordering information.

RESEARCH PRESS
PUBLISHERS

2612 N. Mattis Avenue ◆ Champaign, IL 61822
www.researchpress.com ◆ (800) 519-2707

Visit www.skillstreaming.com for details on research support for the program, sample lessons, and more.